FIFTH EDITION

THE COLLECTOR'S ENCYCLOPEDIA OF DEPRESSION GLASS

By Gene Florence

COLLECTOR BOOKS
P.O. Box 3009
Paducah, KY 42001

The current values in this book should be used only as a guide. They are not intended to set prices, which vary from one section of the country to another. Auction prices as well as dealer prices vary greatly and are affected by condition as well as demand. Neither the Author nor the Publisher assumes responsibility for any losses that might be incurred as a result of consulting this guide.

Additional copies of this book may be ordered from:

COLLECTOR BOOKS
P.O. Box 3009
Paducah, Kentucky 42001
or
Gene Florence
P.O. Box 22186
Lexington, Kentucky 40522

@$17.95 Add $1.00 for postage and handling.

Copyright: Bill Schroeder, Gene Florence, 1982
ISBN: 0-89145-180-3

This book or any part thereof may not be reproduced without the written consent of the Author and Publisher.

ABOUT THE AUTHOR

Gene FLorence, born in Lexington in 1944, graduated from the University of Kentucky where he held a double major in mathematics and English. He taught nine years in the Kentucky school systems at the Junior High and High School levels before his glass collecting "hobby" became his full time job.

Mr. Florence has been interested in "collecting" since childhood, beginning with baseball cards and progressing through comic books, coins, bottles and finally, glassware. He first became interested in Depression glassware after purchasing a set of Sharon dinnerware at a garage sale for $5.00.

He has written several books on glassware: **The Collector's Encyclopedia of Depression Glass**, now in its fifth edition; **The Collector's Encyclopedia of Akro Agate; The Collector's Encyclopedia of Occupied Japan**, Volume I and II, **The Pocket Guide To Depression Glass**, now in its second edition, and **Kitchen Glassware of the Depression Years**.

Should you be in Lexington, he is often found at Grannie Bear Antique Shop located at 120 Clay Avenue. This is the shop he helped his mother set up in what was formerly her children's day care center. The shop derived its name from the term of endearment the toddlers gave her.

Should you know of any unlisted or unusual pieces of glassware IN THE PATTERNS SHOWN IN THIS BOOK, you may write him at Box 22186, Lexington, KY 40522. If you expect a reply, you must enclose a self-addressed, stamped envelope and be patient. His travels and research often cause the hundreds of letters he receives weekly to backlog. He does appreciate your interest, however, and spends many hours answering your letters when time and circumstances permit.

ACKNOWLEDGEMENTS

It seems that in every book some calamity occurs that tops all previous ones. This book was no exception. Some of the glass seen herein survived a fire that gutted the photographer's studio! Thankfully, the fire didn't reach the glass; and glass, being waterproof, wasn't bothered by the drenching from the firemen's hoses.

Further, we spent a long day photographing before realizing that the photographs being taken wouldn't reproduce large enough for the book; so, we had all that packing and unpacking and setting up shots to be done over again.

This book would not be finished yet but for the persistence of Cathy, wife, typist, editor and prodder. We both owe much to John and Trannie Davis, friends who opened their home to us and gave us the freedom (from phone, mail, children) to give total concentration to writing the book. On the home front I need to thank my eleven-year-old son, Chad, for giving an entire summer day to doing paste-up work for me for the book---boring though he deemed it! I thank my seven-year-old loquacious son Marc for managing three DAYS (before deadline) of mouse-like existence! I need to thank "Grannie Bear", Mom, for packing box after box of glass and making endless lists as to what each contained so pieces could be readily located at the studio. Then, there are Dad, Charles, Sib and Marie who care for the home front while we travel.

Glass and information for this book were furnished by Earl and Beverly Hines (who generously lent their rare and unusual collections to be photographed); Kelly and Priscilla McBride, Lois Florence, Kenn and Margaret Whitmeyer, Nancy Maben, Pam Jones, Jim Cooper, Sarah Brown, Virginia Fender, Helen Marshall, Hugh Buzzard of Fostoria Glass Company, Lucille Kennedy of Imperial Glass Company, Lloyd Thrush and Philip Bee of Anchor Hocking.

Too, there were people at the studio who helped unpack, coordinate, wash, powder, set up and take down glass amassed for the photographer. I owe them very special thanks because they WORKED long and hard. They include: Beverly Hines, Laurissa Hyatt, Steve Quertermous, Jane Fryberger, Bill Schroeder and Cathy Florence.

The photographer for the new photographs was Dana Curtis of Curtis and Mays Studios.

There is always the possibility of leaving someone out in a listing of that sort. If I have, it wasn't intentional nor am I unappreciative of your help. It's just that as we go to press on this edition, I've overlooked your gesture of kindness. Forgive me if I have and be happy in the knowledge that many people are enjoying your contribution to this book.

Everyone of us, from the gatherers to the printers, have tried to make this the best book available! We sincerely hope you appreciate our efforts!

FOREWORD

Since the issuance of the past four editions which have gone past the 200,000 mark in circulation, there have been changes in the collecting of Depression Glass. More attention is now being given the cheaper pattens of Depression Glass, or indeed, ANYTHING that is Depression Glass be it a particular pattern or not; and collectors are also becoming aware of the better glassware produced during this same time period. There are several such patterns of Depression ERA glassware included in this book.

Depression Glass as defined in this book is the colored glassware made primarily during the Depression years in the colors of amber, green, pink, blue, red, yellow, white and crystal. There are other colors and some glass included which was made before, as well as after this time; but primarily, the glass within this book was made from the late 1920's through the 1930's. MORE ATTENTION IS BEING GIVEN TO SOME OF THE HAND MADE GLASSWARE now, but MOSTLY THIS BOOK IS CONCERNED WITH THE INEXPENSIVELY MADE GLASSWARE turned out in quantity and sold through the five and dime stores or given away as promotions or inducements to buy other products during that era known as The Depression.

Information for the book has come via research, experience, fellow dealers and collectors and over 350,000 miles of travel in connection with glassware. Too, some of the more interesting information has come from readers who were kind enough to share their photographs and knowledge with me. These gestures I particularly treasure.

PRICING

ALL PRICES IN THIS BOOK ARE RETAIL PRICES FOR MINT CONDITION GLASSWARE. THIS BOOK IS INTENDED TO BE ONLY A GUIDE TO PRICES AS THERE ARE SOME REGIONAL PRICE DIFFERENCES WHICH CANNOT REASONABLY BE DEALT WITH HEREIN.

You may expect dealers to pay from thirty to fifty percent less than the prices quoted. Glass that is in less than mint condition, i.e. chipped, cracked, scratched or poorly molded, will bring very small prices unless extremely rare; and then, it will bring only a small percentage of the price of glass that is in mint condition.

Prices have become pretty well nationally standardized due to national advertising carried on by dealers and due to the Depression Glass Shows which are held from coast to coast. However, **there are still some regional differences in prices due** partly **to glass being more readily available in some areas than in others.** Too, companies distributed certain pieces in some areas that they did not in others. Generally speaking, however, prices are about the same among dealers from coast to coast.

Prices tend to increase dramatically on rarer items and, in general, they have increased as a whole due to more and more collectors entering the field and people becoming more aware of the worth of Depression Glass.

One of the more important aspects of this book is the attempt made to illustrate as well as realistically price those items which are in demand. The desire was to give you the most accurate guide to collectible patterns of Depression Glass available.

MEASUREMENTS

To illustrate why there are discrepancies in measurements, I offer the following sample from just two years of Hocking's catalogue references:

Year	Pitcher Ounces	Flat Tumbler Ounces	Footed Tumbler Ounces
1935	37, 58, 80	5, 9, 13½	10, 13
1935	37, 60, 80	5, 9, 10, 15	10, 13
1936	37, 65, 90	5, 9, 13½	10, 15
1935	37, 60, 90	5, 9, 13½	10, 15

All measurements in this book are exact as to some manufacturer's listing or to actual measurement. You may expect variance of up to ½ inch or 1-5 ounces. This may be due to mold variation or changes made by the manufacturer.

Index

ADAM JEANNETTE GLASS COMPANY, 1932-1934

Colors: Pink, green, crystal, yellow.

Creationists hold that mankind began with "Adam"; so what better place to begin our study of Depression Glass than with a pattern of like name. Indeed, if you study the motif on this generally squared pattern, the leaves, fern-like scrolls, sun rays and profusion of flowers around the border, you receive such a strong impression of a garden that you wonder if perhaps that Biblical viewpoint was the inspiration behind the concept and name of Adam. Unfortunately, who designed the various molds for Depression glass, or what their artistic inspiration was is now purely guesswork.

There have been a few changes in the status quo of this pattern since the fourth edition was published. Those items that were just beginning to become hard to find then (i.e., the vase, the 5½" iced tea tumblers, the cereal bowls in pink and the covered vegetable bowl in green) have become more scarce due to the larger number of collectors entering the field!

Thus far, only one batch of yellow Adam (with those very rare and strange ROUND plates) has surfaced. They were found in 1973 in the basement of a house belonging to a former Jeannette employee and were almost certainly experimental pieces. Surely there were more than 19 pieces made; so, keep a sharp eye open when you shop! Round items have been found in pink, also.

I have heard of another Adam-Sierra patterned butter dish recently. I often get letters from people who THINK they have one. Remember, the Adam pattern is found on the OUTSIDE of the butter top while the Sierra pattern is found on the INSIDE of that SAME top. The base of the butter may be either pattern, but it is usually found on the Adam butter bottom as shown in the picture.

For newcomers to the field, I reiterate that the lids for the sugar and candy dishes are interchangeable; and although a lidless candy may look like a small "ladies" cuspidor, that was not its original purpose. My lady grandmother didn't "chew"; did yours?

The treasured Adam lamps are made from sherbet dishes which were frosted and notched to accommodate a switch. The metal cover and bulb are tough to find separately; you will occasionally find the notched, frosted bottom piece alone. (The lamp is similar to the FLORAL one made by the same company and pictured in that pattern).

To date, there are too few pieces of crystal Adam (pitcher, ash tray, coaster, divided relish, grill plate) found to consider collecting a set. Though these few pieces are quite rare, they don't command great prices because there is so little demand for them.

There have been few drastic jumps in prices in Adam, but their rising trend lends this pattern investment potential! Pink remains the most popular color; of late, I've noticed green catching the eye of more collectors as the prices here have remained steady.

Adam pitchers come with both rounded and squared bases. Only the squared base will contain the motif. The round base has concentric rings.

	Pink	Green		Pink	Green
Ash Tray, 4½"	17.50	15.50	Pitcher, 8", 32 oz.	22.50	27.50
Bowl, 4¾" Dessert	8.50	8.00	Pitcher, 32 oz. Round Base	27.50	
Bowl, 5¾" Cereal	18.00	15.00	Plate, 6" Sherbet	3.50	3.75
Bowl, 7¾"	12.00	12.50	**Plate, 7¾" Square Salad	6.50	7.00
Bowl, 9" Covered	32.50	52.50	Plate, 9" Square Dinner	13.50	13.50
Bowl, 10" Oval	13.50	16.00	Plate, 9" Grill	10.50	10.00
Butter Dish & Cover	65.00	197.50	Platter, 11¾"	9.50	11.50
Butter Dish Combination			Relish Dish, 8" Divided	8.00	9.00
with Sierra Pattern	450.00		Salt & Pepper, 4" Footed	37.50	67.50
Cake Plate, 10" Footed	10.50	15.00	***Saucer, 6" Square	3.00	3.00
Candlesticks, 4" Pair	42.50	57.50	Sherbet, 3"	12.00	15.00
Candy Jar & Cover, 2½"	45.00	57.50	Sugar	8.50	10.50
Coaster, 3¼"	14.00	10.00	Sugar/Candy Cover	12.50	17.50
Creamer	9.00	10.00	Tumbler, 4½"	15.50	14.50
*Cup	13.50	13.00	Tumbler, 5½" Iced Tea	27.50	23.50
Lamp	77.50	77.50	Vase, 7½"	95.00	27.50

*Yellow $80.00
**Round Pink $75.00   Yellow $80.00
***Round Pink $65.00   Yellow $70.00

Please refer to Foreword for pricing information

6

AMERICAN PIONEER   LIBERTY WORKS, 1931-1934

Colors: Pink, green, amber, crystal.

Liberty called their covered pitchers "urns"; so, we'll respect that. These urns have been turning up more and more frequently with the liner plate, as shown in the pattern shot, leading one to think they might have been originally intended as syrup or cream pitchers. In any case, the lid has to be removed before pouring since it totally overlaps the spout.

Luncheon items (cup, saucer, plate, sugar and creamer) are more commonly found than the other pieces pictured in this pattern. The little 2¼", 2 oz. shot glass (pictured in the 4th edition), the wine and water goblets are in scant supply. Several collectors I know would love to have even one in their collection! There are two sizes of covered casserole bowls, an 8¾" and a 9¼". Neither of these bowls is easily found; but how nice you feel when you do turn one up!

There are four styles of vases in pink: a straight edge (only slightly curved outward); a rolled edge (sharply rolled outward like the one pictured on the left of the photograph); a curved inward and a scalloped edge. Only the straight edge and the rolled edge types have been found in green so far.

The tall candy dish is often mistaken for a vase if the lid is missing. The vase flares out slightly at the rim. The candy bottom rises straight upward at the rim. The lids to the candy dishes can be interchanged; however, the plump little 1½ pound candy dish is the hardest of the two to find.

There is a 4½" dish, holding 16 oz. and having a flared rim which I have been calling a rose bowl and which a collector friend feels is a mayonnaise. It missed getting photographed in that veritable sea of glassware we had strewn about the studio this time because we carefully set it aside so it wouldn't get broken! Sorry!

Green tends to be the color favored most by collectors of American Pioneer. Pink is the second choice and crystal takes a back seat altogether. However, that crystal urn pictured is quite rare; so don't pass it by just because crystal is "not your thing". You could use it in trade or sell it and buy what you like.

I had previously stated that the ball-shaped lamp was the only piece I'd ever seen in amber. Please do notice those amber covered urns in BOTH sizes pictured in the pattern shot. They turned up at a Cleveland show!

	Crystal, Pink	Green		Crystal, Pink	Green
Bowl, 5" Handled	7.50	8.50	*Lamp, 5½" Round, Ball		
Bowl, 8¾" Covered	52.50	65.00	Shape	47.50	
Bowl, 9" Handled	9.50	13.50	Lamp, 8½" Tall	52.50	67.50
Bowl, 9¼" Covered	62.50	75.00	**Pitcher, 5" Covered Urn	77.50	117.50
Bowl, 10 3/8" Console	32.50	42.50	***Pitcher, 7" Covered Urn	97.50	127.50
Candlesticks, 6½" Pair	42.50	52.50	Plate, 8"	4.50	4.00
Candy Jar and Cover, 1 lb.	42.00	50.00	Plate, 11½" Handled	8.50	11.50
Candy Jar and Cover, 1½ lb.	52.50	62.50	Saucer	2.00	3.50
Cheese and Cracker Set			Sherbet, 3½"	5.50	8.50
(Indented Platter and Comport)	15.00	17.50	Sherbet, 4¾"	9.50	12.50
Coaster, 3½"	12.50	14.50	Sugar, 2¾"	5.00	6.00
Creamer, 2¾"	6.00	7.00	Sugar, 3½"	5.50	7.50
Creamer, 3½"	5.50	7.00	Tumbler, 5 oz. Juice	10.00	13.50
Cup	4.50	6.50	Tumbler, 4", 8 oz.	12.50	17.50
Dresser Set (2 Cologne,			Tumbler, 5", 12 oz.	15.00	27.50
Powder Jar, on Indented			Vase, 4¼", 16 oz. Footed		
7½" Tray)	77.50		Rose Bowl	37.50	55.00
Goblet, 4", 3 oz. Wine	12.50	17.50	Vase, 7", Four Styles	52.50	70.00
Goblet, 6", 8 oz. Water	15.00	18.50	Whiskey, 2¼", 2 oz.	30.00	32.50
Ice Bucket, 6"	17.50	27.50			

  *Amber $ 57.50
 **Amber $200.00
***Amber $250.00

Please refer to Foreword for pricing information

8

AMERICAN SWEETHEART   MACBETH-EVANS GLASS COMPANY, 1930-1936

Colors: Pink, monax, red, blue; some cremax and color rimmed monax.

Rarer items in this pattern are turning up with more regularity than in the past! For instance, within the past month a 7½", 60 oz. pitcher in American Sweetheart was found for $25.00; a 15½" monax plate turned up for $60.00; and best of all, a 15½" plate and an 18" console bowl in RED (pictured) surfaced at a garage sale for $5.00 each! Don't listen to those doom mongers who say there is nothing rare to be found anymore. It's out there just waiting for a knowledgeable collector!

Cremax, a beige color, is most frequently found in berry sets and lamp shades. That small bowl in the right foreground of the picture is cremax.

Lamp shades sometimes have orange, green, blue or brown panels down the sides. One floor lamp was discovered with a brass base having grooved panels that matched the vertical line panels in the shade. Collectors are hoping to find another one!

Pink shakers continue to be harder to find than the monax shakers although neither is exactly commonplace as reflected in their prices.

Monax sugar lids turn up on occasion; but they are quickly snapped up by diligent collectors. The lid, of course, is the most costly part of the sugar bowl. I realize it does sound odd to the uninformed that you will sell the complete bowl for $156.00 or sell them the sugar bottom for $6.50. Incredulity is the closest I can describe their expressions when told that. Though not as limited as first believed, demand for these lids keeps the price up.

A few more of the tiny, hat shaped bowls in American Sweetheart have been discovered.

The **miniature** version of the large console bowl with its broad, flat rim surfaced recently at a show in North Carolina and caused quite a stir! It's a rare little bowl about 6½" x 1¾" tall; but it's a treasure, so watch for it!

There is a good supply of monax at present; however, certain items in pink are hard to find. So, if pink is your pattern, complete it soon!

No one has found another vase like the one shown here in pink which looks like a glass with a neck on it. So far, this piece is unique---some factory worker's "pet" perhaps.

	Pink	Monax		Pink	Monax
Bowl, 3¾" Flat Berry	20.50		Plate, 15½" Server		150.00
Bowl, 4½" Cream Soup	18.50	35.00	Platter, 13" Oval	15.00	35.00
Bowl, 6" Cereal	8.00	9.50	Pitcher, 7½", 60 oz.	295.00	
Bowl, 9" Round Berry	14.00	32.50	Pitcher, 8", 80 oz.	237.50	
Bowl, 9½" Flat Soup	20.00	34.50	Salt and Pepper, Footed	225.00	210.00
Bowl, 11" Oval Vegetable	22.50	37.50	Saucer	2.50	2.50
Bowl, 18" Console		277.50	Sherbet, 4" Footed	10.50	
Creamer, Footed	6.50	7.00	Sherbet, 4¼" Footed		
Cup	8.50	8.00	(Design Inside or Outside)	8.50	13.50
Lampshade		425.00	Sherbet in Metal Holder (Crystal		
Plate, 6" Bread and Butter	2.50	3.50	Only) 3.00		
Plate, 8" Salad	5.00	6.00	Sugar, Open Footed	6.50	6.50
Plate, 9" Luncheon		7.50	Sugar Cover (Monax Only)*		150.00
Plate, 9¾" Dinner	13.50	13.50	Tidbit 3 Tier, 8", 12" & 15½"		127.50
Plate, 10¼" Dinner	13.50	13.50	Tumbler, 3½", 5 oz.	25.00	
Plate, 11" Chop Plate		11.00	Tumbler, 4", 9 oz.	23.50	
Plate, 12" Salver	9.00	11.00	Tumbler, 4½", 10 oz.	28.00	

*Two style knobs.

Please refer to Foreword for pricing information

11

AMERICAN SWEETHEART (Con't.)

Note the console bowl pictured here. It is the first amberina colored one to turn up. To me it is much prettier than the pure red.

The milky white monax color comes banded in gold or rim blushed with red, pink, green or "smoke" (blue-gray) coloring. Of those trims, the smoke is the most highly prized and the gold rimmed is the least desirable.

Luncheon pieces (cups, saucers, plates) appear more frequently in red American Sweetheart than in blue. Other pieces in these colors appear with equal rarity, however.

Some blue and red sherbets and plates have appeared with the American Sweetheart SHAPE but not having the pattern. These are considered more novel than rare at the moment. Remember if there is no pattern on these then they cannot truly be considered American Sweetheart.

	Red	Blue	Cremax	Smoke & Other Trims
Bowl, 6″ Cereal			7.25	22.50
Bowl, 9″ Round Berry			28.00	57.50
Bowl, 18″ Console	625.00	700.00		
Creamer, Footed	77.50	87.50		40.00
Cup	77.50	87.50		37.50
Lampshade			400.00	
Lamp (Floor with Brass Base)			600.00	
Plate, 6″ Bread and Butter				12.50
Plate, 8″ Salad	65.00	82.50		21.50
Plate, 9″ Luncheon				27.50
Plate, 9¾″ Dinner				40.00
Plate, 12″ Salver	127.50	152.50		
Plate, 15½″ Server	250.00	285.00		
Platter, 13″ Oval				72.50
Saucer	30.00	35.00		12.50
Sherbet, 4¼″ Footed (Design Inside or Outside)				25.00
Sugar, Open Footed	77.50	87.50		40.00
Tidbit, 3 Tier, 8″, 12″ & 15½″	425.00	525.00		

ANNIVERSARY JEANNETTE GLASS COMPANY, 1947-1949

Colors: Pink (recently in crystal and iridescent).

Lately, there has been an upsurge of interest in pink Anniversary. Since the supply of this seems rather limited, this may soon cause a rise in prices. Strictly speaking, this pattern is a "cousin" to Depression Glass having been made in the late forties; however, it's being sought by Depression Glass devotees, so it's included as such.

Larger pieces of Anniversary such as the fruit bowl, candy dish, sandwich server and butter dish, are hard to locate. It will help if you will tell every dealer you see what you're looking for; that way, you'll have help in your looking. This advice holds true for any pattern. Dealers tend to remember what they're specifically asked to find; and mostly, they're glad to help you search for an item.

This listing is from a 1947 Jeannette catalogue. You will notice that what we refer to as a "compote", they called a "comport".

One word of warning: crystal and iridized Anniversary were made as late as 1970! If you like it and want to buy it, that's fine; just don't be duped into believing that the iridized is a form of "Carnival" glass and pay prices best suited to truly old glass.

Caution: As we go to press, I have received reports of a crystal luncheon set now being re-introduced.

	Crystal	Pink		Crystal	Pink
Bowl, 4 7/8" Berry	1.50	2.00	Plate, 6¼" Sherbet	1.25	2.00
Bowl, 7 3/8" Soup	3.00	6.00	Plate, 9" Dinner	3.50	4.50
Bowl, 9" Fruit	7.00	11.00	Plate, 12½" Sandwich Server	4.00	6.50
Butter Dish and Cover	22.00	40.00	Relish Dish, 8"	4.50	6.50
Candy Jar and Cover	15.00	25.00	Saucer	1.00	1.50
*Comport, Open 3 Legged	3.00	6.50	Sherbet, Footed	2.50	4.50
Cake Plate, 12½"	5.50	8.00	Sugar	2.00	4.50
Cake Plate and Cover	10.00	12.50	Sugar Covers	3.00	4.50
Candlestick, 4 7/8" Pair	12.50		Vase, 6½"	6.00	9.00
Creamer, Footed	3.00	6.00	Vase, Wall Pin-up	10.00	12.00
Cup	2.00	4.00	Wine Glass, 2½ oz.	5.50	8.50
Pickle Dish, 9"	3.00	5.00			

*Old form; presently called compote.   Open compote or candy.

AUNT POLLY U.S. GLASS COMPANY, Late 1920's

Colors: Blue, green, iridescent.

A catalogue has now surfaced proving my theory that U.S. Glass did indeed make Aunt Polly as well as her sister patterns of Strawberry and Floral and Diamond.

Shakers, covered sugar and oval bowl remain the most elusive pieces of this pattern. Coffee lovers should notice that company catalogue listings do not mention any cups and saucers for Aunt Polly or her sister patterns.

Most of the pieces listed have shown up in either green or iridescent, but not all have surfaced in both. Until they do, I'll continue to lump those two colors into one listing. To date, a set can only be garnered in the blue.

The iridescent butter is perhaps harder to find than the green; yet the prices for both remain about the same.

The blue color of Aunt Polly is very pleasing to the eye and the pattern itself seems quite durable.

	Green, Iridescent	Blue		Green, Iridescent	Blue
Bowl, 4 3/8" Berry	4.00	4.50	Creamer	15.00	20.00
Bowl, 4¾", 2" High	8.50	11.00	Pitcher, 8", 48 oz.		92.50
Bowl, 7¼" Oval, Handled Pickle	8.50	11.00	Plate, 6" Sherbet	2.50	3.50
			Plate, 8" Luncheon		6.50
Bowl, 7 7/8" Large Berry	10.00	15.00	Salt and Pepper		137.50
Bowl, 8 3/8" Oval	17.50	22.50	Sherbet	7.50	7.00
Butter Dish and Cover	137.50	125.00	Sugar	11.00	13.50
Candy, Cover, Two Handled	22.50	32.50	Sugar Cover	27.50	37.50
			Tumbler, 3 5/8", 8 oz.		12.50
			Vase, 6½" Footed	20.00	25.00

Please refer to Foreword for pricing information

14

AVOCADO, No. 601 INDIANA GLASS COMPANY, 1923-1933

Colors: Pink, green, crystal.   *(See Reproduction Section)*

In my previous book I mentioned that pitchers and salad bowls were turning up in white in this pattern; so, I have included them for you to see this time. I still can't conclusively document that these were made in the 1950's; but it seems logical since Indiana put out numerous other items in this color in that time period.

The drastic jump in prices experienced by Avocado between the third and fourth edition has finally reached a plateau; in some few cases, the prices have lowered somewhat from what they were a few short months ago. Higher prices tend to bring pieces "out of the woodwork" so to speak; and this has recently been true in Avocado. Once collectors have bought up this flurry of supply, the prices may spiral again.

Saucers remain harder to find than the cups. Green pitcher and tumbler sets are almost non-existent in the market. Collectors have them tucked away. Sherbets seem more plentiful than they were first believed to be.

The reproduced pink tumblers and pitcher put out for the Tiara Exclusive Home Products line has depressed the market for the old pink Avocado even though they appeared back in 1973 and tend to be of a more orange hue than the original pink pitcher sets. Someday the glass companies will wake up to the fact that "re-issuing" a product in the original colors does not endear them to the collecting public; rather it may turn them away from their products altogether. So far, the pitcher and tumbler sets are all that Indiana has made for the Tiara line in Avocado. See the Reproduction Section at the back of the book for further comments about these.

A few pieces have turned up with an apple design rather than the avocado; these tend to be viewed more as oddities than anything else. Tiara recently remade these, by the way.

	Pink	Green		Pink	Green
Bowl, 5¼", Two-Handled	17.50	20.00	*Pitcher, 64 ozs.	250.00	400.00
Bowl, 6" Footed Relish	13.50	18.50	Plate, 6¼" Sherbet	6.50	9.50
Bowl, 7" One Handle Preserve	11.50	13.50	**Plate, 8¼" Luncheon	10.00	13.50
Bowl, 7½" Salad	22.50	35.00	Plate, 10¼" Two Handled		
Bowl, 8" Two-Handled Oval	13.50	17.50	Cake	20.00	29.50
Bowl, 8½" Berry	27.50	32.50	Saucer	17.50	20.00
Bowl, 9½", 3¼" Deep	42.50	62.50	Sherbet	42.50	47.50
Creamer, Footed	22.50	27.50	Sugar, Footed	22.50	27.50
Cup, Footed	23.00	25.00	*Tumbler	67.50	97.50

Set of 6 Salad or Dessert Plates

Made of good quality glass. Attractive green pear and leaf design, making a strikingly novel plate in eccentric shape. Diameter, 8½ inches. Weight, packed, 6 pounds.
35N1641—Set of 6..............98c

*Caution on pink. The orangeish-pink is new!
**Apple Design $10.00. Amber has been newly made.

Please refer to Foreword for pricing information

BEADED BLOCK IMPERIAL GLASS COMPANY, 1927-1930's

Colors: Pink, green, crystal, ice blue, vaseline, iridescent, amber, red and opalescent.

Beaded Block is one of those patterns of Depression Glass that will cause you to be informed that you're looking at "Carnival", "Vaseline" or even the older "Pattern" glass. In fact, one antique dealer told me I had really spoiled his liking for this pattern when he found out it was Depression Glass! Until then he'd thought he was dealing in "better' glassware exclusively.

Actually, Beaded Block is "better" glassware than most of the machine molded Depression glass since it had some hand work performed on it to achieve the fluting of the bowls for example. You may also notice that many of the bowls were made by turning up the edges of the plates—something also accomplished by hand.

Some of the opalescent and vaseline colored pieces, which are as pretty as any of the finer glasswares made during that era, tend to command higher prices---sometimes even "out of sight" prices at antique shows. Only you can decide what a particular piece is "worth" to you. When I feel a price is exorbitant, I pass the item by if I can't convince its owner to moderate it.

Imperial called the two-handled "carnival" colored bowl a "jelly" rather than a soup. The taller, footed bowls are "footed jellies" rather than compotes; and the opalescent blue piece in the center is their vase rather than a parfait.

The iridized pink items showing up at the flea markets around the country are of recent vintage. Imperial still makes these today. Some few other pieces of this design have turned up, but they have an "IG" embossed in the bottom, a symbol Imperial has used these last thirty years.

	Crystal*, Pink, Green, Amber	Other Colors		Crystal*, Pink, Green, Amber	Other Colors
Bowl, 4½", 2 Handled Jelly	5.50	12.00	Bowl, 7½" Round, Plain Edge	7.00	12.50
**Bowl, 4½" Round Lily	8.50	14.50	Bowl, 8¼" Celery	8.50	13.00
Bowl, 5½" Square	5.00	7.00	Creamer	8.50	15.00
Bowl, 5½" Blue One Handle	6.50	8.00	Pitcher, 5¼", Pint Jug	117.50	
Bowl, 6" Deep Round	8.00	12.50	Plate, 7¾" Square	4.50	7.50
Bowl, 6¼" Round	6.50	12.50	Plate, 8¾" Round	5.00	10.00
Bowl, 6½" Round	6.50	12.50	Stemmed Jelly, 4½"	6.50	12.50
Bowl, 6½" 2 Handled Pickle	9.50	14.00	Stemmed Jelly, 4½", Flared		
Bowl, 6¾" Round Unflared	8.50	12.00	Top	8.50	15.00
Bowl, 7¼" Round Flared	7.50	14.00	Sugar	9.00	15.00
Bowl, 7½" Round, Fluted			Vase, 6" Bouquet	7.50	15.00
Edges	17.50	19.50			

*All pices except pitcher, 25% to 40% lower.
**Red: $45.00.

"BOWKNOT" UNKNOWN MANUFACTURER, Probably late 1920's

Color: Green.

Even though my wife and a few other people in the world think this is a "darling" pattern, there are still only seven different pieces known to exist at this time. It seems very strange to me that a company would make a cup with no saucer or punch bowl; so, I keep expecting to hear that someone, somewhere has found one or the other.

I've received numerous letters from people who believe they have a creamer or sugar that is "Bowknot" and thus an unlisted piece. Invariable, these have turned out to be Fostoria's "June" pattern which is included in this book for the first time. So, before you write, check your sugar or creamer closely against this pattern and against the "June".

We dusted the embossing on the underside of the plate hoping you could get a better idea of the "Bowknot" pattern.

One bright spot here is that in collecting an eight place setting, you'd only have to buy 56 pieces to complete your set!

	Green			Green
Bowl, 4½" Berry	7.50	Sherbet, Low Footed		7.50
Bowl, 5½" Cereal	9.50	Tumbler, 5", 10 oz.		8.50
Cup	6.50	Tumbler, 5", 10 oz. Footed		8.50
Plate, 7" Salad	5.50			

Please refer to Foreword for pricing information

BLOCK OPTIC, "BLOCK" HOCKING GLASS COMPANY, 1929-1933

Colors: Green, pink, yellow, crystal.

It used to be that Block Optic was recommended to those persons wanting a less expensive pattern to collect; however, so many people have liked this pattern and have begun seeking the harder to get pieces that supply isn't keeping up with demand; and therefore, the prices continue to increase on the harder to find items.

Too, for the sake of collectors of pink Block Optic who are beginning to fuss about the higher prices occuring in various pieces of the green, I am splitting these colors up in this book for more accurate pricing information on each color.

Yellow Block Optic is still very beautiful but in scant supply; and the prices reflect this.

The black stemmed or footed pieces remain unpopular with collectors even though they are relatively scarce.

In gathering the pieces for the photograph, I made an interesting discovery. There are not three styles of creamers and sugars in Block Optic, but five! Notice the two styles of handles on the cone shaped sugars and creamers pictured; the two styles of handles on the shorter sugars; and the flat bottomed sugar and creamer pictured separately. That's just what you needed to go with those four different cup styles (notice shapes and handle variations) and the two different sizes of saucers, right? It is permissible to use the sherbet plates for saucers for the cups as in some cases, they were originally sold that way; and finding the saucers with the cup ring that fits your particular style of cup is getting harder and harder to do.

That squatty, bulbous pitcher on the extreme right has not been listed before and is not easily found in pink. It is 7 5/8" high and holds 68 ounces.

The cone shaped sherbet shown at the right of the butter dish is readily available as are luncheon and sherbet plates. Dinner plates, however, are getting fewer and farther between.

The rectangular butter dish is the only one found in Block Optic pattern to date. If you think you have a round butter dish in Block, please refer to Colonial Block pattern to see if that's the one you have.

The cone shaped mayonnaise pictured at the left of the butter dish has disappeared from the market recently. Scarce, too, are candlesticks, squatty shakers, vases, tumble-ups (a jug with an inverted drinking glass serving as a top), mugs and 4" cocktail glasses (in either pink or green).

Collectors of Block Optic should notice that many of their pieces have shapes similar to the very popular Cameo pattern which was also made by Hocking.

	Green	Yellow	Pink		Green	Yellow	Pink
Bowl, 4¼" Berry	4.00		4.00	Plate, 9" Dinner	10.50	12.50	15.00
Bowl, 5¼" Cereal	6.00	7.50	5.00	Plate, 9" Grill	6.50		9.50
Bowl, 7" Salad	8.50	10.50	7.50	Plate, 10¼" Sandwich	12.00		12.00
Bowl, 8½" Large Berry	9.50	15.00	8.50	Salt and Pepper, Footed	19.50	52.50	39.50
Butter Dish and Cover, 3" x 5"	27.50			Salt and Pepper, Squatty	25.00		
Candlesticks, 1¾" Pr.	22.50		22.50	Sandwich Server, Center Handle	27.50		27.50
Candy Jar and Cover, 2¼"	21.50	37.50	25.00	Saucer, 5¾"	4.50		4.50
Candy Jar Cover, 6¼"	27.50			Saucer, 6 1/8"	4.50	7.50	4.50
Comport, 4" Wide Mayonnaise	12.50			Sherbet, Non Stemmed (Cone)	3.00		
Creamer, Three Styles: Cone				Sherbet, 3¼", 5½ oz.	4.50	7.50	4.00
Shaped, Round Footed and				Sherbet, 4¾", 6 oz.	8.50	10.50	7.50
Flat (5 Kinds)	7.50	8.50	7.50	Sugar, Three Styles: As Creamer	7.50	8.50	7.50
Cup, Four Styles	4.00	5.00	3.50	Tumbler, 3½", 5 oz. Flat	10.00		10.00
Goblet, 4" Cocktail	12.50		11.50	Tumbler, 4", 5 oz. Footed	9.50		11.50
Goblet, 4½" Wine	11.50		10.00	Tumbler, 9 oz. Flat	7.50		7.00
Goblet, 5¾", 9 oz.	11.50		10.00	Tumbler, 9 oz. Footed	10.00	12.00	9.00
Goblet, 7¼", 9 oz. Thin	17.50	15.00	12.00	Tumbler, 10 oz. Flat	10.00		8.50
Ice Bucket	25.00		22.50	Tumbler, 6", 10 oz Footed	12.50	15.00	12.50
Ice Tub or Butter Tub, Open	18.50			Tumble-up Night Set: 3" Tumbler			
Mug, Flat Creamer, No Spout	25.00			Bottle and Tumbler, 6" High	39.50		
Pitcher, 7 5/8", 68 oz., Bulbous	27.50		37.50	Vase, 5¾", Blown	125.00		
Pitcher, 8½", 64 oz.	25.00		25.00	Whiskey, 2½"	12.50		11.50
Pitcher, 8", 80 oz.	30.00		29.50				
Plate, 6" Sherbet	2.00	2.25	1.50				
Plate, 8" Luncheon	3.00	3.75	2.50				

Please refer to Foreword for pricing information

"BUBBLE", "BULLSEYE", "PROVINCIAL"
ANCHOR HOCKING GLASS COMPANY, 1934-1965

Colors: Pink, light blue, dark green, red, crystal.

"Bubble" is the rather apt name given this pattern by collectors over the years. It was originally issued by Hocking in a pink, 8¾" bowl (pictured) called "Bullseye". In 1937, crystal and dark green were introduced. Then, in 1942, after the merger of Anchor and Hocking, the pale blue "Fire King" line was introduced and continued throughout the 40's. This dinnerware was guaranteed to be "heat-proof" and their advertisements stated that this tableware "can be used in the oven, on the table, in the refrigerator". This was certainly a unique feature for Depression Glass as most of it will not stand up to quick changes in temperature. The ruby red pitchers and tumblers were issued in the mid 1960's under the name "Provincial".

Another 9" flanged bowl has been found in Ohio this year; but I have not heard of any other. You see it pictured in the pattern shot. To see a really unique Bubble bowl, however, you need to turn to the Moonstone pattern. That opalescent "bubble" bowl shown still has the original label on it: "Moonstone".

The price and scarcity of the blue creamer keeps pulling the price of the sugar bowl up also. Some dealers are refusing to sell the pieces separately. Sugar bowls are much more plentiful for some obscure reason.

I recently heard of a blue comport, but I was unable to confirm this piece. Keep a weather eye out for it. If you turn it up, I'd appreciate a snapshot.

You may find that 8¾" bowl in almost any color that Anchor Hocking made from jadite to fired-on pink. That same berry bowl in pink was made in abundance; so don't pay a high price for it even if you've never seen pink Bubble before. While visiting the factory I saw bushels of them in storage.

I can find no reference in any of my materials regarding the amber cup shown. Evidently this was experimental or a short lived issue. Some iridized pieces have surfaced in bowls and cups and saucers; I've found no supporting reference on these either. Just be aware that they do exist and are considered to be interesting rather than extremely rare.

Some collectors are buying the crystal stemmed Anchor Hocking pieces with red or green tops to go with their Bubble. These sherbet and goblet shaped pieces were made in the 1950's and have knobby, bubble-like crystal feet.

	Dark Green	Light Blue	Ruby Red		Dark Green	Light Blue	Ruby Red
Bowl, 4" Berry	2.50	6.50		Plate, 6¾" Bread and			
Bowl, 4½" Fruit	2.50	4.50	3.50	Butter	1.50	2.50	
Bowl, 5¼" Cereal	2.50	4.50		Plate, 9 3/8" Grill		6.50	
Bowl, 7¾" Flat Soup		7.50		Plate, 9 3/8" Dinner	4.00	4.50	5.50
Bowl, 8 3/8" Large Berry				Platter, 12" Oval		7.50	
(Pink—$2.50)	6.00	7.50		***Saucer	1.00	2.50	2.50
Bowl, 9" Flanged		32.50		Sugar	4.50	9.50	
Candlesticks (Crystal -				Tidbit (2 Tier)			15.00
$10.00 Pr.)	15.00			Tumbler, 6 oz. Juice			5.50
Creamer	4.50	16.50		Tumbler, 9 oz. Water			5.00
*Cup	2.00	3.00	4.00	Tumbler, 12 oz. Iced Tea			8.50
Lamp, 2 Styles, Crystal Only - 19.50				Tumbler, 16 oz.			
**Pitcher, 64 oz. Ice Lip			32.50	Lemonade			13.50

*Pink — $27.50.
**Crystal — $25.00
***Pink — $17.50.

Please refer to Foreword for pricing information

23

CAMEO, "BALLERINA" or "DANCING GIRL"   HOCKING GLASS COMPANY, 1930-1934

Colors: Green, yellow, pink and crystal with platinum rim.   *(See Reproduction Section)*

Cameo is one of the top five most collectible patterns in Depression Glass and one of the most easily recognized! No one has trouble spotting that "ballerina" or "dancing girl". However, Cameo, as no other pattern, contains a number of rarely seen or one-of-a-kind items that make owning a **complete** set virtually impossible. Naturally, being one of the most desired patterns and having so many rarely found pieces also places this pattern into the "expensive to own" bracket. **Very basic sets can still be gathered** easily without putting too large a dent in your bank account; but be warned that "frill" pieces in Cameo are going to be costly. There's a host of competition for them.

Although there are many Cameo collectors, there has not been such a fevered pitch to obtain the higher priced items as in the past; so there are not many **large** increases in prices this time. There has been a steady rise in all prices instead.

Cameo saucers with an indented ring are perhaps the rarest saucers in Depression Glass; but there is a limit to what most collectors will pay for a saucer.

Other hard to get items include the jam jar, cream soups, decanters with stoppers (also sold as water bottles without stoppers in 1931 catalogue), footed juices and the domino drip tray. The latter item was called thus because it had an inner circle in which the creamer fitted and the outer circle was used to hold (Domino brand?) sugar cubes. One is pictured on the left front of the photograph.

I finally got a picture of the Cameo oil lamp (very rare); unfortunately, it was so poor we couldn't use it. It has a foot, stem, bulbous oil container and a No. 3 burner screws onto it.

Recent finds in Cameo have included a couple of green sandwich servers, a CRYSTAL jam jar and pitcher (shown on rare page in back of book), a cocktail shaker, and a set of six pink water goblets! Thus, rarities ARE being found still; and yes, some people ARE still giving away valuable dishes. I just attended a mall show in Alabama last week and some elderly lady walked past my table and gasped, "You can't MEAN that these old dishes are WORTH anything! Why, I just gave away a whole box load of those green dishes like that (she pointed to Cameo) to the Goodwill Store last week!" After being associated with Depression Glass these past ten years, you tend to think EVERYBODY knows about Depression Glass; nothing could be further from the truth! There's a vast amount of people in these United States who are STILL just as ignorant about the value of Depression Glass as if no books had ever been written on the subject, no shows ever been held or clubs ever been formed or such glass had never been placed in the Smithsonian Institution as a valuable part of our heritage.

I have heard no new reports regarding any other yellow syrup pitcher surfacing in Cameo; the one which has turned up has a very weak Cameo pattern design. I emphasize here that to be considered to be Cameo, pitchers must have the pattern and not just be the SHAPE of Cameo.

Watch for those center handled servers!

As we go to press we understand a private individual is having Cameo shakers made in pink! If possible, we'll get them photographed and/or described in the Reproduction Section at the back.

CAMEO, "BALLERINA" or "DANCING GIRL" (Con't.)

	Green	Yellow	Pink	Crys/ Plat
Bowl, 4¼" Sauce				4.00
Bowl, 4¾" Cream Soup	42.50			
Bowl, 5½" Cereal	12.00	13.50		3.00
Bowl, 7¼" Salad	22.50			
Bowl, 8¼" Large Berry	22.50	32.50		
Bowl, 9" Rimmed Soup	25.00			
Bowl, 10" Oval Vegetable	10.00	17.50		
Bowl, 11", 3 Leg Console	39.00	52.50	17.50	
Butter Dish and Cover	122.50	625.00		
Cake Plate, 10", 3 Legs	12.50			
Cake Plate, 10½" Flat	47.50			
Candlesticks, 4" Pr.	62.50			
Candy Jar, 4" Low and Cover	37.50	47.50	350.00	
Candy Jar, 6½" Tall and Cover	87.50			
Cocktail Shaker (Metal Lid) Appears in Crystal Only				175.00
Comport, 5" Wide Mayonnaise	17.50			
Cookie Jar and Cover	32.50			
Creamer, 3¼"	15.50	12.00		
Creamer, 4¼"	15.00		47.50	
Cup, Two Styles	10.00	6.50	47.50	
Decanter, 10" With Stopper	62.50			
Decanter, 10" With Stopper, Frosted (Stopper Represents ½ Value of Decanter)	21.50			
Domino Tray, 7" With 3" Indentation	52.50			
Domino Tray, 7" With No Indentation			147.50	87.50
Goblet, 3½" Wine	95.00			
Goblet, 4" Wine	42.50		165.00	
Goblet, 6" Water	30.00		100.00	
Ice Bowl or Open Butter, 3" Tall x 5½" Wide	87.50		400.00	175.00
Jam Jar, 2" and Cover	72.50			97.50
Pitcher, 5¾", 20 oz. Syrup or Milk	125.00	177.50		
Pitcher, 6", 36 oz. Juice	35.00			
Pitcher, 8½", 56 oz. Water	32.50			225.00
Plate, 6" Sherbet	2.50	2.00	45.00	1.75
Plate, 7" Salad				3.00
Plate, 8" Luncheon	6.00	2.50	23.00	3.50
Plate, 8½" Square	20.50	55.00		
Plate, 9½" Dinner	10.50	6.00	30.00	
Plate, 10" Sandwich	8.00		30.00	
Plate, 10½" Grill	7.00	6.00	32.50	
Plate, 10½" Grill With Closed Handles	27.50	5.75		
Plate, 11½" With Closed Handles	6.50	5.00		
Platter, 12", Closed Handles	12.50	13.50		
Relish, 7½" Footed, 3 Part	12.50	47.50		
*Salt and Pepper, Footed Pr.	45.00		450.00	
Sandwich Server, Center Handle	1,250.00			
Saucer With Cup Ring	47.50			
Saucer 6" (Sherbet Plate)	2.50	1.75	35.00	
Sherbet, 3 1/8"	9.00	15.00	25.00	
Sherbet, 4 7/8"	20.00	22.50	47.50	
Sugar, 3¼"	9.50	9.50		
Sugar, 4¼"	13.50		42.50	
Tumbler, 3¾", 5 oz. Juice	16.00		55.00	
Tumbler, 4", 9 oz. Water	14.50		55.00	7.50
Tumbler, 4¾", 10 oz. Flat	16.50			
Tumbler, 5", 11 oz. Flat	16.50	22.50	67.50	
Tumbler, 5¼", 15 oz.	27.50			
Tumbler, 3 oz. Footed Juice	35.00		77.50	
Tumbler, 5", 9 oz. Footed	15.50	11.50	72.50	
Tumbler, 5¾", 11 oz. Footed	25.00			
Tumbler, 6 3/8", 15 oz. Footed	150.00			
Vase, 5¾"	87.50			
Vase, 8"	17.50			
Water Bottle (Dark Green) Whitehouse Vinegar	17.50			

*Beware Reproductions

Please refer to Foreword for pricing information

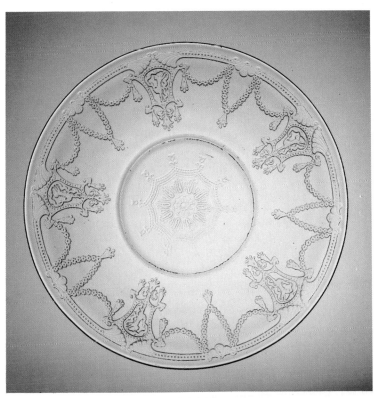

27

CAPRICE   CAMBRIDGE GLASS COMPANY

Colors: Crystal, blue, amethyst, amber, pink.

The inclusion of this pattern has been forced on me as so many people have started collecting it; and it is invariably found at any Depression Glass shows I attend. Strictly speaking, this isn't Depression Glass per se; it's better glass than that. However, it was made during the era that Depression Glass collecting encompasses. So, we include it here as Depression Era glass.

Most people prize the blue color of Caprice more highly than crystal as you'll notice from the prices listed.

Pitchers in amber and amethyst are quite hard to find, particularly the tall 90 oz. Daulton style.

Frankly, I don't yet have the "feel" for this better glassware that I have for the other Depression Glass. I don't know its little idiosyncrasies too well. I'm just learning. So, for now, here's my best shot! (This listing is not complete; but I thought there'd be enough to "be going on").

	Crystal	Pink, Amber, Blue		Crystal	Pink, Amber, Blue
Ash Tray, 2¾", 3 Footed	5.00	7.00	Goblet, 1 oz. Cordial	25.00	45.00
Ash Tray, 3"	5.00	8.00	Goblet, 2½ oz. Wine	20.00	35.00
Ash Tray, 4"	6.00	10.00	Goblet, 3 oz. Cocktail	18.00	35.00
Ash Tray, 5"	7.00	12.00	Goblet, 4½ oz. Oyster		
Bon Bon, 6" Sq., Footed	12.00	18.00	Cocktail	12.00	27.50
Bon Bon, 6" Sq., 2 Handled	12.00	18.00	Goblet, 4½ oz. Claret	15.00	35.00
Bowl, 5", 2 Handled Jelly	10.00	20.00	Goblet, 9 oz. Water	16.00	24.00
Bowl, 6½" Handled, 2 Pt.			Ice Bucket	35.00	50.00
Relish	12.00	19.00	Mayonnaise, 6½", 3 Pc. Set	15.00	25.00
Bowl, 8", 3 Pt. Relish	19.00	29.00	Mayonnaise, 8", 3 Pc. Set	18.00	32.50
Bowl, 10½" Crimped, 4			Oil, 3 oz. w/Stopper	9.50	27.50
Footed	25.00	39.00	Pickle, 9"	7.50	17.50
Bowl, 11", 2 Handled Oval, 4			Pitcher, 32 oz. Ball	32.50	67.50
Footed	25.00	39.00	Pitcher, 80 oz., Ball	47.50	97.00
Bowl, 12½" Bellied, 4 Footed	29.00	42.50	*Pitcher, 90 oz. Tall Daulton		
Bowl, 12½" Crimped, 4			Style	97.50	175.00
Footed	29.00	42.00	Plate, 6½" Bread & Butter	4.00	8.00
Bowl, 13" Crimped, 4 Footed	29.00	42.00	Plate, 6½" Handled Lemon	7.00	15.00
Bowl, 13½", 4 Footed Bail			Plate, 7½" Salad	6.00	11.50
Shallow Cupped	29.00	42.00	Plate, 8" Low Footed	10.00	15.00
Cake Plate, 13" Footed	17.50	32.50	Plate, 8½" Salad	7.50	12.50
Candlestick, 2½" Pair	22.00	38.00	Plate, 9½" Dinner	12.00	25.00
Candlestick, 5" Pair	25.00	40.00	Plate, 11" Cabaret, 4 Footed	20.00	30.00
Candlestick, 7" Pair w/Prism	39.00	55.00	Plate, 11½" Cabaret	22.00	35.00
Candlestick, 2 Lite, Each	30.00	40.00	Plate, 14"	20.00	35.00
Candlestick, 3 Lite, Each	40.00	50.00	Plate, 14" Cabaret, 4 Footed	25.00	35.00
Candy, 6", 3 Footed w/Cover	30.00	50.00	Salt & Pepper, Pair	20.00	50.00
Celery & Relish, 8½", 3 Pt.	21.00	30.00	Saucer	4.00	8.00
Cigarette Jar w/Cover, 3½" x			Sherbet, 6 oz. Low	15.00	25.00
2¼"	19.00	29.00	Sherbet, 6 oz. High	18.00	30.00
Cigarette Jar w/Cover, 4½" x			Sugar, Individual	9.00	14.00
3½"	20.00	32.50	Sugar, Several Styles	8.00	15.00
Coaster, 3½"	3.50	10.00	Tray, For Sugar and Creamer	8.00	12.00
Comport, 7" Low Footed	15.00	22.00	Tray, 6" Oval	4.00	9.50
Comport, 7" Tall	18.00	30.00	Vase, 5" Ivy Bowl	20.00	32.50
Creamer, Individual	10.00	15.00	Vase, 8" Ivy Bowl	27.50	47.50
Creamer, Several Styles	8.00	15.00	Vase, 6"	19.50	30.00
Cup	7.00	20.00	Vase, 7½"	25.50	37.50
Decanter w/Stopper, 36 oz.	37.50	67.50	Vase, 9½"	32.50	47.50

*Amethyst — $350.00

Please refer to Foreword for pricing information

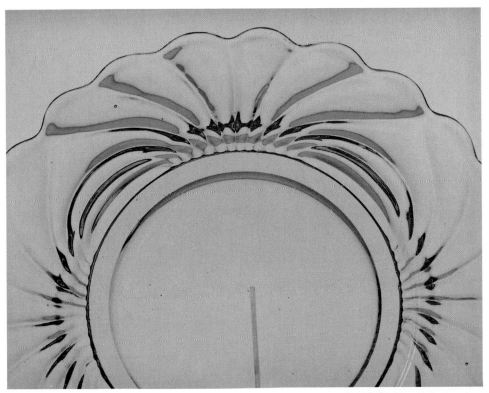

CHERRY BLOSSOM JEANNETTE GLASS COMPANY, 1930-1939

Colors: Pink, green, delphite (opaque blue), crystal, jadite (opaque green), red.
(See Reproduction Section)

In order to show a complete range of pieces in Cherry Blossom, I have included both the picture taken for the last book and the one made for this one. I realize there is some duplication, particularly with the 9" pink platter and the red bowl; but how often do you get to see those pieces even once?

Cherry Blossom is another of the top five most desirable patterns in Depression Glass. It, like Cameo, is easily recognized and has an abundance of pieces to collect. It, too, is readily available; there seems to be a lot of it around. All these reasons combine to make this pattern a prime target for the reproduction artisan, however; and some pieces have been reproduced. Most of these reproductions are shown and discussed at length at the back of the book. I will discuss the child's pieces here as they have obtained a sort of tolerance since their appearance in 1973.

First to appear was a child's cherry cup with a slightly lop-sided handle and having the cherries hanging upside down when the cup was held in the right hand. (This defiance of gravity was due to the inversion of the design when the mold, taken from an original cup, was inverted to create the outside of the "new" cup). After I reported this error, it was quickly corrected by re-inverting the inverted mold. These later cups were thus improved in design but slightly off color. The saucers tended to have slightly off center designs, too. Next came the "child's" butter dish which was never made by Jeannette. It was essentially the child's cup without a handle turned upside down over the saucer and having a little glob of glass added as a knob for lifting purposes. You could get this item in pink, green, light blue, cobalt, gray-green, and iridescent carnival colors.

I get more letters about two pieces in Cherry Blossom than any other pattern. That two handled green tray in the center of the top picture is listed as tray, 10½" sandwich. A similar tray has been found without handles; and another tray has been found divided by a circular middle and having raised divisions running off the center circle. Look for these last two pieces as they are real "finds".

The second piece I get letters about is the crystal, two handled bowl pictured in the lower photo. This is a very common piece which sells in the $10.00 - $12.00 range.

An amber sugar has now been found to go with the amber cup and saucer; so possibly a creamer and plates may exist making a unique child's set!

The green shakers shown here as well as the pink ones on the next page are the original! The pink pair is **one of the two pairs known to exist**. See the Reproduction Section for a discussion of how to identify the old shakers from those newly made. Remember too that the butter dishes, pitcher and tumblers in the all over pattern (AOP), scalloped bottom, have also been reproduced and are pictured and discussed in that same section. Luckily, reproductions, to date, are rather poorly made and easily spotted by the informed collector. Being informed and subscribing to a good monthly trade publication will keep you out of the hands of the unscrupulous. Be wary of too good a deal, also. I've had people write me and tell of dealers telling them that so and so is listed in the book for $300.00, but they'll let it go for $20.00. Now, who in their right mind would deal like that?

Prices of Cherry Blossom have generally creeped higher with the cereal bowl and grill plates jumping considerably since the last book.

Hopefully, somebody will find another piece of red cherry like the bowl, plate or tumbler shown; or perhaps another piece of translucent green will appear like the plate shown in the right foreground. There's always the feeling that at that next market or garage sale another unknown piece will surface!

The letters AOP in the price listing refer to pieces having an "all over pattern"; PAT means "pattern at the top" only.

See page 32 for prices.

CHERRY BLOSSOM (Con't.)

	Pink	Green	Delphite	Jadite
Bowl, 4¾" Berry	7.50	9.00	10.00	
Bowl, 5¾" Cereal	19.50	17.50		
Bowl, 7¾" Flat Soup	30.00	32.50		
*Bowl, 8½" Round Berry	12.50	14.50	39.50	
Bowl, 9" Oval Vegetable	15.00	16.50	41.50	
Bowl, 9" 2 Handled	13.50	16.50	12.50	275.00
Bowl, 10½", 3 Leg Fruit	32.50	35.00		275.00
Butter Dish and Cover	60.00	72.50		
Cake Plate (3 Legs) 10¼"	15.00	16.00		
Coaster	10.50	9.50		
Creamer	10.00	12.00	16.00	
Cup	12.00	13.00	14.00	
Mug, 7 oz.	137.50	127.50		
Pitcher 6¾" AOP, 36 oz. Scalloped or Round Bottom	30.00	37.50		
Pitcher, 8" PAT, 42 oz. Flat	27.50	32.50		
Pitcher, 8" PAT, 36 oz. Footed	30.00	42.50	80.00	
Plate, 6" Sherbet	4.50	5.00	8.50 (design on top)	
Plate, 7" Salad	12.50	13.00		
**Plate, 9" Dinner	10.50	13.50	11.00	30.00
Plate, 9" Grill	15.50	15.50		
Plate, 10" Grill		35.00		
Platter, 9" Oval	625.00			
Platter, 11" Oval	18.50	20.00	30.00	
Platter, 13" and 13" Divided	32.00	35.00		
Salt and Pepper (Scalloped Bottom)	900.00	600.00		
Saucer	4.00	3.50	4.25	
Sherbet	9.50	10.50	10.00	
Sugar	8.00	10.00	16.00	
Sugar Cover	12.00	12.00		
Tray, 10½" Sandwich	12.50	15.00	13.00	
Tumbler, 3¾", 4 oz. Footed AOP, Round or Scalloped	11.00	14.50	16.00	
Tumbler, 4½", 9 oz. Round Foot AOP	22.50	25.00	16.50	
***Tumbler, 4½", 8 oz. Scalloped Foot AOP	22.50	25.00	16.50	
Tumbler, 3½", 4 oz. Flat PAT	12.00	12.00		
Tumbler, 4¼", 9 oz. Flat PAT	12.00	16.50		
Tumbler, 5", 12 oz. Flat PAT	27.50	35.00		

*Yellow — $350.00.   Red — $375.00.
**Translucent Green, Red — $165.00
***Red — $175.00

CHERRY BLOSSOM — CHILD'S JUNIOR DINNER SET

	Pink	Delphite
Creamer	20.00	21.50
Sugar	20.00	21.50
Plate, 6"	7.25	8.25 (design on bottom)
Cup	17.50	20.00
Saucer	4.00	4.50
14 Piece Set	137.50	167.50

Original box sells for $10.00 extra with these sets.

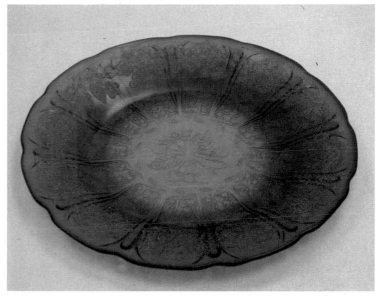

CHINEX CLASSIC

MACBETH-EVANS DIVISION OF CORNING GLASS WORKS, Late 1930's · Early 1940's

Colors: Ivory, ivory decal decorated.

There are few collectors of Chinex due mostly to its relative scarcity. It's hard to get excited about collecting something you rarely see no matter how attractive it is!

The castle decaled pieces are true "finds" in Chinex.

The 7" soup bowl has surged in price recently!

Chinex has an embossed scroll-like design in the dishes which distinguishes it from the plainer Cremax pattern. However, this scrolling is found only on the lid of the butter dish and not in the base. The base has only the pie crust type edging which often causes people to think they've discovered a Cremax butter bottom.

The decaled butter has the same decal on the inside base as around the top of the butter. Don't pass any butter dishes by in Chinex Classic. There's always a market for them!

	Browntone or Plain Ivory	Decal Decorated*
Bowl, 5¾" Cereal	3.50	4.50
Bowl, 7" Flat Soup	11.50	12.00
Bowl, 9" Vegetable	9.50	12.50
Butter Dish	50.00	62.50
Creamer	4.50	7.00
Cup	3.50	4.50
Plate, 6¼" Sherbet	2.00	2.50
Plate, 9¾" Dinner	3.50	5.00
*Plate, 11½" Sandwich or Cake	6.50	8.00
Saucer	2.00	3.50
Sherbet, Low Footed	6.50	9.00
Sugar, Open	4.00	7.00

*Castle decal about 20% higher in most areas.

CIRCLE   HOCKING GLASS COMPANY, 1930's

Colors: Green, pink.

This is a minor pattern of Hocking's that I have had a lot of fun with since the last book because I keep turning up unlisted pieces! I have added the following pieces to those listed previously: rounded cup, 8" bowl, water goblet, 4¾" sherbet and dinner plate as well as the color pink!

The flat bottomed cup near the center is found on a saucer without an indent while the rounded cup on the left takes a saucer with a cup ring. Thus far, the rounded cup seems more scarce than the flat bottomed version.

Pink Circle appears very infrequently; and I have litte idea yet as to just how rare the bi-colored crystal sherbet with the green stem is. Help me look! Who knows what we can turn up yet in this pattern!

	Green/Pink		Green/Pink
Bowl, 4½"	2.50	Plate, 9½" Dinner	4.00
Bowl, 8"	5.00	Saucer	1.00
Creamer	4.00	Sherbet, 3 1/8"	3.50
Cup (2 Styles)	2.50	Sherbet, 4¾"	4.50
Decanter, Handled	16.00	Sugar	4.00
Goblet, 4½" Wine	3.50	Tumbler, 4 oz. Juice	3.50
Goblet, 8 oz. Water	5.50	Tumbler, 8 oz. Water	4.00
Pitcher, 80 oz.	16.00	Vase, Hat Shape	15.00
Plate, 6" Sherbet	2.00		

Please refer to Foreword for pricing information

CLOVERLEAF   HAZEL ATLAS GLASS COMPANY, 1930-1936

Colors: Pink, green, yellow, crystal, black.

Cloverleaf is an attractive pattern, but one that is rather hard to accumulate in a short period of time. If you choose this pattern to collect, you'll learn the virtue of patience.

The 8″ bowl in yellow seemingly does not exist. I meant only to remove the yellow bowl from the listing in the 4th edition; but somehow all the 8″ bowls were removed; and yes , I got letters! All bowls in Cloverleaf are hard to find with the exception of the 4″ bowl in green and pink.

Flat tumblers seem to be disappearing faster than the footed ones. Of course, in yellow, there are few flat tumblers!

Little black Cloverleaf has appeared on the market recently and thus prices have tended to remain the same. This is not due to its being any less valuable than before; rather it is due to most of the black having disappeared into people's collections. No one has yet found a black Cloverleaf candy, but keep looking. Hazel Atlas lists a black candy dish and I have found one which had the correct ovide shape; but there was no pattern on it. So, whether they made one with the pattern on it or not is still anyone's guess.

Remember that the black Cloverleaf sherbet plate and saucer are the same size; however, the sherbet plate carries the design in the center while the saucer does not.

In my travels, the 7″ bowl seems to be more difficult to find than the 8″ bowl.

	Pink	Green	Yellow	Black
Ash Tray 4″, Match Holder in Center				52.50
Ash Tray 5¾″, Match Holder in Center				67.50
Bowl, 4″ Dessert	9.00	12.50	15.00	
Bowl, 5″ Cereal		13.50	20.00	
Bowl, 7″ Deep Salad		19.50	35.00	
Bowl, 8″		35.00		
Candy Dish and Cover		35.50	92.50	
Creamer, 3 5/8″ Footed		6.50	12.50	9.50
Cup	5.00	5.00	11.50	7.50
Plate, 6″ Sherbet		3.50	4.50	17.50
Plate, 8″ Luncheon	4.75	4.75	10.00	10.50
Plate, 10¼″ Grill		15.00	17.50	
Salt and Pepper, Pair		22.50	82.50	52.50
Saucer	2.00	2.50	3.00	3.00
Sherbet, 3″ Footed	4.50	4.00	7.50	10.00
Sugar, Footed, 3 5/8″		6.00	9.50	9.50
Tumbler, 4″, 9 oz. Flat		22.50		
Tumbler, 3¾″, 10 oz. Flat Flared	12.50	19.50		
Tumbler, 5¾″, 10 oz. Footed		15.00	22.50	

Design highlighted in photographs to emphasize pattern.

COLONIAL, "KNIFE AND FORK"   HOCKING GLASS COMPANY, 1934-1936

Colors: Pink, green, crystal, opaque white.

The longer I'm around Depression Glass the more convinced I am that the Colonial designer managed to achieve a timeless elegance with this arched and columned pattern. You never seem to tire of it.

The discovery of the Colonial mugs created quite a stir among collectors. I included a picture of one of the 15 known pink ones last time; so, I'm treating you to a picture of one of the 3 known green ones in this book!

No new reports of any beaded edged pitchers (shown) have been forthcoming; yet I'm very doubtful that only one exists! So, keep looking!

Prices on the 15 oz., flat lemonade tumblers have shot out of sight; and the rapid rise in cost of some of the bowls (5½" cereal, 7" soup and 3 7/8" small berry) is enough to make collectors wince. Dinner plates are valuable commodities to own, also.

You can see the 4", 9 oz. water tumbler in ROYAL RUBY Colonial on the rare page at the back of the book. Someone dug this up, cracked and chipped. I further mutilated it by catching it with my sleeve at a show where I was very cramped for space and smashing it into further pieces. Anyway, it's an interesting piece; and I just know there are others out there to be found!

As in several Hocking patterns, cups are outnumbering saucer/sherbet plates (i.e., no cup ring).

The spooner pictured on the far right in pink is taller than the sugar (shown in green to its left). Lidless sugar bowls are often mistaken as spooners by novice collectors. Notice how far the spooner handle is from the bottom edge of the bowl.

The butter or cheese dish top will fit the wooden cheese server. The cheese top stands ½" shorter than the butter lid, however.

The 3" sherbet in pink has edged ahead of the round 3 3/8" size in price. I have yet to hear of a 3" sherbet in green or crystal. If you find it, let me know!

For you who have asked, I'm pricing the crystal as listed by Hocking; however, I've yet to see all these pieces in my travels.

The white Colonial-like cup and saucer pictured now has a matching plate to accompany it. I can't verify it as Hocking made. So, it's just "interesting".

	Pink	Green	Crystal		Pink	Green	Crystal
Bowl, 3¾" Berry	22.50			Plate, 6" Sherbet	2.50	3.00	1.50
Bowl, 4½" Berry	6.00	7.50	2.50	Plate, 8½" Luncheon	4.50	5.00	2.50
Bowl, 5½" Cereal	22.50	32.50	7.50	Plate, 10" Dinner	17.50	32.50	9.50
Bowl, 4½" Cream Soup	27.50	29.50		Plate, 10" Grill	12.50	17.50	6.50
Bowl, 7" Low Soup	22.50	30.00	8.00	Platter, 12" Oval	10.00	12.50	7.50
Bowl, 9" Large Berry	10.00	12.50	7.50	Salt and Pepper, Pair	95.00	97.50	42.50
Bowl, 10" Oval Vegetable	10.50	15.00	8.50	Saucer (White 3.00) (Same as			
Butter Dish and Cover	425.00	40.00	27.50	Sherbet Plate)	2.00	2.50	1.50
Cheese Dish (As Shown)		72.50		Sherbet, 3"	7.50		
Creamer, 5", 8 oz. (Milk				Sherbet, 3 3/8"	5.50	8.50	3.00
Pitcher)	10.50	13.50	6.00	Spoon Holder or Celery	67.50	72.50	32.50
Cup (White 7.00)	5.00	8.00	4.75	Sugar, 5"	9.00	10.00	5.00
Goblet, 3¾", 1 oz. Cordial		19.50	10.00	Sugar Cover	15.00	10.00	6.00
Goblet, 4", 3 oz. Cocktail	14.50	16.50		Tumbler, 3", 5 oz. Juice	8.00	12.00	5.00
Goblet, 4½", 2½ oz. Wine	14.50	17.50		**Tumbler, 4", 9 oz. Water	7.50	13.50	6.00
Goblet, 5¼", 4 oz. Claret	13.00	15.00		Tumbler, 10 oz.	11.00	16.50	7.00
Goblet, 5¾", 8½ oz. Water	16.50	17.50	10.00	Tumbler, 12 oz. Iced Tea	17.50	25.00	8.00
Mug, 4½" 12 oz.	125.00	250.00		Tumbler, 15 oz. Lemonade	22.50	55.00	10.00
Pitcher, 7", 54 oz. Ice Lip or				Tumbler, 3¼", 3 oz. Footed	9.00	12.50	6.00
None	30.00	32.50	17.50	Tumbler, 4", 5 oz. Footed	12.50	18.50	7.00
*Pitcher, 7¾", 68 oz. Ice Lip or				Tumbler, 5¼", 10 oz. Ftd.	12.50	16.50	8.00
None	32.50	45.00	20.00	Whiskey, 2½", 1½ oz.	6.50	8.50	3.50

*Beaded top in pink $295.00
**Royal Ruby $25.00

Please refer to Foreword for pricing information

COLONIAL BLOCK HAZEL ATLAS GLASS COMPANY

Colors: Early 1930's, green and pink; 1950's, white.

This pattern's major claim to fame lies in its butter dish. It's the one usually substituted in Block Optic pattern, causing someone to wonder if it's "Block" or not. Well, it is; but it's Colonial Block rather than Block Optic. The butter for Block Optic is rectangular.

This pattern has so few pieces that collectors are adding the U.S. Glass pitcher and tumbler as "go with" items for Colonial Block. Thus, they are pictured here along with the Colonial Block to show you how well they do blend with the pattern. Would YOU have known the difference if I hadn't pointed it out? The pitcher presently sells for about $20.00 and the goblet for about $8.00. If it weren't for their chameleon ability to fit this pattern, the pitcher and goblet would be worth considerably less as just Depression Glass with no particular patttern.

	Pink, Green	White
Bowl, 4"	4.00	
Bowl, 7"	10.00	
Butter Dish	25.00	
Candy Jar w/Cover	22.50	
Creamer	7.50	5.50
Sugar	6.50	4.50
Sugar Lid	4.50	3.00

COLONIAL FLUTED, "ROPE" FEDERAL GLASS COMPANY, 1928-1933

Colors: Green, crystal.

To paraphrase Mr. Twain, "the reports of a dinner plate have been greatly exaggerated!" There is a similar pattern made by Federal and marked with their F in a shield marking that has the same type panels as Colonial Fluted pattern but which lacks the roping effect along the edge. Therefore, all these so-called dinner plates do not belong to this pattern. There is another version which shows up with the roping design but which does not have the panels. This isn't Colonial Fluted either. However, since there is so little of this pattern to be found, it would be perfectly permissible to blend all three types if you wished to do so!

In crystal, I've only seen a few cups, saucers and plates with decals (hearts, spades, diamonds and clubs) indicating their use as a bridge set. Unhappily, I passed the set by the first time and have never yet been given a second opportunity to see it.

The scratch marks, but no chips, invariably found on pieces of this pattern indicate two things: it was widely used and very durable!

If you look closely, you can see the F in the shield mark on the saucer at the back. This was Federal's trademark.

	Green		Green
Bowl, 4" Berry	3.50	Plate, 6" Sherbet	1.50
Bowl, 6" Cereal	4.50	Plate, 8" Luncheon	2.50
Bowl, 6½" Deep Salad	8.00	Saucer	1.50
Bowl, 7½" Large Berry	8.50	Sherbet	4.00
Creamer	4.00	Sugar	3.00
Cup	2.50	Sugar Cover	6.50

Please refer to Foreword for pricing information

COLUMBIA FEDERAL GLASS COMPANY, 1938-1942

Colors: Crystal, pink.

Columbia is a pretty pattern, indeed, a "dressy" pattern which for some reason has caught few collectors' eyes. It's still rather inexpensive for a Depression pattern; so, perhaps you should consider it. There's quite a bit of flash glare in this picture; it's much more attractive when you see it "live".

Since there are only four different pieces to find in pink, you'd think that an easy task. Not so! Pink Columbia is in scant supply as many who've looked for it will tell you.

The cereal and soup bowls are difficult to locate in crystal with the snack set not far behind.

Butter dishes are often found with various flashed-on colors decorating the tops. I've seen blue, iridescent, red, purple, amethyst and green flashed tops; perhaps you will find other colors!

	Crystal		Crystal	Pink
Bowl, 5" Cereal	5.00	Cup	3.00	7.00
Bowl, 8" Low Soup	6.50	Plate, 6" Bread & Butter	1.50	3.50
Bowl, 8½" Salad	6.50	Plate, 9½" Luncheon	3.00	10.50
Bowl, 10½" Ruffled Edge	10.00	Plate, 11¾" Chop	5.50	
Butter Dish and Cover	15.50	Saucer	1.00	5.00
Ruby Flashed (17.50)		Snack Plate	12.50	
Other Flashed (16.00)				

CORONATION, "BANDED FINE RIB", "SAXON" HOCKING GLASS COMPANY, 1936-1940

Colors: Pink, crystal, royal ruby.

Interest in Coronation was revitalized recently with the discovery of a new piece, the 68 oz., 7¾" pitcher shown on the rare page in the back of the book! There's certain to be more of these found, possibly by you!

Heretofore, the only real distinction Coronation enjoyed was in being the source of confusion between Lace Edge and Coronation tumblers. People were constantly getting the cheaper Coronation tumbler in the mail instead of the more costly Lace Edge ones they'd ordered. The rays of the Coronation tumbler travel well up the glass. The rays of the Lace Edge tumbler do not.

Antique dealers who do not sell much Depression Glass have been trying to sell the Royal Ruby berry sets at some rather high prices. As late as 1975, over 600 of these berry sets were discovered in an old warehouse in the original Hocking packaging. Hocking promoted a whole line of Royal Ruby products in the early 1940's.

You will find no ruby saucer to match the Royal Ruby Coronation cup because this item was promoted residing on a crystal saucer.

	Pink	Ruby Red		Pink	Ruby Red
Bowl, 4¼" Berry	3.00	4.50	Plate, 8½" Luncheon	3.50	5.00
Bowl, 6½" Nappy	3.50	6.50	Saucer (Same as 6" Plate)	1.50	
Bowl, 8" Large Berry	6.50	10.50	Sherbet	3.00	4.00
Cup	3.00	4.50	Tumbler, 5", 10 oz. Footed	7.50	
Plate, 6" Sherbet	1.50				

Please refer to Foreword for pricing information

CREMAX MACBETH-EVANS DIVISION OF CORNING GLASS WORKS, Late 1930's · Early 1940's

Color: Cremax.

Actually, this pattern is rare; but there is so little of it around that little interest is stimulated toward collecting it. Don't pass by a piece of this because you don't collect it!

As with Chinex, the pieces with the castle decal are the most prized. One collector told me she had almost completed a set of the floral decal and was using it every day and enjoying it "a thousand times more than that old melamine"! We're raising whole generations of children who have never eaten from anything but plastic dishes!

There is no butter dish in Cremax although the base to the Chinex butter is similar to the Cremax pattern.

This PATTERN is called Cremax. However, Macbeth-Evans also used cremax to describe the beige-like COLOR used in some of its patterns such as American Sweetheart, Dogwood and Petalware. Be aware of this overlapping of meaning.

	Cremax	Decal Decorated		Cremax	Decal Decorated
Bowl, 5¾" Cereal	2.50	4.00	Plate, 9¾" Dinner	3.50	5.00
Bowl, 9" Vegetable	5.50	7.50	Plate, 11½" Sandwich	4.00	6.50
Creamer	3.00	5.50	Saucer	1.50	1.50
Cup	3.00	3.50	Sugar, Open	3.00	5.50
Plate, 6¼" Bread and Butter	1.50	2.50			

CUBE, "CUBIST" JEANNETTE GLASS COMPANY, 1929-1933

Colors: Pink, green, crystal, ultramarine.

As in many of Jeannette's patterns, there is a great variance in shades of pink from very light to an orange tinted pink. This is not unusual even though it may disturb some collectors. It merely shows a lack of scientific and exacting controls under which the glassware was made back then.

Pitchers and tumblers have really jumped in price due to their relative scarcity; but other pieces have enjoyed only moderate gains.

Except for the 2" creamer and sugar abundantly found in crystal, there have hardly been enough other pieces found to make that color collectible. Fostoria's "American" pattern is often mistaken as Cube. However, though the design is similar, there is no comparison in the quality of the glass. The Fostoria glassware is much better, clearer glass.

	Pink	Green		Pink	Green
Bowl, 4½" Dessert	3.50	4.00	Plate, 8" Luncheon	2.50	4.00
Bowl, 4½" Deep	3.50	5.00	Powder Jar and Cover, 3 Legs	10.50	15.00
*Bowl, 6½" Salad	6.00	10.00	Salt and Pepper, Pr.	20.00	22.50
Butter Dish and Cover	42.50	45.00	Saucer	1.50	2.00
Candy Jar and Cover, 6½"	18.50	22.50	Sherbet, Footed	4.00	5.50
Coaster, 3¼"	3.50	4.50	**Sugar, 2"	2.00	
**Creamer, 2"	2.00		Sugar, 3"	3.50	5.50
Creamer, 3"	4.50	6.00	Sugar/Candy Cover	6.00	8.00
Cup	3.50	6.00	Tray for 3" Creamer and Sugar, 7½" (Crystal Only)	4.00	
Pitcher, 8¾", 45 oz.	122.50	127.50			
Plate, 6" Sherbet	1.50	2.50	Tumbler, 4", 9 oz.	17.50	27.50

*Ultramarine — $27.50.
Amber — $3.00.   **Please refer to Foreword for pricing information

"CUPID" PADEN CITY GLASS COMPANY, 1930's

Colors: Pink, green, light blue.

Little did I realize what I was getting into when I included this pattern in the last book. Everyone whose name is "Angel", "Love" or anything similar is now trying to collect this pattern. I really don't blame them. It is perfectly beautiful.

Only the 4¾" ice tub (like the one shown in Peacock & Rose) is new to the listing. If you find other unlisted pieces, like a cup and saucer, for instance, I'd appreciate your sharing the information.

Due to the mad scramble to collect Cupid in whatever piece or color to appear on the market, the prices have increased rather dramatically. However, no other piece of blue has appeared at any price as yet. We KNOW there's more out there! It just needs bringing out!

The center handled trays were called sandwich trays by Paden City; the handled bowls were called candy trays. In either case, you had to get your hand right down in the middle of things if you picked the dish up by that center handle.

	Pink, Green & Blue
Bowl, 8½" Oval Footed	27.50
Bowl, 9¼" Footed Fruit	25.00
Bowl, 9¼" Center Handled	30.00
Bowl, 11" Console	29.50
Candlestick, 5" Wide, Pair	27.50
Comport, 6¼"	19.50
Creamer, 4½" Footed	22.50
Ice Bucket, 6"	42.50
Ice Tub, 4¾"	35.00
Mayonnaise, 6" Diameter, Fits on 8" Plate	37.50
Plate, 10½"	20.00
Sugar, 4¼" Footed	22.50
Tray, 10½" Center Handled	25.00
Tray, 10 7/8" Oval, Footed	30.00
Vase, 8¼" Elliptical	47.50

"DAISY", NUMBER 620 INDIANA GLASS COMPANY

Colors: Crystal, 1933; amber, 1940; dark green and milk glass, 1960's - 1970's.

Indiana made this under a line number; collector's have given it its name of "Daisy".

The truly Depression era crystal Daisy is hardly noticed by collectors. Rather, they seek the amber color made during the war years. In this color, cereals, tumblers, sherbets and the 9 3/8" deep berry bowl are very hard to locate as their prices indicate.

The avocado green color and the milk white colors are a 1960's - early 1970's issue; so be aware of that. These were marketed under the name "Heritage", which is not to be confused with Federal's "Heritage" pattern. One dealer was shipped the Indiana "Heritage" in green and in the original box, thinking he was getting the very rare green "Heritage" by Federal. Imagine his dismay when the eagerly anticipated box arrived!

A few collectors are beginning to buy the newer green color; that's fine as long as you know it's newer glass and are paying accordingly.

	Green, Crystal	Amber		Green, Crystal	Amber
Bowl, 4½" Berry	2.00	6.00	Plate, 9 3/8" Dinner	2.50	5.00
Bowl, 4½" Cream Soup	3.00	6.00	Plate, 10 3/8" Grill	3.50	9.00
Bowl, 6" Cereal	5.00	16.50	Plate, 11½" Cake or		
Bowl, 7 3/8" Deep Berry	4.00	9.00	Sandwich	5.00	8.50
Bowl, 9 3/8" Deep Berry	5.00	18.50	Platter, 10¾"	5.00	9.50
Bowl, 10" Oval Vegetable	5.00	11.50	Relish Dish, 3 Part, 8 3/8"	7.50	12.50
Creamer, Footed	3.50	5.50	Saucer	1.00	1.50
Cup	2.00	4.00	Sherbet, Footed	2.50	6.00
Plate, 6" Sherbet	1.00	2.00	Sugar, Footed	3.00	5.00
Plate, 7 3/8" Salad	1.50	5.50	Tumbler, 9 oz. Footed	5.00	11.50
Plate, 8 3/8" Luncheon	1.50	4.50	Tumbler, 12 oz. Footed	9.00	25.00

DIANA FEDERAL GLASS COMPANY, 1937-1941

Colors: Pink, amber, crystal.

Because there are a number of swirling patterns in Depression Glass, Diana is often confused with other patterns. Generally speaking, if the bottom of the piece you're considering is swirled also, you're viewing a piece of Diana.

Few people have elected to collect this pattern and therefore, the prices have remained steady for some time. If your funds are limited, you might do well to seriously consider this.

Frosted pieces similar to the bowl pictured keep turning up. An entire set of frosted Diana surfaced recently in pink!

Shaker and candy dish collectors have depleted the supply of those items.

A set of pink demitasse cups and saucers have been found with a wire rack like the crystal one pictured.

	Amber, Crystal, Pink****		Amber, Crystal, Pink****
*Ash Tray, 3½"	3.00	Plate, 5½" Child's	3.00
Bowl, 5" Cereal	3.50	Plate, 6" Bread and Butter	1.50
Bowl, 5½" Cream Soup	5.00	Plate, 9½" Dinner	4.50
Bowl, 9" Salad	6.50	Plate, 11¾" Sandwich	5.00
Bowl, 11" Console Fruit	6.50	Platter, 12" Oval	6.50
Bowl, 12" Scalloped Edge	7.50	***Salt and Pepper, Pr.	27.50
**Candy Jar and Cover, Round	17.50	Saucer	1.50
Coaster, 3½"	3.50	Sherbet	5.00
Creamer, Oval	3.50	Sugar, Open Oval	3.50
Cup	4.00	Tumbler, 4 1/8", 9 oz.	8.50
Cup, 2 oz. Demi-tasse		Junior Set: 6 Cups, Saucers	
and 4½" Saucer Set	4.50	and Plates with Round	
		Rack	37.50

*Green — $3.00
**Amber — $22.50
***Amber — $62.50
****Crystal 30% Less

Please refer to Foreword for pricing information

DIAMOND QUILTED, "FLAT DIAMOND"

IMPERIAL GLASS COMPANY, Late 1920's - Early 1930's

Colors: Pink, blue, green, crystal, black.

The blue punch bowl I hoped for in this still remains a dream; but wouldn't one be fabulous in that color blue?

Most of the blue and black pieces of Diamond Quilted have the quilting effect on the inside of the dish, including that elusive ice bucket! The black plate shows a smooth exterior with the pattern being underneath. You have to pick the piece up and examine the under side. Sugars and creamers have the pattern on the interior.

Hazel Atlas made a pitcher and tumbler set in blue, pink and green that is often confused with Diamond Quilted pattern. These sets are heavy and have the quilting effect stopping in a straight line before it reaches the top of the dish.

A few pieces of red and amber have shown up; but none recently.

While studying old catalogues at a recent visit to Imperial, I learned that the candle holders come in two styles: the flat bottom type shown and a rolled edge type which to my knowledge has never turned up. So, look for those!

	Pink, Green	Blue, Black		Pink, Green	Blue, Black
Bowl, 4¾" Cream Soup	6.50	10.00	Mayonnaise Set: Ladle,		
Bowl, 5" Cereal	4.00	6.50	Plate, 3 Footed Dish	15.00	
Bowl, 5½" One Handle	5.00	8.50	Pitcher, 64 oz.	22.50	
Bowl, 7" Crimped Edge	5.50	9.50	Plate, 6" Sherbet	2.00	3.00
Bowl, Rolled Edge Console	13.50	22.50	Plate, 7" Salad	3.50	5.50
Cake Salver, Tall 10"			Plate, 8" Luncheon	3.50	9.50
Diameter	27.50		Punch Bowl and Stand	250.00	
Candlesticks (2 Styles), Pr.	8.50	20.00	Plate, 14" Sandwich	8.50	
Candy Jar and Cover, Ftd.	15.00	25.00	Sandwich Server,		
Compote and Cover, 11½"	35.00		Center Handle	13.50	22.50
Creamer	5.50	8.50	Saucer	1.50	3.25
Cup	3.00	5.50	Sherbet	3.50	7.50
Goblet, 1 oz. Cordial	5.00		Sugar	5.50	8.50
Goblet, 2 oz. Wine	5.00		Tumbler, 9 oz. Water	5.00	
Goblet, 3 oz. Wine	6.00		Tumbler, 12 oz. Iced Tea	6.50	
Goblet, 6", 9 oz.			Tumbler, 6 oz. Footed	5.00	
Champagne	7.50		Tumbler, 9 oz. Footed	8.50	
Ice Bucket	37.50	52.50	Tumbler, 12 oz. Footed	10.00	
			Vase, Fan, Dolphin Handles	19.50	30.00
			Whiskey, 1½ oz.	5.50	

Covered Bowl—6⅜ in. diam., deep round shape with 3 artistic feet, dome cover, fine quality brilliant finish **pot glass**, allover block diamond design, transparent Rose Marie and emerald green.
1C5603—Asstd. ½ doz. in carton, 20 lbs.
Doz $6.95

1C989—3 piece set, 2 transparent colors (rose and green), good quality, 10½ in. rolled rim bowl, TWO 3½ in. wide base candlesticks. Asstd. 6 sets in case, 30 lbs............SET (3 pcs) **65c**

Please refer to Foreword for pricing information

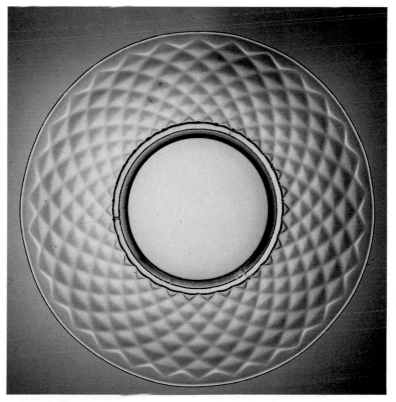

51

DOGWOOD, "APPLE BLOSSOM", " WILD ROSE"
MACBETH-EVANS GLASS COMPANY, 1929-1932

Colors: Pink, green, some crystal, monax, cremax and yellow.

Dogwood, always extremely popular with collectors, has had some new additions since the last book. A 3¾" pink coaster and a cremax cake plate were discovered in the Pittsburgh area; a 4¾" wine goblet came from Ohio. Actually, the wine was not made by Macbeth-Evans, but, like some of the U.S. Glass pieces showing up with Dogwood designs on them, it's a close first cousin.

Strangely enough, the 3" footed creamer has almost doubled in price. These have become less plentiful than the footed sugar or the thin creamer and sugar.

Beginning collectors should know that **pink** cups, creamers and sugars come in both thick and thin variety.

The monax salver has turned out to be more plentiful than first thought.

The yellow bowl and an 8" plate are the only two pieces of yellow Dogwood known. Green and pink sherbets, the pink platter and the large 10¼" fruit bowls have nearly disappeared from the market. It still bothers me to tell how very rare the platter is knowing I once bought four and turned down two with minor chips for less than $10.00 each! You don't see that many in an entire year of shows now!

Dogwood pitchers with the silk screened design are rarely seen. Two of the rarest are shown: the American Sweetheart style pink and the green Dogwood. Do you suppose there could be an American Sweetheart style green pitcher?

I have seen an 11" cake plate in pink Dogwood, the size of the one pictured in "S" Pattern. It has to be considered a rare piece.

Plain, unpatterned pitchers and tumblers in the Dogwood or "S" Pattern SHAPE blend with either pattern but are not considered to BE either pattern.

Some frosted green Dogwood bowls were drilled through and used as lamp shades. What a waste!

Pink grill plates are found with the Dogwood design all over or just at the rim.

Luncheon plates abound; dinner plates get fewer and farther between.

	Pink	Green	Monax, Cremax
*Bowl, 5½" Cereal	12.50	15.00	15.00
Bowl, 8½" Berry	27.50	55.00	39.50
Bowl, 10¼" Fruit	137.50	77.50	
Cake Plate, 11" Heavy Solid Foot	147.50		
Cake Plate, 13" Heavy Solid Foot	52.50	47.50	125.00
Creamer, 2½" Thin	8.50	32.50	
Creamer, 3¼" Thick	12.50		
Cup, Thin or Thick	7.50	13.50	35.00
Pitcher, 8" 80 oz. Decorated	95.00	425.00	
Pitcher, 8" 80 oz. (American Sweetheart Style)	437.50		
Plate, 6" Bread and Butter	3.50	4.00	20.00
*Plate, 8" Luncheon	4.00	5.00	
Plate. 9¼" Dinner	14.50		
Plate, 10½" Grill AOP or Border Design Only	12.50	10.50	
Plate, 12" Salver	17.50		23.50
Platter, 12" Oval (Rare)	227.50		
Saucer	4.00	5.00	15.00
Sherbet, Low Footed	15.50	37.50	
Sugar, 2½" Thin	7.50	32.50	
Sugar, 3¼" Thick	8.50		
Tumbler, 3½", 5 oz. Decorated	72.50		
Tumbler, 4" 10 oz. Decorated	19.50	45.00	
Tumbler, 4¾", 11 oz. Decorated	23.50	55.00	
Tumbler, 5", 12 oz. Decorated	27.50	65.00	
Tumbler, Etched Band	9.00		

*Yellow — $45.00   **Please refer to Foreword for pricing information**

DORIC JEANNETTE GLASS COMPANY, 1935-1938

Colors: Pink, green, delphite, yellow.

The green Doric footed pitcher finally makes an appearance on the rare page at the back of the book. The equally rare 5″, 36 oz. delphite one is shown here next to the yellow footed Doric pitcher. This yellow pitcher came from the same group of glass the yellow Adam did in 1973.

To save myself several dozen letters, I would like to say that the 3 part iridized candy has been made as recently as the 1970's. It may have been made earlier, but it is not too old and was selling a few years ago in the local dish barn for 79¢.

The 4½″, 9 oz. tumblers and cereal bowls are getting hard to find. In fact, the supply of Doric has been drastically reduced in markets of late. The price is not the problem; the quantity of glass is not there from which to choose.

The sugar and candy lids in this pattern are **not** interchangeable. The candy lid is taller and more cone shaped.

The Doric cake plate is footed.

Delphite Doric is hard to find except for the sherbets.

	Pink	Green	Delphite
Bowl, 4½″ Berry	4.50	5.50	25.00
Bowl, 5″ Cream Soup		125.00	
Bowl, 5½″ Cereal	15.50	17.50	
Bowl, 8¼″ Large Berry	8.50	10.00	75.00
Bowl, 9″ Two Handled	9.50	9.50	
Bowl, 9″ Oval Vegetable	9.50	10.50	
Butter Dish and Cover	52.50	62.50	
Cake Plate, 10″, Three Legs	12.00	11.50	
Candy Dish and Cover, 8″	22.50	22.50	
*Candy Dish, Three Part	4.50	5.00	4.00
Coaster, 3″	8.50	10.00	
Creamer, 4″	6.50	8.00	
Cup	5.00	6.00	
Pitcher, 6″, 36 oz. Flat	22.00	27.00	275.00
Pitcher, 7½″, 48 oz. Footed	197.50	350.00	
(Also in Yellow at $500.00)			
Plate, 6″ Sherbet	2.50	3.00	
Plate, 7″ Salad	12.50	11.50	
Plate, 9″ Dinner (Serrated 35.00)	6.50	7.50	
Plate, 9″ Grill	6.50	10.00	
Platter, 12″ Oval	10.00	10.50	
Relish Tray, 4″ x 4″	4.50	6.50	
**Relish Tray, 4″ x 8″	5.50	8.50	
Salt and Pepper, Pr.	23.00	27.50	
Saucer	2.00	2.50	
Sherbet, Footed	6.50	7.50	4.75
Sugar	8.00	8.50	
Sugar Cover	9.00	15.00	
Tray, 10″ Handled	6.50	9.50	
Tray, 8″ x 8″ Serving	7.50	8.50	
Tumbler, 4½″, 9 oz.	22.50	37.50	
Tumbler, 4″, 11 oz. Flat	14.00	18.00	
Tumbler, 5″, 12 oz.	15.00	18.00	

*Candy in metal holder — $37.50. Iridescent
 made recently.
**Trays in metal holder as shown — $27.50

Please refer to Foreword for pricing information

DORIC & PANSY   JEANNETTE GLASS COMPANY, 1937-1938

Colors: Pink, crystal, green ultramarine.

One of the problems with a pattern that has high priced and hard to find items is that prices reach a point where they scare away new collectors. Unfortunately, Doric and Pansy is one of those patterns. I still firmly believe that good patterns of Depression Glass have enormous investment potential. So, don't let today's price scare you away from good, long term investments.

Many of the shakers are weakly struck and do not have a strong pattern design. They need to have SOME design, however, to be labeled Doric & Pansy. I've seen a few that had only shape and color and in all honesty, they couldn't truly be called Doric and Pansy shakers.

Beginners should notice from the picture that the ultramarine color varies widely. Matching sets thus become a problem to be reckoned with.

Crystal Doric & Pansy is rarely found; but there are few collectors, so the price stays down.

Only the child's set and the berry set have been found in pink.

	Green, Teal	Pink, Crystal		Green, Teal	Pink, Crystal
Bowl, 4½" Berry	8.50	6.00	Plate, 7" Salad	25.00	
Bowl, 8" Large Berry	57.50	17.50	Plate, 9" Dinner	15.00	4.75
Bowl, 9" Handled	22.50	9.50	Salt and Pepper, Pr.	357.50	
Butter Dish and Cover	657.50		Saucer	4.00	2.25
Cup	12.50	6.50	Sugar, Open	157.50	57.50
Creamer	157.50	57.50	Tray, 10" Handled	17.50	
Plate, 6" Sherbet	8.00	6.00	Tumbler, 4½", 9 oz.	32.50	

DORIC AND PANSY
"PRETTY POLLY PARTY DISHES"

	Teal	Pink		Teal	Pink
Cup	22.50	15.00	Creamer	27.50	20.00
Saucer	4.25	3.25	Sugar	27.00	20.00
Plate	8.00	6.00	14 Piece Set	182.50	135.00

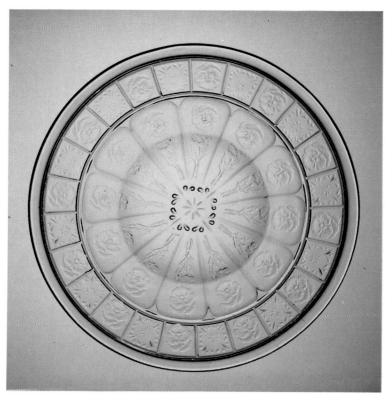

57

ENGLISH HOBNAIL   WESTMORELAND GLASS COMPANY, 1920's - 1970's

Colors: Crystal, pink, amber, turquoise, cobalt, green, blue, red.

Collectors need to be aware that shortly after the fourth edition appeared with the red English Hobnail pitcher on the cover, Westmoreland made 17 pieces of red for LeVay Distributing Company---including the pitcher. The one shown on that cover was cracked and broken, but it was at least old. You need to know all this before you pay high prices for red pieces.

Also, the light amber colored sherbet in the lower part of the picture was made in the 1960's; so all amber pieces priced here in this list are for the older, dark amber color. This is why I do not price any crystal. Westmoreland is still in business and who knows what they'll choose to make next. If they make red for one customer, perhaps cobalt blue for someone else?

Even though this is a beautiful pattern and much you find in it is older than I am, it's still a "collect at your own risk" pattern as far as I'm concerned.

To help you distinguish English Hobnail from Miss America, notice that English Hobnail has a center motif with rays of varying distance from the center. Hobnail tips are more rounded, giving the English Hobnail a smoother feel when touched. English Hobnail goblets flair slightly at the rim. Miss America goblets don't flair at the rim and have a set of three rings above the hobs before entering a plain glass rim.

	Cobalt, Amber, Turquoise*, Pink, Green		Cobalt, Amber, Turquoise*, Pink, Green
**Ash Tray, Several Shapes	18.50	Goblet, 5 oz. Claret	13.00
Bowls, 4½", 5" Square		**Goblet, 6¼", 8 oz.	15.00
and Round	8.50	Grapefruit, 6½" Flange Rim	12.50
Bowl, Cream Soup	12.50	Lamp, 6¼" Electric	52.50
Bowls, 6" Several Styles	9.50	**Lamp, 9¼"	90.00
Bowls, 8" Several Styles	15.50	Lampshade, 17" Diameter	
**Bowls, 8" Footed and		(Crystal)	100.00
Two Handled	37.50	Marmalade and Cover	27.50
**Bowls, 11" and 12"		Pitcher, 23 oz.	77.50
Nappies	35.00	Pitcher, 39 oz.	92.50
Bowls, 8", 9" Oval Relish	15.00	Pitcher, 60 oz.	127.50
Bowl, 12" Oval Relish	16.50	Pitcher, ½ Gal. Straight	
Candlesticks, 3½" Pair	27.50	Sides	122.50
Candlesticks, 8½" Pair	42.50	**Plate, 5½", 6½" Sherbet	3.00
Candy Dish, ½ lb.		Plate, 7¼" Pie	3.50
Cone Shaped	40.00	**Plate, 8" Round or Square	6.00
Candy Dish and Cover,		Plate, 10" Dinner	15.50
Three Feet	52.50	Salt and Pepper, Pair,	
Celery Dish, 9"	15.00	Round or Square Bases	52.50
Celery Dish, 12"	17.50	Salt Dip, 2" Footed and	
**Cigarette Box	20.00	with Place Card Holder	15.00
**Cologne Bottle	22.50	Saucer	3.00
Creamer, Footed or Flat	13.50	**Sherbet	10.50
Cup	11.50	Sugar, Footed or Flat	13.50
Decanter, 20 oz. with		Tumbler, 3¾", 5 oz. or 9 oz.	11.50
Stopper	52.50	Tumbler, 4", 10 oz. Iced Tea	13.50
Demitasse Cup and Saucer	22.50	Tumbler, 5", 12 oz. Iced Tea	16.00
Egg Cup	22.50	Tumbler, 7 oz. Footed	12.00
Goblet, 1 oz. Cordial	15.50	Tumbler, 9 oz. Footed	13.50
Goblet, 2 oz. Wine	12.50	Tumbler, 12½ oz. Footed	18.00
Goblet, 3 oz. Cocktail	12.50	Whiskey, 1½ oz. and 3 oz.	16.00

*Add about 50% more for Turquoise
**Cobalt double price listed

Please refer to Foreword for pricing information

FAIRFAX FOSTORIA GLASS COMPANY, 1927 - 1944

Colors: Blue, orchid, amber, rose, green, topaz; some ruby and black.

This Fostoria pattern is actually the blank upon which other Fostoria patterns included in the book (June, Trojan, Versailles) are etched. Notice the panelled indentations which are typical of those patterns. Observe, too, that some cups are footed. (Our Round Robin cups had something in common with this better glassware made during the Depression Era). We don't really call this glassware Depression Glass per se. It wasn't your typical give-away type glass. However, it was made during the same time span as our dear Depression Glass and it is appearing at Depression Glass shows as "Depression ERA" glassware.

There are several hard to find items in Fairfax. These include the pitchers, footed oils, the salad dressing bottle and the covered butter dish.

Naturally, being perfectly plain, there is not quite the demand for Fairfax as there is for the etched patterns mentioned previously; but many collectors find that the topaz yellow and the azure blue make serenely beautiful table settings.

Before I go further, I need to explain that those whipped cream pails at the back of the photograph are not Fairfax pattern but Pioneer which is another plainer Fostoria pattern. However, since we had these little Fostoria pails, which are quite good items to find, I slipped them in this plain pattern picture so you'd have some idea of what to look for as a "whipped cream pail". The first time I heard about them, I didn't have the faintest idea what they looked like.

Some Fairfax was made in ruby and black; you might watch for the few pieces to be found in these colors.

	Blue, Orchid	Amber, Rose	Green, Topaz		Blue, Orchid	Amber, Rose	Green, Topaz
Ash Tray	20.00	12.00	16.00	Ice Bucket	40.00	25.00	30.00
Baker, 9" Oval	25.00	15.00	20.00	Lemon Dish, 2 Handled	5.00	4.00	4.00
Baker, 10½" Oval	30.00	20.00	25.00	Mayonnaise	7.50	5.00	6.50
Bon Bon	8.00	6.00	7.00	Mayonnaise Ladle	4.50	3.50	4.00
Bouillon, Footed	8.00	5.00	6.00	Mayonnaise Plate, 7"	4.00	2.50	3.00
Bowl, 5" Fruit	6.00	4.00	5.00	Oil, Footed	70.00	45.00	55.00
Bowl, 6" Cereal	8.50	5.00	7.00	Pickle, 8½"	10.00	6.00	8.00
Bowl, 7" Soup	10.00	6.00	8.00	Pitcher	100.00	65.00	85.00
Bowl, 8" Round Nappy	15.00	10.00	12.00	Plate, 6" Bread & Butter	3.00	2.00	2.50
Bowl, Large Handled				Plate, 7" Salad	4.00	3.00	3.50
Dessert	12.00	8.00	10.00	Plate, 8" Salad	5.00	3.50	4.00
Bowl, 12"	16.00	12.00	14.00	Plate, 9" Dinner	7.50	5.00	6.00
Bowl, 12" Centerpiece	18.00	12.00	15.00	Plate, 10" Dinner	10.00	7.00	8.00
Bowl, 13" Oval Centerpiece	20.00	15.00	17.50	Plate, 10" Grill	10.00	7.00	8.00
Bowl, 15" Centerpiece	24.00	17.50	20.00	Plate, 12" Bread	12.00	8.00	10.00
Butter Dish w/Cover	75.00	55.00	65.00	Plate, 13" Chop	12.00	8.00	10.00
Cake Plate, 10", 2 Handled	16.00	10.00	13.00	Platter, 10½" Oval	20.00	15.00	17.50
Candlestick, Plattened Top,				Platter, 15" Oval	25.00	18.00	22.00
Pair	20.00	16.00	18.00	Relish, 8½"	10.00	7.00	8.00
Candlestick, 3" Pair	20.00	16.00	18.00	Relish, 11½"	12.00	8.00	10.00
Canape Plate	5.00	3.00	4.00	Salad Dressing Bottle		45.00	55.00
Celery, 11½"	14.00	10.00	12.00	Sauce Boat	25.00	18.00	22.00
Cheese & Cracker Set	20.00	16.00	18.00	Sauce Boat Plate	10.00	7.00	8.00
Comport, 7"	10.00	5.00	7.50	Saucer, After Dinner	6.00	4.00	5.00
Cream Soup, Footed	10.00	8.00	9.00	Saucer	4.00	2.50	3.00
Cream Soup Plate, 7"	3.00	2.50	3.00	Shaker, Footed Pair	40.00	27.50	32.50
Creamer, Flat		6.00	8.00	Sugar, Flat		7.00	8.00
Creamer, Footed	10.00	6.00	8.00	Sugar, Footed	10.00	7.00	8.00
Creamer, Tea	10.00	6.00	8.00	Sugar Cover	20.00	16.00	18.00
Cup, After Dinner	12.00	8.00	10.00	Sugar, Tea	10.00	7.00	8.00
Cup, Flat	5.00	3.00	4.00	Sweetmeat	8.00	6.00	7.00
Cup, Footed	6.00	4.00	5.00	Tray, 11" Center Handle	15.00	10.00	12.50
Flower Holder, Oval	10.00	6.00	8.00	Whipped Cream Bowl	8.00	5.00	6.50

Please refer to Foreword for pricing information

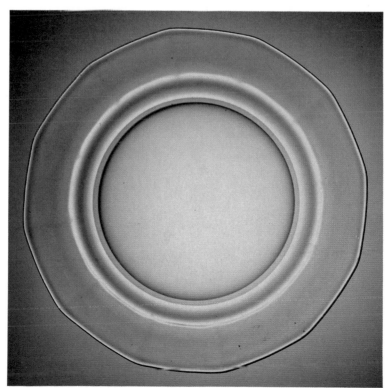

FIRE-KING DINNERWARE "PHILBE" HOCKING GLASS COMPANY, 1937-1938

Colors: Pink, green, blue, crystal.

This is a difficult pattern to collect and it is getting priced beyond the average collector's means; but it is a beautiful pattern, particularly in blue; and every collector needs to recognize it because you wouldn't want to pass a valuable piece you found, even if you don't personally collect it. Someone else does and the money you make from the sale of a good piece of glass can buy you what **you** like!

Notice that the large blue pitcher, flat tumbler, cereal and salad plate all have platinum rims. The two footed tumblers were omitted in the large picture; so they are included as a pattern shot.

The pitchers shown, plus a pink one are all that I can trace so far. If you find another, let me know. All five of these pitchers have come from Ohio and not far from Lancaster where they were originally made.

Unfortunately, the picture of the 7¼" goblet in "Philbe" (similar to the blue Mayfair goblet) did not reproduce well enough for the book. It's a beauty! Most pieces of "Philbe" are shaped like those in Cameo except for this 7¼" goblet.

I've found a green low candy bottom in case someone out there turns up a lid! It's quite similar in shape to the low candy in Cameo.

	Crystal	Pink, Green	Blue
Bowl, 5½" Cereal	10.00	30.00	40.00
Bowl, 7¼" Salad	15.00	40.00	60.00
Bowl, 10" Oval Vegetable	15.00	37.50	55.00
Candy Jar, 4" Low, with Cover	75.00	127.50	157.50
Cookie Jar with Cover	100.00	150.00	250.00
Creamer, 3¼" Footed	25.00	37.50	57.50
Cup	20.00	47.50	75.00
Goblet, 7¼", 9 oz. Thin	37.50	117.50	150.00
Pitcher, 6", 36 oz. Juice	150.00	300.00	450.00
Pitcher, 8½", 56 oz.	250.00	350.00	500.00
Plate, 6" Sherbet	10.00	15.00	25.00
Plate, 8" Luncheon	12.00	17.50	30.00
Plate, 10" Heavy Sandwich	15.00	20.00	35.00
Plate, 10½" Salver	15.00	20.00	35.00
Plate, 10½" Grill	12.00	17.50	30.00
Plate, 11 5/8" Salver	12.00	17.50	32.50
Platter, 12" Closed Handles	15.00	27.50	50.00
Saucer, 6" (Same as Sherbet)	10.00	15.00	25.00
Sugar, 3¼" Footed	25.00	37.50	57.50
Tumbler, 4", 9 oz. Flat Water	25.00	77.50	97.50
Tumbler, 3½" Footed Juice	30.00	87.50	110.00
Tumbler, 5¼", 10 oz. Footed	20.00	30.00	35.00
Tumbler, 6½", 15 oz. Footed Iced Tea	25.00	32.50	32.50

FIRE-KING OVEN GLASS ANCHOR HOCKING GLASS CORPORATION, 1941-1950's

Colors: Pale blue, crystal, beige.

It took three times of photographing this pattern to get the blue color! The prices for some of these pieces have really increased since it was first introduced in the Pocket Guide. Too, in my book **Kitchen Glassware of the Depression Years** this is shown as one of the patterns that can be collected in sets. Since the crystal has not begun to be as collectible as the blue color, you may figure its value at 1/2 to 1/3 the value of the blue pieces at present. This is also true of the opaque Fire-King.

The large covered roaster and the juice saver pie plate are already becoming difficult pieces to find.

The uncovered casseroles were called "bakers" while the ones sold with lids were called "casseroles". The bottom pieces remain the same. Thus, a one pint casserole without its top becomes a one pint baker.

A child's "Sunny Suzy Glass Baking Set" sells for about $25.00-35.00 in the original box in answer to all those who wanted to know. (One was pictured in the 4th edition).

There are four different custard cups and two distinct styles of coffee mugs. Some mugs are very thick; others are rather thin.

The 16 oz. measuring bowl with lip and the tri-spouted measuring cup are two of the handiest items ever manufactured for the kitchen!

	Blue		Blue
Baker, 1 pt., Round or Square	2.50	Measuring Bowl, 16 oz.	8.00
Baker, 1 qt.	3.00	Nurser, 4 oz.	6.00
Baker, 1½ qt.	3.25	Nurser, 8 oz.	8.00
Baker, 2 qt.	4.50	Pie Plate, 4 3/8" Individual	2.75
Cake Pan (Deep), 8¾" (Roaster)	10.00	Pie Plate, 5 3/8" Deep Dish	4.00
Casserole, 1 pt., Knob Handle Cover	4.00	Pie Plate, 8 3/8"	4.50
Casserole, 1 qt., Knob Handle Cover	6.00	Pie Plate, 9"	5.00
Casserole, 1½ qt., Knob Handle Cover	7.00	Pie Plate, 9 5/8"	5.50
Casserole, 2 qt., Knob Handle Cover	10.00	Pie Plate, 10 3/8" Juice Saver	12.00
Casserole, 1 qt., Pie Plate Cover	7.00	Perculator Top, 2 1/8"	2.50
Casserole, 1½ qt., Pie Plate Cover	9.00	Refrigerator Jar & Cover, 4½" x 5"	4.00
Casserole, 2 qt., Pie Plate Cover	12.00	Refrigerator Jar & Cover, 5 1/8" x 9 1/8"	10.00
Casserole, 10 oz., Tab Handle Cover	7.00	Table Server, Tab Handles (Hot Plate)	7.50
Coffee Mug, 7 oz., 2 Styles	12.00	Utility Bowl, 6 7/8"	4.50
Cup, 8 oz. Measuring, 1 Spout	5.00	Utility Bowl, 8 3/8"	5.50
Cup, 8 oz., Measuring, 3 Spout	8.00	Utility Bowl, 10 1/8"	6.50
Custard Cup, 5 oz.	1.50	Utility Pan, 10½" Rectangular	6.00
Custard Cup, 6 oz., 2 Styles	2.00	Utility Pan, 8 1/8" x 12½"	8.00
Loaf Pan, 9 1/8" Deep	7.00		

FLORAGOLD, "LOUISA"   JEANNETTE GLASS COMPANY, 1950's

Colors: Iridescent, some shell pink, ice blue, crystal and red-yellow combinations.

The big news for Floragold collectors is that there is now a smaller square butter dish to search for in their travels! It measures 5½" across and is 3" tall! (The normal butter is 6¼" across and 3½" tall). This was discovered in the Pittsburg area and we photographed it here beside the regular sized butter dish for comparison purposes. Notice that the knobs are very different; so you could spot these at a distance once you know what to look for. A price is yet to be determined for the smaller butter dish.

One question I'm often asked is if there is really a difference in the 10 oz. and 11 oz. tumblers. I assume there is an ounce difference but I have been unable to again lay hands on said tumblers to measure ounces and diameter although they are pictured. What about it, collectors? The 15 oz. tumbler is tough to locate!

The golden color of this glassware has been sprayed on over crystal. Many people think that the name refers to this color. The pattern itself is a take-off of an older Carnival glass pattern known as "Louisa". That rose bowl you see in the center of the picture IS a Carnival glass "Louisa" piece. Now, I could claim I set that there for purposes of comparison. However, the truth is I bought it thinking I had a wonderful Floragold "find" and included it in the picture before I did my homework. We teachers refer to those episodes as "learning experiences".

The saucer/sherbet plates are much more difficult to locate than cups which were also sold by the dozen with the pitchers or a bowl and called "egg nog sets".

A recent report has come to my ear of a tid-bit in Floragold made from two ruffled bowls set around a wooden post.

The other colors listed at the top are all rather recent issue and are found mostly as 5¼" candy dishes or comports.

	Iridescent		Iridescent
Bowl, 4½" Square	3.50	Pitcher, 64 oz.	18.00
Bowl, 5½" Round Cereal	15.00	Plate, 5¾" Sherbet	5.00
Bowl, 5½" Ruffled Fruit	3.50	Plate, 8½" Dinner	14.00
Bowl, 8½" Ruffled Fruit	4.00	Plate or Tray, 13½"	11.50
Bowl, 9½" Deep Salad	22.50	Indent on 13½" Plate	30.00
Bowl, 12" Ruffled Large Fruit	6.50	Platter, 11¼"	12.50
Butter Dish and Cover, ¼ lb. Oblong	14.00	Salt and Pepper, Plastic Tops	30.00
Butter Dish and Cover, Round	32.50	Saucer, 5¼" (No Ring)	5.00
Candlesticks, Double Branch Pr.	27.50	Sherbet, Low Footed	7.50
Candy or Cheese Dish and Cover,		Sugar	3.00
6¾"	27.50	Sugar Lid	5.00
Candy, 5¼" Long, 4 Feet	4.50	Tumbler, 10 oz. Footed	8.50
Coaster/Ash Tray, 4"	4.50	Tumbler, 11 oz. Footed	11.00
Creamer	5.00	Tumbler, 15 oz. Footed	35.00
Cup	3.50	Vase or Celery	62.50

FLORAL, "POINSETTIA" JEANNETTE GLASS COMPANY, 1931-1935

Colors: Pink, green, delphite, jadite, crystal, amber, red, yellow.

The green and crystal Floral flower frogs reported in the last book are now pictured atop their respective vases in the rare page at the end of the book. A new find is represented by the flat bottomed crystal pitcher also shown on that page.

A minor oddity is being noted in the Floral platters in both pink and green. The normal platter has a smooth rim whereas the rim of the other has indentations much like the design of the 11" platter in Cherry Blossom.

As in other Jeannette patterns, sugar and candy lids are interchangeable.

The Floral dresser set on the next page consists of: one 4¼" powder dish, two 3" powder dishes resting on the 9¼" tray. Only one complete set has turned up; however, quite a few lone trays have surfaced.

Floral jadite cannisters are pictured in the **Kitchen Glassware of the Depression Years** book under the section on cannisters.

Other rare items discovered in the Floral pattern include the following:
- a) a set of **delphite** Floral
- b) a yellow, two part relish
- c) an amber plate, cup and saucer
- d) green juice pitchers with ground bottoms, 23 and 24 oz. (shown)
- e) footed vases in green and crystal, flared at the rim
- f) a crystal lemonade pitcher
- g) a Floral lamp (shown)
- h) a green grill plate (shown)
- i) an eight sided vase with a solid, round foot
- j) a pink, ruffled edge berry bowl and master berry bowl
- k) pink and green Floral ice tubs
- l) an oval vegetable with cover

	Pink	Green	Delphite	Jadite
Bowl, 4" Berry (Ruffled 35.00)	7.50	8.00	22.50	
Bowl, 5½" Cream Soup		95.00		
Bowl, 7½" Salad (Ruffled 45.00)	8.50	10.00	45.00	
Bowl, 8" Covered Vegetable	20.00	22.50	37.50 (no cover)	
*Bowl, 9" Oval Vegetable	8.50	10.50		
Butter Dish and Cover	60.00	67.50		
Canister Set: Coffee, Tea, Cereal, Sugar, 5¼" Tall Set				55.00
Candlesticks, 4" Pr.	40.00	57.50		
Candy Jar and Cover	22.50	25.00		
Creamer, Flat	7.00	8.50	55.00	
Coaster, 3¼"	6.50	7.50		
Comport, 9"	250.00	250.00		
†Cup	6.50	7.00		
Dresser Set (As Shown)		925.00		
Frog for Vase (Also Crystal)		550.00		
Ice Tub, 3½" High Oval	357.50	357.50		
Lamp	77.50	77.50		
Pitcher, 5½", 23 or 24 oz.		447.50		
Pitcher, 8", 32 oz. Footed Cone	17.50	22.50		
Pitcher, 10¼", 48 oz. Lemonade	137.50	157.50		
Plate, 6" Sherbet	3.00	3.00		
Plate, 8" Salad	5.50	6.00		
†Plate, 9" Dinner	9.00	10.00	45.00	

	Pink	Green	Delphite	Jadite
Plate, 9" Grill		37.50		
Platter (Like Cherry Blossom)	32.50	32.50		
Platter, 10¾" Oval	8.50	10.00	75.00	
Refrigerator Dish and Cover, 5" Square	37.50	42.50		12.50
††Relish Dish, Two Part Oval	6.50	8.00		
Salt and Pepper, 4" Footed Pair	27.50	32.50		
Salt and Pepper, 6" Flat	27.50			
†Saucer	5.00	5.50		
Sherbet	7.50	8.50	65.00	
Sugar	6.50	7.00	45.00 (open)	
Sugar/Candy Cover	7.50	12.00		
Tray, 6" Square, Closed Handles	8.50	9.00		
Tumbler, 4½", 9 oz. Flat		150.00		
Tumbler, 3½", 3 oz. Footed		85.00		
Tumbler, 4", 5 oz. Footed Juice	10.50	11.00		
Tumbler, 4¾", 7 oz. Footed Water	9.50	11.00	100.00	
Tumbler, 5¼", 9 oz. Footed Lemonade	22.50	23.00		
Vase, 3 Legged Rose Bowl		357.50		
Vase, 3 Legged Flared (Also in Crystal)		350.00		
Vase, 6 7/8" Tall (8 Sided)		350.00		

†These have now been found in amber and red.
††This has been found in yellow.
*Covered in green — 87.50

Please refer to Foreword for pricing information

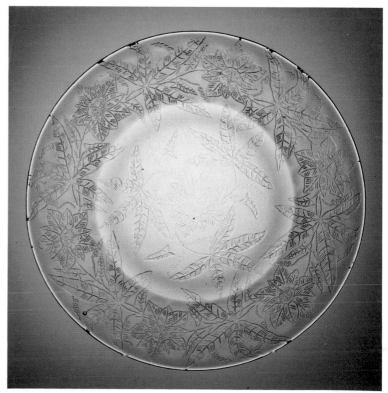

FLORAL AND DIAMOND BAND U.S. GLASS COMPANY, Late 1920's

Colors: Pink, green, irridescent and black.

A newly discovered item is an iridized Floral and Diamond butter dish to accompany the iridized pitcher shown here. The crystal pitcher went almost unnoticed on the rare page of the 4th edition; but I've not heard of another being found yet!

As is true of Strawberry and Aunt Polly pattern made by this same company, there are no cups and saucers in this pattern.

Floral and Diamond is more reminiscent of earlier Pattern glass than Depression glass. It's heavier in shape, appearance and feel.

The iridized pieces are known to Carnival glass collectors by the name "Mayflower".

There appears to be more green available than pink; and the green often varies in hue, a characteristic of many Depression glasswares due to the imprecise methods of firing the glass back then.

I am splitting the two prices of pink and green as there are finally pricing differences to be noted between the two colors.

	Green	Pink			Green	Pink
Bowl, 4½″ Berry	4.50	4.00		*Pitcher, 8″, 42 oz.	65.00	57.50
Bowl, 5¾″ Handled Nappy	6.00	5.50		Plate, 8″ Luncheon	11.00	9.50
Bowl, 8″ Large Berry	8.50	7.50		Sherbet	3.50	3.50
Butter Dish and Cover	67.50	57.50		Sugar, Small	5.00	5.00
Compote, 5½″ Tall	7.50	6.50		Sugar, 5¼″	7.50	7.50
Creamer, Small	5.50	5.00		Sugar Lid	22.50	17.50
Creamer, 4¾″	9.50	9.50		Tumbler, 4″ Water	8.50	7.50
				Tumbler, 5″ Iced Tea	13.50	13.00

*Iridescent — $125.00
   Crystal — $100.00

Seven-Piece Berry Set
You'll really be most satisfied with the purchase of this set. It's very attractive, and affords a fitting and stylish addition to your present pieces. In green pressed glass, with diamond and floral design. Large bowl, 8 inches in diameter, and six sauce dishes to match, 4½ inches in diameter.
35N6838—Weight, packed, 7 pounds. Per set......**68c**

Seven-Piece   Water Set
Made from green pressed glass, with a floral and diamond design. You'll find that the sparkling scintillating pitcher and glasses are a set you'll be mighty proud to own when serving cold drinks. 3-pint pitcher. Six 8-ounce tumblers.
35N6837—Weight, packed, 12 pounds. Per set.**$1.18**

Five-Piece Table Set
Heavy pressed glass in light green, with pressed diamond and floral design. Creamer, covered sugar bowl and covered butter dish. Weight, packed, 9 pounds.
35N6836..........**65c**

71

FLORENTINE NO. 1, "OLD FLORENTINE", "POPPY NO. 1"

HAZEL ATLAS GLASS COMPANY, 1932-1935

Colors: Pink, green, crystal, yellow, cobalt.

A frequent question asked me is how to tell the difference between Florentine No. 1 and Florentine No. 2. It helps to know that Florentine No. 1 was first advertised as Florentine Hexagonal as opposed to Florentine Round. A second characteristic is that only Florentine No. 1 has serrated edges; and they occur on both flat and footed pieces.

Before we go further, I need to point out that there are eight pieces of Florentine No. 2 pattern down the left side of this Florentine No. 1 picture. I did this deliberately, not for comparison purposes, though they serve as that, but because at the time this was taken, we were switching only the Florentine No. 1 picture in the book from black and white to color; and I saw this as a means of showing the colors in Florentine No. 2, also. Do, please, be properly appreciative of all the color photographs in this book. It costs a king's ransom to do the book in full color; but it's a thousand times better than the original black and white version! Those Florentine No. 2 pieces include the four cobalt items, the unusual large and small berry bowls in pink and the two blown flat bottomed tumblers holding 6 oz. and measuring 3½" tall.

There are nine sets of sugars and creamers in Florentine No. 1! Ruffled creamers seem to be in shorter supply than the sugars.

I've recently noticed that prices of crystal Florentine are catching up with the green!

Please notice, John, that I included in the listing the 3¼", 5 oz. tumbler in green that I left out last time after you'd told me about it! Not only professors are absent minded at times!

I did see at a show in Denver the very rare cobalt blue pitcher in Florentine No. 1. It's a pretty pitcher! Where there's one, there's bound to be another. Watch for it!

Notice the unusual Florentine iced tea pictured at the right rear of the photograph. It's from a Floral iced tea mold, but it has the Florentine pattern on it. No, the same companies did NOT make the two patterns! The only explanation lies in our knowledge that glass companies used to exchange molds on occasion---a practice which further muddies the waters of research for people like me!

	Crystal, Green	Yellow	Pink	Blue
Ash Tray, 5½"	16.50	24.00	24.00	
Bowl, 5" Berry	6.00	6.50	7.50	12.50
Bowl, 6" Cereal	7.50	8.50	10.00	
Bowl, 8½" Large Berry	13.50	17.50	20.00	
Bowl, 9½" Oval Vegetable & Cover	27.50	32.50	35.00	
Butter Dish and Cover	97.50	125.00	157.50	
Coaster/Ash Tray, 3¾"	12.00	13.50	20.00	
Creamer	6.50	8.50	9.50	
Creamer, Ruffled	16.50	22.50	20.00	42.50
Cup	4.50	5.50	6.00	
Pitcher, 6½", 36 oz. Footed	30.00	37.50	35.00	400.00
Pitcher, 7½", 54 oz. Flat, Ice Lip or None	37.50	127.50	97.50	
Plate, 6" Sherbet	3.00	3.50	3.00	
Plate, 8½" Salad	4.50	8.00	8.50	
Plate, 10" Dinner	7.50	11.00	12.50	
Plate, 10" Grill	7.00	9.50	10.00	
Platter, 11½" Oval	8.50	12.50	13.50	
Salt and Pepper, Footed	22.50	37.50	40.00	
Saucer	2.00	3.00	3.00	
Sherbet, 3 oz. Footed	4.50	6.50	7.50	
Sugar	5.00	6.50	8.50	
Sugar Cover	10.00	11.50	11.00	
Sugar, Ruffled	15.00	20.00	17.50	39.50
Tumbler, 3¼", 5 oz. Footed	7.50			
Tumbler, 3¾", 5 oz. Footed Juice	7.00	12.00	13.00	
Tumbler, 4¾", 10 oz. Footed Water	10.50	14.50	17.50	
Tumbler, 5¼", 12 oz. Footed Iced Tea	12.00	18.50	20.00	
Tumbler, 5¼", 9 oz. Lemonade (Like Floral)			42.50	

Please refer to Foreword for pricing information

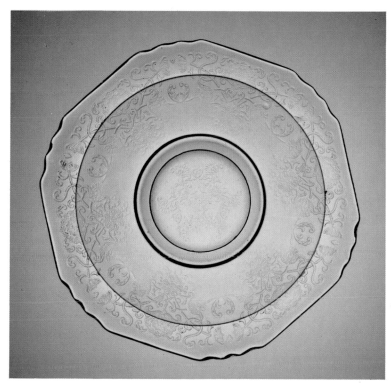

FLORENTINE NO. 2, "POPPY NO. 2"

HAZEL ATLAS GLASS COMPANY, 1934-1937

Colors: Pink, green, crystal, some cobalt, amber, ice blue.

All those hard to find pitchers in one picture should command your attention here! If they aren't enough to rivet your interest, then try that RUFFLED yellow plate in the foreground! Notice that the handles on the pitchers to the left have Florentine No. 1 type handles. However, they've been found boxed with Florentine No. 2 type tumblers; so, we include them here. They would obviously go with either pattern. The bulbous pitchers on the right are few and far between; but as luck would have it, the crystal one was found on the way to the photographer's studio! (You KNOW it's IMPOSSIBLE to PASS small shops along the way!)

If you've reached this point without having read the information about Florentine No. 1 pattern, turn back and read the first two paragraphs since they contain information pertinent to this pattern, also.

The tops to the butter dishes and the oval vegetable bowls are interchangeable between the two patterns. The crystal butter dish in both patterns is the hardest fo find although this is not reflected in the prices yet.

A few odd pieces in other colors exist. An ice blue pitcher (pictured on the 2nd edition cover page at the back) was found in Mexico for $3.00. A dark amber color has surfaced in cup, saucer, sherbet and tumbler (pictured in 4th edition). A few items in cobalt have turned up, though some, like the shaker on the preceding page are not true cobalt, but color fired-on over crystal. I've even seen an orange fired-on shaker.

The 6¼" plate with indent for the custard cup is readily found in crystal or yellow; but I've never seen one in green. The custard cup, itself, is hard to locate in yellow or crystal.

I've encountered some lidless candy bottoms (with borrowed ladles) masquerading as mayonnaise sets lately! That lid is tough to find!

There are TWO sizes of footed, cone shaped pitchers in Florentine No. 2. The usually found one measures 7 1/8" tall and holds between 28-29½ oz. when filled to overflowing. The RARELY FOUND one is shorter, chubbier and measures only 6¼" tall and holds only 24-25½ oz.

The pattern shot shows a Federal Madrid shape sherbet with a Hazel Atlas Florentine No. 2 design. This piece was also found in a Mexican flea market.

	Crystal, Green	Pink	Yellow	Blue		Crystal, Green	Pink	Yellow	Blue
Bowl, 4½" Berry	7.00	9.00	12.50		Plate, 6¼" with Indent	12.00		20.00	
Bowl, 4¾" Cream Soup	8.50	8.50	12.50		Plate, 8½" Salad	4.50	5.00	6.00	
Bowl, 5" Cream Soup, or Ruffled					Plate, 10" Dinner	7.50	11.00	9.00	
Nut		8.00		27.50	Plate, 10¼" Grill	6.00		7.00	
Bowl, 5½"	13.50		22.50		Platter, 11" Oval	9.50	10.00	10.00	
Bowl, 6" Cereal	11.50	13.50	19.50		Platter, 11½" for Gravyboat			27.50	
Bowl, 8" Large Berry	13.50	16.50	15.50		Relish Dish, 10", 3 Part or Plain	7.50	14.00	12.50	
Bowl, 9" Oval Vegetable and					††Salt and Pepper, Pr.	30.00		35.00	
Cover	27.50		37.50		Saucer (Amber: 15.00)	2.00		3.00	
Bowl, 9" Flat	15.00				Sherbet, Footed (Amber: 37.50)	6.00		7.50	
*Butter Dish and Cover	77.50		110.00		Sugar	4.50		6.50	
Candlesticks, 2¾" Pair	30.00		35.00		Sugar Cover	8.50		12.50	
Candy Dish and Cover	62.50	97.50	125.00		Tray, Condiment for Shakers,				
Coaster, 3¼"	9.00	13.50	15.00		Creamer and Sugar (Round)			40.00	
Coaster/Ash Tray, 3¾"	11.50		17.50		Tumbler, 3½", 5 oz. Juice	6.00	8.00	12.50	
Coaster/Ash Tray, 5½"	15.00		25.00		Tumbler, 3½", 6 oz. Blown	8.50			
Comport, 3½" Ruffled	10.00	6.00	15.00	42.50	†††Tumbler, 4", 9 oz. Water	8.50	8.50	12.50	47.50
Creamer	6.00		6.50		Tumbler, 5", 12 oz. Iced Tea	12.50		22.50	
Cup (Amber 35.00)	5.00		6.00		Tumbler, 3¼", 5 oz. Footed	7.50		8.00	
Custard Cup or Jello	25.00		37.50		Tumbler, 4", 5 oz. Footed	8.00		9.50	
Gravy Boat			30.00		Tumbler, 4½", 9 oz. Footed	9.50		10.50	
Pitcher, 6¼", 24 oz. Cone Footed			79.50		Tumbler, 5", 12 oz. Footed	12.50		22.50	
†Pitcher, 7½", 28 oz. Cone Footed	17.50		18.50		Vase or Parfait, 6"	17.00		37.50	
Pitcher, 7½", 54 oz.	37.50	97.50	127.50						
Pitcher, 8", 76 oz.	67.50		127.50						
Plate, 6" Sherbet	2.00		3.00						

* Crystal — $97.50

†Blue — $400.00
††Fired-on Orange or Blue, Pr. — 25.00 **Please refer to Foreword for pricing information**
†††Amber: — 47.50

FLOWER GARDEN WITH BUTTERFLIES, "BUTTERFLIES AND ROSES"

U.S. GLASS COMPANY, Late 1920's

Colors: Pink, green, blue-green, canary yellow, crystal, amber, black.

There's a beautiful blue, heart shaped candy dish in this pattern that my wife keeps hoping to find; otherwise, she's pretty content with the few pieces shown here that she's managed to collect. The pink saucer still needs a cup; but she has fun looking for this!

We got a call from one lucky couple who bought a whole set of this pattern at a sale for $25.00 or $30.00. They wanted to know was it REALLY worth the prices listed in my book that someone had lent them! I enjoy people still finding bargains like that TODAY! It lends zest to the hunt!

The only new pieces I can confirm are the mayonnaise set with the ladle and a 7¼" salad plate. I might mention that a ladle in that color blue is extremely hard to find! I didn't even have one that color for the whole page of ladles featured in the Kitchenware book!

My mother did find one plate in Flower Garden that DIDN'T have even a piece of a butterfly on it. Usually, somewhere in that jumble of flowers you'll find at least one butterfly!

	All Colors		All Colors
Ash Tray, Match-Pack Holders	115.00	Cup	72.50
Bowl, Rolled Edge Console,		Mayonnaise Set, 3 Piece	47.50
2 Styles	40.00	Plate, 7"	9.00
Candlesticks, 4" Pair	32.50	Plate, 8", Two Styles	10.00
Candlesticks, 8" Pair	47.50	Powder Jar, Footed	27.50
Candy Dish and Cover, 8"	42.50	Powder Jar, Flat	22.50
Candy Dish, Heart Shaped	157.50	Sandwich Server, Center Handle	45.00
Candy Dish, 6" Open	13.50	Saucer	32.50
Cheese and Cracker Set		Sugar, Open	47.50
(4" Compote, 10" Plate)	37.50	Tray, 5½" x 10" Oval	27.50
Cigarette Box, 2½" x 3½"		Tray, 11¾" x 7¾" Rectangular	32.50
(Black)	52.50	Vase, 6"	57.50
Cologne Bottle, 7½" Tall Footed	27.50	Vase, 7" (Black)	77.50
Console Bowl, 10" Footed	37.50	Vase, 10"	59.50
Creamer	47.50		

Design on Black highlighted to emphasize pattern.

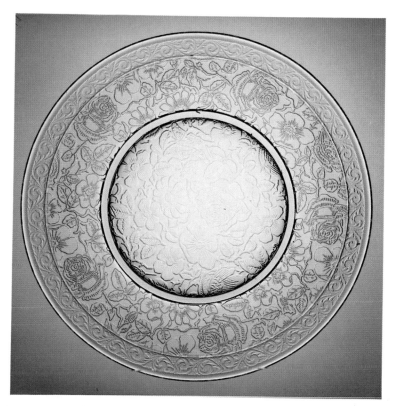

FOREST GREEN ANCHOR HOCKING GLASS COMPANY CORPORATION, 1950-1957

Color: Green.

Actually, the collecting of Forest Green is only beginning. It was a later pattern and many of the younger collectors associate it with their childhood memories. As I said when I first started including it in my book, it really isn't Depression Glass, but so many people are collecting it that I've been forced to include it. One dealer put it rather succinctly, "It's not the best pattern in the world, but it sells well---especially at Christmas!"

Little Forest Green is difficult to get at this time with the possible exception of the 3 quart pitcher. Tumblers are abundant, both decorated and plain. The former are a bit higher priced.

I put in the green Bubble creamer and sugar to remind you that, just as in Royal Ruby, there are other Hocking patterns made in Forest Green color. This dinnerware per se consists of the square shaped pieces.

Notice the mixing bowls pictured at the back.

	Green		Green
Ash Tray	2.50	Platter, Rectangular	8.50
Batter Bowl	5.00	Saucer	1.25
Bowl, 4¾" Dessert	3.00	Sugar, Flat	2.50
Bowl, 6" Soup	5.00	Tumbler, 5 oz.	1.50
Bowl, 7 3/8" Salad	5.50	Tumbler, 10 oz.	2.50
Creamer, Flat	3.00	Vase, 4" Ivy	2.00
Cup	2.00	Vase, 6 3/8"	3.50
Mixing Bowl Set, 3 Piece	12.50	Vase, 9"	4.00
Pitcher, 22 oz.	8.50		
Pitcher, 3 qt. Round	15.00		
Plate, 6 5/8" Salad	1.25		
Plate, 8 3/8" Luncheon	2.50		
Plate, 10" Dinner	7.50		

FORTUNE HOCKING GLASS COMPANY, 1937-1938

Colors: Pink, crystal.

The name given this pattern by collectors was definitely mischance! It is neither worth a fortune nor do collectors consider themselves fortunate in discovering a piece! Yet, it really isn't bad looking; it just never has caught on with collectors.

Luncheon plates are the hardest item to find; and pitchers and candy dishes are sought by "item" collectors.

	Pink, Crystal		Pink, Crystal
Bowl, 4" Berry	2.50	Cup	3.00
Bowl, 4½" Dessert	3.50	Plate, 6" Sherbet	2.00
Bowl, 4½" Handled	3.50	Plate, 8" Luncheon	4.00
Bowl, 5¼" Rolled Edge	4.00	Saucer	2.00
Bowl, 7¾" Salad or Large Berry	4.50	Tumbler, 3½", 5 oz. Juice	3.00
Candy Dish and Cover, Flat	12.50	Tumbler, 4", 9 oz. Water	4.00

Please refer to Foreword for pricing information

"FRUITS" HAZEL ATLAS AND OTHER GLASS COMPANIES, 1931-1933

Colors: Pink, green, crystal.

"Fruits" pattern encompasses glass made by several companies showing one or many fruit designs. The cherries only tumblers are particularly desirable to collectors because they match the pitcher that's been found. Berry bowls are hard to find.

A new 5", 12 oz. flat tumbler in green turned up at the Charlotte show. The iridized tumblers, usually with pear designs, are NOT Carnival glass and are worth about $7.00, not the $15.00 I've seen. Crystal and iridized tumblers are frequently found; only the pink and green seem less plentiful.

Item collectors drive up the prices of pitchers, candy dishes, butter dishes, etc., in all patterns.

	Pink, Green		Pink, Green
Bowl, 5" Cereal	10.50	Sherbet	5.50
Bowl, 8" Berry	30.00	Tumbler, 3½" Juice	7.00
Cup	4.00	Tumbler, 4" (One Fruit)	7.50
Pitcher, 7" Flat Bottom	35.00	Tumbler, 4" (Combination	
Plate, 8" Luncheon	4.00	of Fruits)	8.50
Saucer	2.50	Tumbler, 5", 12 oz.	20.00

HARP JEANNETTE GLASS COMPANY, 1954-1957

Colors: Crystal, crystal with gold trim, shell pink, ice blue.

This is another of the later patterns that Depression collectors are forcing me to include. Collecting this now is understandable since all eight pieces can still be found and purchased inexpensively; yet they have some of the collectible mystique about them.

A light blue cake stand keeps turning up; but I have heard of no other pieces being found in the blue. You can also find a shell pink cake stand which was made by Jeannette during their surge of promoting shell pink in the 1950's.

I have added the two-handled, rectangular tray to the listing which can also be found in shell pink.

	Crystal		Crystal
Ash Tray/Coaster	3.00	Plate, 7"	2.50
Coaster	2.00	Saucer	1.25
Cup	3.00	Tray, 2 Handled Rectangular	12.50
*Cake Stand, 9"	10.00	Vase, 6"	6.50

*Ice blue or shell pink $10.00

GEORGIAN, "LOVEBIRDS"   FEDERAL GLASS COMPANY, 1931-1936

Colors: Green, crystal.

In 1977, Georgia's Peach State Depression Glass Club made arrangements for a setting of this pattern to be donated to the Smithsonian Institution in President Jimmy Carter's name and thereby struck a mighty blow toward preserving this American made glassware as part of our national heritage. (For a picture of "The President's Table" and a more detailed account of this club's coup, see the 4th edition). The resultant publicity created a host of new collectors of Georgian; and a pattern that had been in abundant supply immediately felt the effects of this surge of new collectors.

New collectors tend to mix up "Lovebirds" with "Parrot". First of all, "Parrot" has a squared shape and features only birds. The Georgian "Lovebirds" is round and alternates birds with baskets of flowers. It also has a garland encircling each piece.

The dinner plates come with full design as shown in the pattern shot or with only the garland and center motif---no birds or baskets. Tumblers have ONLY BASKETS in their design.

Sugar lids are NOT interchangeable; and the larger lid is much harder to find.

You can see how the Georgian walnut lazy susan would look by referring to the one pictured in the Madrid pattern.

The 6½" bowl pictured in front is twice as hard to find as the one shown behind it. Both have doubled in price in the last year. All prices have jumped in this pattern!

A spoutless 4" creamer has turned up and is being called a "mug".

	Green		Green
Bowl, 4½" Berry	4.50	†Hot Plate, 5" Center Design	27.50
Bowl, 5¾" Cereal	9.50	Plate, 6" Sherbet	3.00
Bowl, 6½" Deep	37.50	Plate, 8" Luncheon	5.50
Bowl, 7½" Large Berry	32.50	Plate, 9¼" Dinner	14.50
Bowl, 9" Oval Vegetable	37.50	Plate, 9¼" Center Design Only	12.50
Butter Dish and Cover	57.50	Platter, 11½" Closed Handled	35.00
Cold Cuts Server, 18½" Wood with		Saucer	2.50
Seven 5" Openings for 5" Coasters	375.00	Sherbet	7.00
Creamer, 3" Footed	7.50	Sugar, 3" Footed	7.00
Creamer, 4" Footed	8.50	Sugar, 4" Footed	8.00
Cup	6.50	Sugar Cover for 3"	10.00
		Sugar Cover for 4"	17.50
		Tumbler, 4", 9 oz. Flat	27.50
		Tumbler, 5¼", 12 oz. Flat	37.50

†Crystal: 18.50

Please refer to Foreword for pricing information

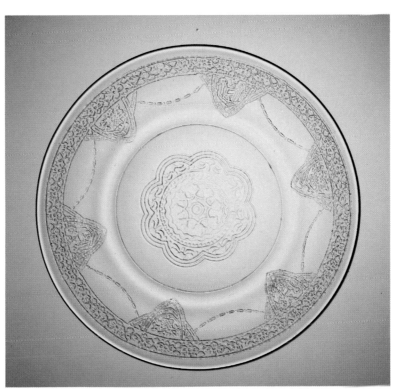

83

HERITAGE FEDERAL GLASS COMPANY, Late 1930's · 1960's

Colors: Crystal, some pink, blue, green.

People ignoring Heritage as a pattern to collect should reconsider. It makes a fantastic table display! Naturally, everyone would LIKE to find a set in any of the colors; but so far, that isn't feasible. Since finding the green berry set in Ohio in 1974, I've never seen another piece in color (and that covers a lot of miles and a few million pieces of glass)!

I received a snapshot in the mail of a blue saucer in Heritage that a lady found at a garage sale in Georgia. So, Southerners, look sharp!

The larger berry bowl, sandwich plate and sugar and creamer are the harder pieces to find.

	Crystal	Pink	Blue Green
Bowl, 5" Berry	4.00	12.50	27.50
Bowl, 8½" Large Berry	11.00	37.50	57.50
Bowl, 10½" Fruit	10.00		
Cup	2.50		
Creamer, Footed	9.00		
Plate, 8" Luncheon	4.00		
Plate, 9¼" Dinner	5.00		
Plate, 12" Sandwich	7.00		
Saucer	2.00		
Sugar, Open Footed	8.00		

HEX OPTIC, "HONEYCOMB" JEANNETTE GLASS COMPANY, 1928-1932

Colors: Pink, green.

We can now confirm that the "ice bucket with a lip" is in fact a bucket reamer. There are two complete ones pictured in my new Kitchenware book. In fact, kitchenware items, such as the stacking set and mixing bowls, are creating more interest in this pattern than the regular pieces!

Hex Optic tends to show the heavy usage this utilitarian line received over the years. It was obviously durable. Notice that the handles in this pattern are closed.

The iridized pieces found in tumblers, oil lamps and pitchers are from the late 1950's and early 1960's, as is the teal colored tumbler also being found.

A sunflower motif found in the bottom of the 5", 32 oz. pitcher is an typical Jeannette trademark found in many of their kitchenware lines. This does not indicate this is a Sunflower pitcher.

	Pink, Green		Pink, Green
Bowl, 4¼" Ruffled Berry	2.00	Plate, 8" Luncheon	4.50
Bowl, 7½" Large Berry	5.00	Platter, 11" Round	5.00
Bowl, 7¼" Mixing	4.50	Refrigerator Dish, 4"x4"	4.00
Bowl, 8¼" Mixing	6.00	Refrigerator Stack Set, 3 Pc.	
Bowl, 9" Mixing	7.00	w/Handles	15.00
Bowl, 10" Mixing	9.00	Salt and Pepper, Pr.	15.00
Bucket Reamer	17.50	Saucer	1.50
Butter Dish and Cover, Rectangular 1 lb. Size	17.50	Sugar, 2 Styles of Handles	3.50
		Sherbet, 5 oz. Footed	3.00
Creamer, 2 Style Handles	3.50	Tumbler, 3¾", 9 oz.	3.50
Cup, 2 Style Handles	2.50	Tumbler, 5¾" Footed	4.00
Ice Bucket, Metal Handle	7.50	Tumbler, 7" Footed	5.00
Pitcher, 5", 32 oz. Sunflower Motif in Bottom	10.00	Whiskey, 2", 1 oz.	3.00
Pitcher, 9", 48 oz. Footed	25.00		
Plate, 6" Sherbet	1.50		

Please refer to Foreword for pricing information

HOBNAIL HOCKING GLASS COMPANY, 1934-1936

Colors: Crystal, pink.

Creating glassware with hobbed designs has been done by numerous glass companies. The listing shown here refers only to those items made by Hocking during the time period indicated.

Because of the dearth of pieces available in Hocking's pink Hobnail, however, a number of collectors are buying the Macbeth-Evans "Hobnail" pitcher and tumblers shown to go with their pink Hocking collections. Hence its inclusion in this photograph.

If you collect this, you will probably have to ask dealers for it specifically since this is often one of the patterns left at home when packing for a show. They tend to take the "showier" Moonstone pattern to the glass shows they attend.

Collectors tell me that only luncheon sets come trimmed in red and that matching sugars and creamers are hard to find! Usually, trimmed pieces take a back seat with collectors; but Hobnail is the exception to that rule. Numerous people have mentioned they were searching for the red trimmed Hobnail.

	Pink	Crystal		Pink	Crystal
Bowl, 5½" Cereal		2.50	Saucer (Sherbet Plate		
Bowl, 7" Salad		1.75	in Pink)	1.50	1.00
Cup	2.00	2.00	Sherbet	2.50	2.00
Creamer, Footed		2.50	Sugar, Footed		2.50
Decanter and Stopper, 32 oz.		12.50	Tumbler, 5 oz. Juice		3.00
Goblet, 10 oz. Water		4.00	Tumbler, 9 oz., 10 oz. Water		4.00
Goblet, 13 oz. Iced Tea		5.00	Tumbler, 15 oz. Iced Tea		5.00
Pitcher, 18 oz. Milk		10.00	Tumbler, 3 oz. Footed Wine		5.00
Pitcher, 67 oz.		15.00	Tumbler, 5 oz. Footed Cordial		3.75
Plate, 6" Sherbet	1.50	1.00	Whiskey, 1½ oz.		4.00
Plate, 8½" Luncheon	2.00	1.50			

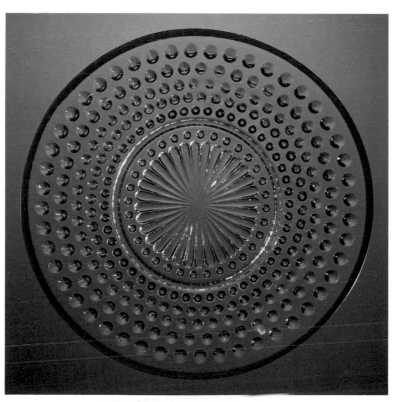

HOLIDAY, "BUTTONS AND BOWS" JEANNETTE GLASS COMPANY, 1947-1949

Colors: Pink, iridescent; some shell pink opaque and crystal.

It constantly amazes me that this later than Depression era pattern has pieces that are harder to find than patterns made years before over an equal time period. The answer, of course, lies in the popularity of the design. "Daisy and Button" patterned dishes were selling well long before Holiday was manufactured.

The cake plate, console bowl, footed iced teas and small milk pitchers are considered "finds" of first importance by many collectors.

There are two styles of cups. Cups which fit the center rayed saucers will not fit the plain centered saucers.

In the 1950's, the platter, footed juice and small milk pitcher were iridized and a shell pink console bowl was also produced. Even a few crystal items have turned up which evidently missed the iridizing spray. These pieces are considered to be more novel than rare.

	Pink		Pink
Bowl, 5 1/8″ Berry	5.00	Plate, 6″ Sherbet	2.50
Bowl, 7¾″ Soup	19.50	Plate, 9″ Dinner	7.50
Bowl, 8½″ Large Berry	12.50	Plate, 13¾″ Chop	52.50
Bowl, 9½″ Oval Vegetable	9.50	Platter, 11 3/8″ Oval	8.50
Bowl, 10¾″ Console	57.50	Sandwich Tray, 10½″	8.00
Butter Dish and Cover	29.50	Saucer, Two Styles	2.50
Cake Plate, 10½″, 3 Legged	47.50	Sherbet	4.50
Candlesticks, 3″ Pair	45.00	Sugar	4.00
Creamer, Footed	5.00	Sugar Cover	6.50
Cup, Two Sizes	4.00	Tumbler, 4″, 10 oz. Flat	12.00
Pitcher, 4¾″, 16 oz. Milk	35.00	Tumbler, 4″, Footed	22.50
Pitcher, 6¾″, 52 oz.	22.50	Tumbler, 6″, Footed	42.50

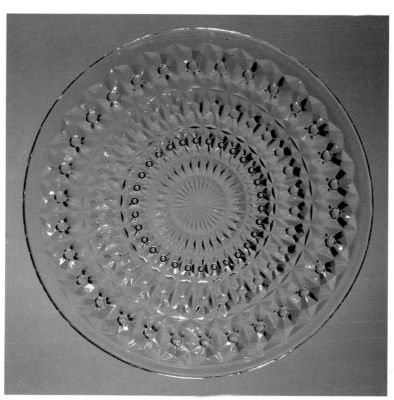

HOMESPUN, "FINE RIB" JEANNETTE GLASS COMPANY, 1939-1940

Colors: Pink, crystal.

With patience and careful searching, this is still a pattern that can be gathered without mortgaging the car.

The 96 oz. pitcher does not contain the waffle design that characterizes many of the Homespun pieces. Therefore, it is often confused with Hazel Atlas's "Fine Rib" cobalt pitcher and tumblers. Homespun was not made in cobalt; rather, look for a large, tilted pitcher in crystal or pink with ribs as shown here.

For years I've asked for confirmation of the child's set tea pot in crystal like the one shown here in pink. To date, none has been forthcoming! Therefore, I still list only twelve pieces in the crystal child's set.

The footed, 5 oz. 4" tumbler for juice or wine and the platter appear frequently causing me to believe they may have been promoted together as a set.

	Pink, Crystal		Pink, Crystal
Bowl, 4½", Closed Handles	4.00	Platter, 13", Closed Handles	7.00
Bowl, 5" Cereal	7.50	Saucer	2.00
Bowl, 8¼" Large Berry	8.50	Sherbet, Low Flat	5.00
*Butter Dish and Cover	37.50	Sugar, Footed	5.50
Coaster/Ash Tray	4.00	Tumbler, 4", 9 oz. Water	6.00
Creamer, Footed	6.00	Tumbler, 5¼", 13 oz. Iced Tea	11.50
Cup	3.50	Tumbler, 4", 5 oz. Footed	7.00
Pitcher, 96 oz.	27.50	Tumbler, 6¼", 9 oz. Footed	8.50
Plate, 6" Sherbet	2.00	Tumbler, 6½", 15 oz. Footed	12.50
Plate, 9¼" Dinner	7.50		

*Crystal: 57.50

HOMESPUN CHILD'S TEA SET

	Pink	Crystal		Pink	Crystal
Cup	21.50	13.25	Tea Pot	21.50	
Saucer	6.25	5.00	Tea Pot Cover	35.00	
Plate	8.75	6.75	Set: 14 Pieces	197.50	
			Set: 12 Pieces		100.00

INDIANA CUSTARD, "FLOWER AND LEAF BAND" INDIANA GLASS COMPANY

Colors: Ivory or custard, early 1930's; white, 1950's.

A few collectors have found this pattern to their liking in the last couple of years; and the supposedly common pieces such as cups, soups, cereals and bowls just about disappeared! A friend of mine told me to look for him some cups and saucers; and that's all I did. Look! Suddenly there were none to be found!

The sherbet has long been known to be difficult. Many collectors have sets except for the sherbets which may well be the rarest sherbets in Depression glass. Any appearing on the market are soon snatched up, even at that $65.00 price tag!

	French Ivory		French Ivory
Bowl, 4 7/8" Berry	5.00	Plate, 5¾" Bread and Butter	4.00
Bowl, 5¾" Cereal	10.00	Plate, 7½" Salad	7.50
Bowl, 7½" Flat Soup	14.50	Plate, 8 7/8" Luncheon	8.50
Bowl, 8¾" Large Berry	17.50	Plate, 9¾" Dinner	12.50
Bowl, 9½" Oval Vegetable	19.50	Platter, 11½" Oval	20.00
Butter Dish and Cover	47.50	Saucer	5.00
Cup	22.50	Sherbet	65.00
Creamer	10.00	Sugar	7.50
		Sugar Cover	12.50

Please refer to Foreword for pricing information

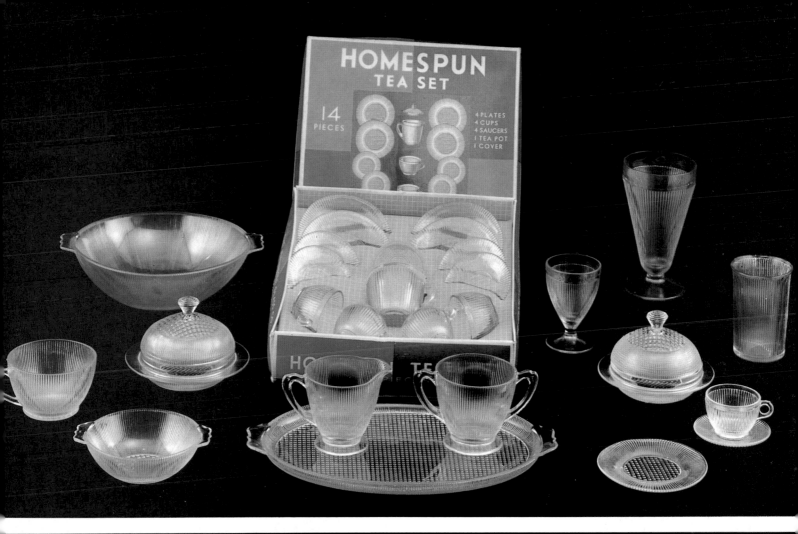

IRIS, "IRIS AND HERRINGBONE" JEANNETTE GLASS COMPANY, 1928-1932; 1950's; 1970's

Colors: Crystal, iridescent, some pink; recently red-yellow and blue-green combinations.

The flat soup bowl in crystal Iris has jumped faster in price and percentage of increase than any bowl in Depression Glass. From $17.50 to $62.50 is a big leap; but it's become very apparent that these bowls are in short supply even at that price!

The 9½" scalloped fruit bowl in pink shown on the rare page is the first new piece in pink to surface in some time. I've heard report of other pieces in pink or green, but the bowl and the 9" vase are the only pieces I've seen.

The nut sets with nut picks and the fruit sets with knives which were made from the 11" bowl are getting to be good items to own. It used to take my Grannie Bear Antique shop ages to sell one; now we have people wanting to find them!

Remember the new vases and candy bottoms which are appearing in a red-yellow, blue-green combination sprayed on over crystal do not have the rayed bottom design of the old; so there's no reason to confuse them. Only these items have been made recently.

The lack of demitasse saucers was explained by an ad from a 1947 magazine showing cups being promoted on plain copper saucers for "al fresco dining".

Collectors pay little attention to the satinized pieces, including the rarely found 7" plate!

	Crystal	Iridescent		Crystal	Iridescent	Pink, Green
Bowl, 4½" Berry, Beaded Edge	20.00	5.00	Goblet, 5¾", 4 oz.	9.00		
Bowl, 5" Ruffled Sauce	4.50	4.50	Goblet, 5¾", 8 oz.	11.50		
Bowl, 6" Cereal	19.50		Pitcher, 9½" Footed	17.50	22.50	
Bowl, 7½" Soup	62.50	17.50	Plate, 5½" Sherbet	4.50	3.50	
Bowl, 8" Berry, Ruffled	9.50	8.50	Plate, 8" Luncheon	27.50		
Bowl, 8" Berry, Beaded Edge	27.50	9.50	Plate, 9" Dinner	24.50	15.00	
*Bowl, 9½" Salad	8.00	7.50	Plate, 11¾" Sandwich	9.50	9.00	
Bowl, 11" Ruffled Fruit	8.50	6.00	Saucer	3.50	3.00	
Bowl, 11" Fruit, Straight Edge	22.50		Sherbet, 2½" Footed	10.00	6.50	
Butter Dish and Cover	25.00	30.00	Sherbet, 4" Footed	8.00		
Candlesticks, Pr.	15.00	19.50	Sugar	4.50	5.50	
Candy Jar and Cover	47.50		Sugar Cover	5.50	5.50	
Coaster	27.50		Tumbler, 4" Flat	30.00		
Creamer, Footed	4.00	5.00	Tumbler, 6" Footed	9.50	9.50	
Cup	7.00	6.50	Tumbler, 7" Footed	12.50	11.50	
**Demitasse Cup	14.00	25.00	Vase, 9"	12.50	12.50	37.50
**Demitasse Saucer	20.00	37.50				
Fruit or Nut Set	25.00					
Goblet, 4" Wine	10.50	12.00				
Goblet, 4½" Wine	10.50					

*Pink — $37.50
**Ruby, Blue, Amethyst priced as Iridescent

93

JUBILEE LANCASTER GLASS COMPANY, Early 1930's

Color: Yellow.

I've gotten letter after letter wanting to know what this pattern was; so, I got busy and rounded some up to include it in the book. Jubilee is really very attractive with its floral etchings and it comes in the most beautiful yellow color imaginable! You don't often see this, but when you do, it's usually in luncheon sets. It's also a pattern that sells itself.

There are two different goblets in Jubilee: a 6", 10 oz. which is usually found and a 6 1/8", 12½ oz. which was unknown until recently. It's doubtful that it is very plentiful. Time will tell.

The mayonnaise set originally had a ladle with it; but you seldom find the ladle today. Any serving pieces in this pattern are hard to get!

If you're looking for a really pretty pattern to collect in yellow, you can't go wrong with this!

	Yellow
Bowl, 9" Handled Fruit	27.50
Cheese & Cracker Set	22.50
Creamer	10.00
Cup	5.50
Goblet, 6", 10 oz.	15.00
Goblet, 6 1/8", 12½ oz.	22.50
Mayonnaise & Plate	25.00
w/Original Ladle	30.00
Plate, 7" Salad	4.00
Plate, 8¾" Luncheon	7.50
Plate, 13" Sandwich	15.00
Saucer	2.00
Sugar	10.00
Tray, 11", 2 Handled Cake	13.50
Tray, Center Handled Sandwich	17.50

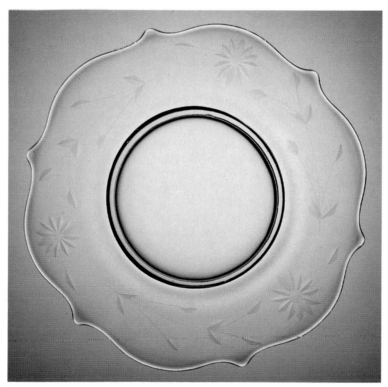

95

JUNE FOSTORIA GLASS COMPANY, 1928-1944

Colors: Crystal, "Azure" blue, "Topaz" yellow, "Rose" pink.

This is one of the Fostoria patterns that is highly collected in every color. Blue is the most desirable color to own; the pink seems to be more scarce with prices comparable to those of yellow.

Doing a show in Tennessee recently, a lady walking by the table stopped and exclaimed, "Is that June? That's my pattern! I got that when we married 37 years ago!" She was amazed to even see it out for sale; and delighted to know it was very collectible!

Choice pieces to own include pitchers, shakers with those difficult to find glass lids, footed oils, cordials, grapefruits with liners and the 2½ ounce tumblers. At present, all these items can still be found, perhaps not as reasonably as you'd wish. Most items, considering their age, collectibility and investment potential, are VERY reasonable as compared to the prices they ask for new crystal in the department stores today!

	Crystal	Blue	Rose, Topaz		Crystal	Blue	Rose, Topaz
Ash Tray	20.00	30.00	30.00	Grapefruit Liner	17.50	32.50	27.50
Baker, 9" Oval	30.00	50.00	45.00	Ice Bucket	45.00	85.00	75.00
Bon Bon	12.00	19.00	17.00	Ice Dish	20.00	40.00	35.00
Bouillon, Footed	12.00	18.00	16.00	Ice Dish Liner (Tomato,			
Bowl, 5" Fruit	10.00	20.00	16.50	Crab, Fruit)	5.00	10.00	10.00
Bowl, 6" Cereal	15.00	25.00	22.00	Lemon Dish	14.00	22.00	18.00
Bowl, 7" Nappy	15.00	22.50	20.00	Mayonnaise	20.00	35.00	30.00
Bowl, 7" Soup	16.50	27.50	22.50	Mint Dish	10.00	18.00	14.00
Bowl, Large Hdld. Dessert	16.00	32.00	24.00	Nappy, 6" Footed	10.00	20.00	15.00
Bowl, 10"	20.00	45.00	35.00	Oil, Footed	150.00	300.00	250.00
Bowl, 10" Grecian	30.00	55.00	45.00	Oyster Cocktail	16.00	28.00	22.00
Bowl, 11" Centerpiece	20.00	40.00	30.00	Parfait	20.00	30.00	25.00
Bowl, 12" Centerpiece,				Pitcher		375.00	295.00
Several Styles	20.00	45.00	35.00	Plate, 6" Bread & Butter	4.00	6.00	5.00
Bowl, 13" Oval Centerpiece	30.00	55.00	45.00	Plate, 7" Salad	5.00	10.00	8.00
Cake Plate, 10" Hdld.	20.00	40.00	30.00	Plate, 8" Luncheon	5.00	10.00	8.00
Canape Plate	10.00	15.00	12.50	Plate, 9" Dinner	8.00	16.00	14.00
Candlestick, 2" Pair	25.00	35.00	30.00	Plate, 10" Dinner	16.00	30.00	25.00
Candlestick, 3" Pair	25.00	40.00	32.50	Plate, 10" Grill	16.00	30.00	25.00
Candlestick, 3" Pair Grecian	20.00	35.00	30.00	Plate, 13" Chop	20.00	40.00	35.00
Candlestick, 5" Pair	24.00	39.00	32.00	Platter, 12"	20.00	40.00	35.00
Candy, 3 Pt. w/Cover	40.00	80.00	70.00	Platter, 15"	22.50	50.00	42.50
Candy, ½ lb. w/Cover	40.00	80.00	70.00	Relish, 8½"	14.00	20.00	18.00
Celery, 11½"	25.00	40.00	35.00	Salad Dressing Bottle	100.00	200.00	150.00
Cheese & Cracker Set	25.00	40.00	32.50	Sauce Boat	25.00	50.00	40.00
Comport, 5"	18.00	30.00	25.00	Sauce Boat Liner	5.00	15.00	10.00
Comport, 6"	20.00	30.00	25.00	Saucer, After Dinner	6.00	10.00	8.00
Comport, 7"	22.00	37.50	32.50	Saucer	4.00	7.50	5.00
Comport, 8"	24.00	40.00	35.00	Shaker, Footed Pair	50.00	100.00	75.00
Cream Soup, Footed	12.00	28.00	18.50	Sherbet, High	17.50	27.50	24.00
Cream Soup Plate, 7"	4.00	9.00	6.50	Sherbet, Low	15.00	24.00	19.00
Creamer, Footed	12.00	20.00	16.00	Sugar, Footed	12.00	20.00	16.00
Creamer, Tea	15.00	24.00	20.00	Sugar Cover	30.00	60.00	50.00
Cup, After Dinner	20.00	40.00	30.00	Sugar Pail	50.00	90.00	80.00
Cup, Footed	15.00	25.00	20.00	Sugar, Tea	15.00	24.00	20.00
Decanter	100.00	200.00	175.00	Tray, 11" Center Handled	20.00	40.00	30.00
Finger Bowl	15.00	24.00	20.00	Tumbler, 2½ oz.	20.00	35.00	30.00
Goblet, Claret	30.00	42.50	35.00	Tumbler, 5 oz.	15.00	25.00	20.00
Goblet, Cocktail	24.00	30.00	28.00	Tumbler, 9 oz.	12.50	25.00	18.00
Goblet, Cordial	30.00	60.00	50.00	Tumbler, 12 oz.	15.00	28.00	22.00
Goblet, Water	20.00	30.00	27.50	Vase, 8"	35.00	115.00	97.50
Goblet, Wine	20.00	45.00	35.00	Vase, 8½", Footed Fan	30.00	60.00	50.00
Grapefruit	25.00	45.00	35.00	Whipped Cream Bowl	11.00	18.00	15.00
				Whipped Cream Pail	50.00	90.00	80.00

Please refer to Foreword for pricing information

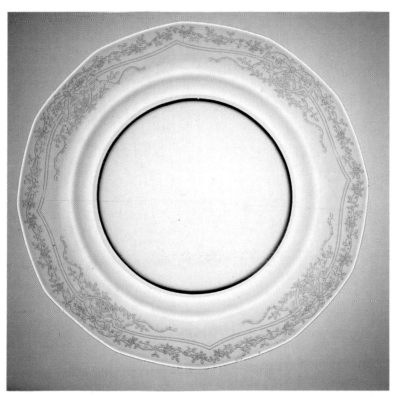

97

LACE EDGE, "OPEN LACE"   HOCKING GLASS COMPANY, 1935-1938

Colors: Pink, some crystal.

This year there are two new pieces in Lace Edge to report, an ash tray and a 9" large comport shown in the pattern shot! I know two of the ash trays have been found and I have received confirming pictures on two more 9" comports. Exciting, isn't it! Prices for the two items have not really been established yet. One ash tray sold for $60.00 and the other for considerably less than that. Only time and the avidity of Lace Edge collectors will establish prices for these items.

For those who have not seen the 7" vase, it is shaped similar to the large Cameo or Princess vase and is perfectly plain except for the lacing at the top.

The vase, console bowl and candlesticks are found satinized about ten times more frequently than they're found unfrosted. Though I've seen high prices on the satinized pieces, they are worth considerably less than those same pieces unfrosted.

Certain pieces of Lace Edge get confused with other patterns. Cups are confused with Queen Mary cups; and footed tumblers are often confused with Coronation tumblers. Rays climb higher on those other patterns than they do on the Lace Edge counterparts. Rays on Lace Edge tumblers hardly reach mid glass.

There are many other companies that made lace edged pieces. Hocking made this Lace Edge pattern only in pink and a little crystal. Therefore, if you have blue, green, yellow or black pieces with a laced edge, they were made by some other company and do not belong to this pattern.

Because of the open area effecting the laced edge design, this pattern damages easily! Repeating information given in the Foreword of the book on pricing, the prices shown here reflect retail prices for MINT condition glassware. Mint glass means as near the condition in which it was first minted as possible with no flakes, chips, cracks, dings or chunks! DO NOT PAY retail prices for damaged glassware!

	Pink*		Pink*
**Bowl, 6 3/8" Cereal	7.50	Plate, 7¼" Salad	10.00
Bowl, 7¾" Salad	11.50	Plate, 8¾" Luncheon	9.50
Bowl, 9½" Plain or Ribbed	10.00	Plate, 10½" Dinner	15.00
***Bowl, 10½", 3 Legs	97.50	Plate, 10½" Grill	9.50
Butter Dish or Bon Bon		Plate, 10½" 3 Part Relish	15.00
with Cover	40.00	Plate, 13", 4 Part Solid Lace	12.50
***Candlesticks, Pr.	97.50	Platter, 12¾"	15.00
Candy Jar and Cover, Ribbed	27.50	Platter, 12¾", 5 Part	13.50
Comport, 7"	10.00	Relish Dish, 7½", 3 Part Deep	27.50
Comport and Cover, Footed	20.00	Saucer	5.50
Cookie Jar and Cover	32.50	***Sherbet, Footed	35.00
Creamer	10.00	Sugar	10.00
Cup	12.00	Tumbler, 3½", 5 oz. Flat	6.50
Fish Bowl, 1 gal. 8 oz.		Tumbler, 4½", 9 oz. Flat	7.50
(Crystal Only)	13.50	Tumbler, 5", 10½ oz. Footed	27.50
Flower Bowl, Crystal Frog	15.00	Vase, 7"	177.50

*Satin or frosted items 50% lower in price
**Officially listed as cereal or cream soup
***Price is for absolute mint condition

99

LAKE COMO HOCKING GLASS COMPANY, 1934-1937

Color: White with blue decoration.

Many collectors would like to have a set of this very attractive pattern; however, very little of it has turned up! Surely it wasn't all broken.

Shakers and regular cups have been difficult for me to locate. The St. Dennis cup is shown in this photograph.

	White		White
Bowl, 6" Cereal	4.00	Plate, 9¼" Dinner	4.50
Bowl, 9¾" Vegetable	6.50	Platter, 11"	8.50
Creamer, Footed	4.50	Salt & Pepper, Pr.	17.50
Cup, Regular	3.00	Saucer	1.50
Cup, St. Denis	6.00	Saucer, St. Denis	2.00
Plate, 7¼" Salad	3.00	Sugar, Footed	4.50

LAUREL McKEE GLASS COMPANY, 1930's

Colors: French ivory, jade green, white opal and poudre blue.

Since more people are searching for Depression Glass than ever before, new items are being found all the time. In Laurel, two new pieces have appeared: an 8" flat soup and an 8 3/8" grill plate!

People who already own the beloved Scottie Dog decal child's dishes are fortunate. They are seldom seen any more and coveted by many. Color rimmed child's dishes come also in orange and blue in addition to the red and green shown.

Poudre (powder) blue colored Laurel is rarely seen; but sets in ivory and green can still be gathered. This isn't a plentiful pattern; but there are relatively few collectors of Laurel at the moment, a combination which usually gives enormous investment potential to a pattern. I sold a set of Laurel to a lady recently, not for investment purposes, however, but because the green color exactly "matched" the green in her new floral placemats!

Hardest pieces to find are the three legged console bowl, tumblers, shakers and candlesticks. Don't pass those when you're shopping even if they aren't your pattern! Somebody will be delighted to buy them from you---or trade with you for something you want!

The cheese dish bottom is the 7½" salad plate.

	White Opal, Jade Green	French Ivory	Poudre Blue		White Opal, Jade Green	French Ivory	Poudre Blue
Bowl, 5" Berry	3.00	4.00	6.50	Plate, 6" Sherbet	2.50	3.25	4.00
Bowl, 6" Cereal	4.00	5.00	7.50	Plate, 7½" Salad	2.75	5.00	7.50
Bowl, 6", Three Legs	6.00	7.50		Plate, 9 1/8" Dinner	4.50	5.00	9.00
Bowl, 8" Soup		12.50		Plate, 9 1/8" Grill	3.00	4.00	7.00
Bowl, 9" Large Berry	8.50	11.50	15.00	Platter, 10¾" Oval	12.50	15.00	17.50
Bowl, 9¾" Oval Vegetable	12.00	15.00	21.50	Salt and Pepper	42.50	32.50	
				Saucer	2.00	2.50	4.00
Bowl, 10½", Three Legs	20.00	25.00	32.50	Sherbet	6.00	9.00	
Bowl, 11"	15.00	25.00	25.00	Sugar, Short	6.00	7.00	12.50
Candlestick, 4" Pair	15.00	20.00	25.00	Sugar, Tall	7.50	8.00	12.50
Cheese Dish and Cover	37.50	47.50		Tumbler, 4½", 9 oz. Flat		20.00	
Creamer, Short	6.00	7.00		Tumbler, 5", 12 oz. Flat		27.50	
Creamer, Tall	7.50	8.00	12.50				
Cup	4.00	5.00	10.00				

CHILDREN'S LAUREL TEA SET

	Plain	Decorated Rims	Scotty Dog Decal
Creamer	17.50	27.50	32.50
Cup	12.50	17.50	22.50
Plate	7.50	12.00	15.00
Saucer	5.50	7.50	10.00
Sugar	17.50	27.50	32.50
14 Piece Set	135.00	167.50	257.50

Please refer to Foreword for pricing information

LINCOLN INN FENTON GLASS COMPANY, Late 1920's

Colors: Amethyst, cobalt, black, red, green, pink, crystal, jade (opaque), green.

That exciting amber Lincoln Inn water pitcher shown here for the very first time measures 7¼″ to the spout and holds 46 ounces! You will notice that it's a larger version of the creamer.

Goblets and tumblers are the easiest pieces to find in this pattern---an unusual turn of events in a Depression glass pattern. Cereal and fruit bowls, straight sided and very shallow, appear to be the harder items to locate with shakers being an absolute nemesis for most Lincoln Inn collectors. Green shakers are shown for those of you who have never seen them.

We overturned the red plate in the pattern shot and the photograph so you could see the pattern. Occasionally, you'll notice an amberina (yellow/red) cast to some pieces of red you find---particularly in the stemware.

Red and cobalt blue, happily, are the easiest colors to find in Lincoln Inn. I particularly like the ice blue color as it's reminiscent of the Mayfair blue which first attracted me to Depression Glass.

	Blue, Red	All Other Colors
Ash Tray	10.00	4.00
Bon Bon, Handled Square	10.00	6.00
Bon Bon, Handled Oval	10.00	6.00
Bowl, 5″ Fruit	5.00	3.50
Bowl, 6″ Cereal	7.00	4.50
Bowl, 6″ Crimped	8.00	5.00
Bowl, Handled Olive	8.00	5.00
Bowl, Finger	7.50	6.00
Bowl, 9¼″ Footed	12.50	10.00
Bowl, 10½″ Footed	17.50	12.50
Candy Dish, Footed Oval	10.00	6.50
Comport	8.00	5.00
Creamer	15.00	10.00
Cup	9.50	6.50
Goblet, Water	15.00	10.00
Goblet, Wine	12.00	8.00
Nut Dish, Footed	10.00	6.00
Pitcher, 7¼″, 46 oz.		300.00
Plate, 6″	3.50	2.00
Plate, 8″	5.50	3.50
Plate, 9¼″	7.50	5.50
Plate, 12″	12.50	8.50
Salt/Pepper, Pair	125.00	75.00
Saucer	2.50	1.75
Sherbet, 4¾″	12.00	7.00
Sugar	15.00	10.00
Tumbler, 4 oz. Flat Juice	10.00	6.00
Tumbler, 5 oz. Footed	11.00	7.00
Tumbler, 7 oz. Footed	12.00	7.50
Tumbler, 9 oz. Footed	12.50	8.50
Tumbler, 12 oz. Footed	15.00	10.00
Vase, 12″ Footed	57.50	37.50

Please refer to Foreword for pricing information

LORAIN, "BASKET", No. 615" INDIANA GLASS COMPANY, 1929-1932

Colors: Green, yellow; some crystal.

In my last book I stated that prices for Lorain had gotten so high that people had to be "basket cases" to collect it. Yet, if they'd bought it at third book prices, they were laughing all the way to the bank! I believe I could still say the same thing regarding people who bought it at **fourth** book prices!

I only record prices; I don't set them. So, don't hold me responsible for the escalation in price on the 8" deep berry bowl! People who collect this pattern know that the supply of these bowls is quite limited; and they're willing to pay high prices to have them in their sets. Don't we ALL wish we'd gotten them at the 1974 price of $7.00.?

I have dropped the 9 3/8" dinner and 11½" cake plate from the listing. Serious collectors have convinced me these aren't to be found.

The luminescent yellow color of Lorain draws most collectors. Crystal Lorain is rarely seen. However, some crystal snack sets (rectangular with an off center indent for cups) have turned up with flashed borders in primary colors of red, yellow, blue and green.

Saucers in mint condition are harder to find than the cups.

The sherbet with "Lorain" design and a "Lace Edge" border in avocado green or white are of recent origin.

	Crystal, Green	Yellow		Crystal, Green	Yellow
Bowl, 6" Cereal	20.00	37.50	Plate, 10¼" Dinner	22.50	35.00
Bowl, 7¼" Salad	22.50	32.50	Platter, 11½"	16.50	25.00
Bowl, 8" Deep Berry	57.50	87.50	Relish, 8", 4 Part	12.00	19.50
Bowl, 9¾" Oval Vegetable	22.50	32.50	Saucer	3.00	3.50
Creamer, Footed	10.00	15.00	Sherbet, Footed	12.00	22.50
Cup	7.00	9.00	Snack Tray, Crystal/Trim	10.00	
Plate, 5½" Sherbet	3.50	4.50	Sugar, Footed	10.00	13.50
Plate, 7¾" Salad	6.50	10.00	Tumbler, 4¾", 9 oz. Footed	12.50	16.00
Plate, 8 3/8" Luncheon	12.50	19.00			

Please refer to Foreword for pricing information

MADRID FEDERAL GLASS COMPANY, 1932-1939

Colors: Green, pink, amber, crystal, "Madonna" blue.

There has been an upsurge in the collecting of old Madrid since the demise of Federal! Because I am approached daily by so many people new to collecting Depression Glass, I am repeating practically verbatim two paragraphs from my last book regarding the re-issue of Madrid by Federal; so, if you read the 4th edition, skip the next two paragraphs.

Ostensibly as their contribution to the Bi-Centennial celebration in 1976, Federal Glass Company redesigned molds to make their "Recollection" glassware. Their "Recollection" was a new, sharper molded **Madrid** pattern in AMBER glass with a tiny little '76 date marking in the design of each piece. The amber color was a hair darker than the old. Since the glass was marked, there was little reason for collectors of amber Madrid to panic; but they had to be a little more careful that they didn't buy new butter tops on old butter bottoms. (The new butter top mold marks run through the North and South poles of the knob while the old mold marks form an equator around the middle of the butter top knob). You could get a twenty piece starter set, 4 dinners, salads, cups, saucers and soups for $19.00. The butter and cover cost you $6.00.

Shortly thereafter, Federal Glass Company went out of business; and many of the local discount stores offered the butter dishes at the close out price of $1.99 early in 1979. Even at this, "Recollection" was no bargain as an investment! Many major department stores sold it; so, there must be millions of the new pieces. Consequently, it's a waste of money. Two hundred years from now it MIGHT have some worth. On the other hand, dishes and collecting may both be passé by then. Who knows?

A few crystal butter dish tops found their way onto the market after Federal closed. These were found both unmarked and marked '76. All you have to remember is to look at the knob to tell old from new. (See explanation in paragraph two). I've had no reports of bottoms to these dishes being found.

The crystal juice pitcher seen on the rare page at the back is the only one I have ever seen or heard about. Nearly all of Federal's crystal pitchers are harder to find than colored ones.

You should check the sugar lid very carefully for chips around the pointed edges and knob. Too, many people are now repairing chipped glass. I'm not against this. It allows more of the glass to be salvaged and thereby, affords more of us an opportunity to own and enjoy it. However, I AM against having repaired glass represented to me as "mint". If a piece has been repaired, it is **not** "mint"---even when it looks BETTER than it originally came as it sometimes does. It is still REPAIRED glass; and the customer needs to know that.

Because the amber gravy boat and platter have most often shown up in the state of Iowa, it would seem some items were only distributed regionally. Those walnut lazy susans have turned up in Kentucky, Virginia and West Virginia. I have discovered that the Kroger Company gave amber Madrid for premiums in my area in the early 1930's.

	Crystal, Amber	Pink	Green	Blue
Ash Tray, 6" Square	112.50		77.50	
Bowl, 4¾" Cream Soup	7.50			
Bowl, 5" Sauce	4.00	5.50	5.00	6.50
Bowl, 7" Soup	7.50		9.00	10.00
Bowl, 8" Salad	10.00		15.00	20.00
Bowl, 9 3/8" Large Berry	12.50	17.50		
Bowl, 9½" Deep Salad	17.50			
Bowl, 10" Oval Vegetable	10.00	11.50	12.50	17.50
††Bowl, 11" Low Console	8.50	7.00		
†Butter Dish and Cover	57.50		62.50	
††Candlesticks, 2¼" Pair	13.50	12.50		
Cookie Jar and Cover	27.50	21.50		
Creamer, Footed	5.50		8.00	9.50
Cup	4.50	5.50	5.50	9.50
Gravy Boat and Platter	650.00			
Hot Dish Coaster	25.00		27.50	
Hot Dish Coaster w/Indent	27.50		27.50	
Jam Dish, 7"	15.00		12.50	20.00
Jello Mold, 2 1/8" High	6.50			
†††Pitcher, 5½", 36 oz. Juice	25.00			
Pitcher, 8", 60 oz. Square	27.50	30.00	97.50	127.50
Pitcher, 8½", 80 oz.	45.00		175.00	
Pitcher, 8½", 80 oz. Ice Lip	45.00		175.00	
Plate, 6" Sherbet	2.50	3.00	2.50	5.00
Plate, 7½" Salad	7.50	7.50	7.00	11.00
Plate, 8 7/8" Luncheon	4.50	5.00	7.00	12.00
Plate, 10½" Dinner	23.00	23.00	25.00	35.00
Plate, 10½" Grill	7.50		12.50	
Plate, 10¼" Relish	7.50	7.50	9.00	
††Plate, 11¼" Round Cake	8.50	8.50	16.50	
Platter, 11½" Oval	8.50	8.50	11.00	15.00
Salt/Pepper, 3½" Footed	52.50		72.50	107.50
Salt/Pepper, 3½" Flat	35.00		52.50	
Saucer	2.00	2.50	3.00	4.00
Sherbet, Two Styles	5.00		6.50	9.00
Sugar	6.50		7.50	9.50
Sugar Cover	22.50		24.00	50.00
Tumbler, 3 7/8", 5 oz.	10.50		27.50	15.00
Tumbler, 4¼", 9 oz.	10.00	10.50	16.50	16.00
Tumbler, 5½", 12 oz., 2 Styles	14.50		22.50	18.50
Tumbler, 4", 5 oz. Footed	14.50		37.50	
Tumbler, 5½", 10 oz. Footed	17.50		27.50	
Wooden Lazy Susan, 7 Hot Dish Coasters	450.00			

†Crystal — $250.00
††(Iridescent priced slightly higher)
†††Crystal — $150.00

Please refer to Foreword for pricing information

MANHATTAN, "HORIZONTAL RIBBED" ANCHOR HOCKING GLASS COMPANY, 1938-1941

Colors: Pink, crystal; some green and ruby.

Please do notice that Manhattan plate in Royal Ruby that turned up in Ohio along with several other pieces including the juice pitcher!

Many dealers are now beginning to carry crystal Manhattan to Depression Glass shows; and, as more collectors are buying up the available supply, the prices are edging upward! It used to be when you **asked** for Manhattan at shows, that was the pattern that the dealer had left back in his shop. No more!

People who bought the 2nd Pocket Guide noticed that I omitted quite a few pieces in pink from my listing. Until someone can show me cups and saucers and dinner plates in pink, I'm omitting them from the listing here, also.

The relish tray, with ruby, crystal or pink inserts, remains a big seller no matter what color inserts it has. However, collectors tend to favor the ruby colored inserts.

The small 42 oz. pitcher in pink is probably the hardest item to find.

The covered candy and the little wine pictured are nice items to go with Manhattan pattern. When the candy was first pictured, I failed to price it. Boy! Did I get letters about that omission!

Apple green tumblers have surfaced. Where is the pitcher?

	Crystal	Pink		Crystal	Pink
Ashtray, 4″	4.00		Relish Tray, 14″, 5 Part	8.00	13.50
Bowl, 4½″ Sauce	4.50	5.00	*Relish Tray Insert	3.00	4.00
Bowl, 5 3/8″ Berry			Pitcher, 42 oz.	12.50	22.50
with Handles	4.00	4.50	Pitcher, 80 oz. Tilted	17.50	30.00
Bowl, 7½″ Large Berry	5.00	6.00	Plate, 6″ Sherbet	2.00	
Bowl, 8″, Closed Handles	8.50	9.50	Plate, 8½″ Salad	4.50	5.00
Bowl, 9″ Salad	7.50	9.00	Plate, 10¼″ Dinner	5.50	
Bowl, 9½″ Fruit	12.50	15.00	Plate, 14″ Sandwich	7.50	8.00
Candlesticks, 4½″			Salt/Pepper, 2″ Pr.		
(Double) Pr.	7.50		(Square)	11.50	25.00
Candy Dish, 3 Legs	3.50	5.00	Saucer	2.00	
Candy Dish and Cover	15.00		Sherbet	4.00	5.00
Coaster, 3½″	2.00	3.00	Sugar, Oval	3.00	5.00
Comport, 5¾″	6.50	7.50	**Tumbler, 10 oz. Footed	6.00	7.50
Creamer, Oval	3.00	5.00	Vase, 8″	6.00	
Cup	6.50		Wine, 3½″	6.00	
Relish Tray, 14″, 4 Part	6.50	8.50			

**Green — $5.50
*Ruby - $2.50

Please refer to Foreword for pricing information

108

MAYFAIR FEDERAL GLASS COMPANY, 1934

Colors: Crystal, amber, green.

In today's market, Federal's Mayfair is the best example I know of a really scarce pattern without overwhelming prices! It's an attractive pattern; but the limited supply has discouraged many from even trying to accumulate it; so, prices have remained down.

Federal's Mayfair enjoyed a limited run at the factory because Hocking had already patented the "Mayfair" name. Rather than change the name of the pattern, Federal re-designed their mold into what ultimately became the Rosemary pattern shown elsewhere in the book.

There are "transitional" pieces which bridge the gap between Mayfair and Rosemary, however. I include these transitional pieces with the regular Mayfair because their prices conform more with the prices of the less frequently found Mayfair than they do with the more commonly found Rosemary.

Looking closely at the green (handle-less) sugar, the green cup, the green and amber cream soups and the amber creamer on the extreme right of the photograph, you will notice they're not quite Mayfair due to the fact that the arches do not contain the waffle design caused by interlocking smaller arches. Neither are these transitional pieces Rosemary because that pattern allows arches only at the rims of the pieces, leaving the bottom half of each piece perfectly plain glass.

For some reason the green tumbler is seen more often than any other piece of Mayfair. Was it a premium item with soap, oats or flour?

	Amber	Crystal	Green
Bowl, 5″ Sauce	4.00	3.00	5.00
Bowl, 5″ Cream Soup	12.50	9.00	12.50
Bowl, 6″ Cereal	12.00	6.00	13.50
Bowl, 10″ Oval Vegetable	12.50	9.00	13.50
Creamer, Footed	9.00	7.00	8.50
Cup	5.00	3.50	6.50
Plate, 6¾″ Salad	3.50	2.25	4.50
Plate, 9½″ Dinner	9.50	6.50	8.50
Plate, 9½″ Grill	9.00	7.00	7.50
Platter, 12″ Oval	12.50	9.00	13.50
Saucer	2.00	1.25	2.00
Sugar, Footed	9.00	7.00	8.50
Tumbler, 4½″, 9 oz.	10.00	6.50	13.50

Please refer to Foreword for pricing information

MAYFAIR, "OPEN ROSE"   HOCKING GLASS COMPANY, 1931-1937

Colors: Ice blue, pink; some green, yellow, crystal.   *(See Reproduction Section)*

Mayfair may well be THE most popular in Depression Glass! It enjoyed a long run at the factory and was made into a variety of pieces. The pattern was popular with the public and via premiums and coupons, nearly everybody was able to own some of it. My wife's aunt remembered buying cookies from the grocery in her Mayfair cookie jar. A lady in Chattanooga recently told me she was almost certain her hat shaped bowl came from a soap coupon deal. Indeed, numerous people have become collectors of this pattern due to inheriting a partial set.

Rare items command a lot of attention from advanced collectors. Rare items in a major pattern such as Mayfair command high prices. Therefore, items such as the unique FOOTED shaker, ROUND cups, THREE FOOTED bowls, sugar LIDS, decanter (came with bath salts) STOPPERS, unusual sized wines, pieces in the rarely found YELLOW and GREEN colors create awed attention by collectors. Newcomers to the field should carefully study the price listings for clues to the rarer items to be located in this pattern, most of which have been pictured and discussed at length in previous issues of the book.

I hope you enjoyed the picture of blue Mayfair on the cover. For those of you who have followed all five editions, you know that I have shown very little blue Mayfair although it's what I originally "collected". That collection had to be sold to finance the glass included in the first book. I sold blue Mayfair in order to buy Raindrops, Bow Knot, Rose Cameo, etc. After that, even seeing it was hurtful. It was as if I had sold rubies to purchase gravel.

Now that you can see the blue fully pictured for the first time, I want to show you another SHADE of blue never shown before. The juice pitchers are both blue Mayfair, but one is more like Federal's "Madonna" blue. The odd blue pitcher has a ground bottom which probably indicates it was an earlier piece. Perhaps we will find other items in this softer blue color!

Although they were thought to be uncollectible as a SET by some, those yellow and green pieces of Mayfair are popping up more and more. In fact, the yellow candy dish is practically unsalable at today's prices because the few collectors for yellow and green Mayfair already have one or **two**! Now hear this! A twelve piece place setting of green Mayfair turned up recently in Ohio---including stemmed pieces in various sizes! So, sets of green and yellow ARE possible; all it takes is luck and money.

Since nearly all pieces of Mayfair found in the green and yellow colors suffer some damage, collectors of it have begun to theorize that Hocking may have abandoned these colors due to breakage. Somehow, those colors in the glass, though fantastic to see, weren't as durable as the pink and blue. This, however, brings me to another point. DON'T ALLOW AMATEURS TO REPAIR RARE GLASS! I have seen too many pieces recently "fixed" beyond any hope of their achieving their true worth! In the hands of an expert, a repaired piece can retain its value; in the hands of a butchering amateur, even a supposedly rare piece can fast become a worthless piece of junk!

Satinized pieces of Mayfair are frequently found, usually having little pink roses painted thereon--- unless they've encountered the dishwasher! With or without the roses, there are very few collectors for the camphoric acid ("satinized") pieces; so, their value is less than half that of regular Mayfair.

Several more sugar lids have been reported including one bought for 24¢! They still number fewer than 100 found, however; so, they retain their price!

There seem to be quite a few of the 4", 2½ oz. wines listed last time. Judging from the letters I received, they appear to run about one of those to every four of the standard wine.

Crystal shakers and juice pitchers sell for about half the prices listed for pink.

Thankfully, there are no new reproductions to discuss. See the section at the back of the book for ways to recognize the newly manufactured shot glass. It really isn't hard to spot!

See Page 114 for Prices.

MAYFAIR, "OPEN ROSE" (Con't.)

	Pink*	Blue	Green	Yellow
Bowl, 5" Cream Soup	27.50			
Bowl, 5½" Cereal	11.00	17.50	47.50	37.50
Bowl, 7" Vegetable	14.00	27.50	85.00	85.00
Bowl, 9", 3 1/8" High, 3 Leg Console	1,750.00			
Bowl, 9½" Oval Vegetable	13.50	29.50	75.00	75.00
Bowl, 10" Vegetable	12.00	32.50		85.00
Bowl, 10" Same Covered	45.00	67.50		200.00
Bowl, 11¾" Low Flat	29.50	37.50	18.00	77.50
Bowl, 12" Deep Scalloped Fruit	30.00	40.00	20.00	87.50
Butter Dish and Cover or 7" Covered Vegetable	40.00	195.00	750.00	750.00
Cake Plate, 10" Footed	15.00	35.00	49.50	
Candy Dish and Cover	30.00	115.00	400.00	275.00
Celery Dish, 9" Divided			85.00	85.00
**Celery Dish 10" or 10" Divided	14.50	22.50	75.00	75.00
Cookie Jar and Lid	25.00	117.50	450.00	450.00
Creamer, Footed	11.00	40.00	125.00	125.00
Cup	9.00	30.00	95.00	95.00
Decanter and Stopper, 32 oz.	72.50			
Goblet, 3¾", 1 oz. Liqueur	337.50		337.50	
Goblet, 4", 2½ oz.	67.50			
Goblet, 4", 3½ oz. Cocktail	45.00		250.00	
Goblet, 4½", 3 oz. Wine	45.00		250.00	
Goblet, 5¼", 4½ oz. Claret	367.50		367.50	
Goblet, 5¾", 9 oz. Water	32.50		250.00	
Goblet, 7¼", 9 oz. Thin	77.50	72.50		
Pitcher, 6", 37 oz.	25.00	67.50	350.00	350.00
Pitcher, 8", 60 oz.	30.00	72.50	300.00	300.00
Pitcher 8½", 80 oz.	45.00	97.50	350.00	350.00
Plate, 6" (Often Substituted as Saucer)	6.50	9.50	45.00	45.00
Plate, 6½" Round Sherbet	7.50			
Plate, 6½" Round, Off Center Indent	17.50	18.50	60.00	
Plate, 8½" Luncheon	12.00	18.00	50.00	50.00
Plate, 9½" Dinner	32.50	35.00	75.00	75.00
Plate, 9½" Grill	20.00	20.00	50.00	50.00
Plate, 11½" Handled Grill				75.00
Plate, 12" Cake w/Handles	22.00	35.00	22.00	
***Platter, 12" Oval, Open Handles	12.50	27.50	100.00	100.00
Platter, 12½" Oval, 8" Wide, Closed Handles				157.50
Relish, 8 3/8", 4 part or Non-Partitioned	15.50	27.50	95.00	90.00
Salt and Pepper, Flat Pair	35.00	150.00	500.00	500.00
Salt and Pepper, Footed Pair	2,000.00			
Sandwich Server, Center Handle	22.50	37.50	17.50	85.00
Saucer (Cup Ring)	17.50			
Saucer (See 6" Plate)				
Sherbet, 2¼" Flat	65.00	47.50		
Sherbet, 3" Footed	10.00			
Sherbet, 4¾" Footed	42.50	37.50	125.00	125.00
Sugar, Footed	13.50	37.50	125.00	125.00
Sugar Lid	600.00		700.00	700.00
Tumbler, 3½", 5 oz. Juice	22.00	65.00		
Tumbler, 4¼", 9 oz. Water	17.50	57.50		
Tumbler, 4¾", 11 oz. Water	50.00	67.50	150.00	
Tumbler, 5¼", 13½ oz. Iced Tea	25.00	62.50		
Tumbler, 3¼", 3 oz. Footed Juice	45.00			
Tumbler, 5¼", 10 oz. Footed	22.50	65.00		150.00
Tumbler, 6½", 15 oz. Ftd. Iced Tea	25.00	75.00	175.00	
Vase (Sweet Pea)	69.50	50.00	145.00	
Whiskey, 2¼", 1½ oz.	55.00			

*Frosted or satin finish items slightly lower
**Divided Pink Celery — $47.50
***Divided Crystal — $12.50

Please refer to Foreword for pricing information

MISS AMERICA (DIAMOND PATTERN) HOCKING GLASS COMPANY, 1935-1937

Colors: Crystal, pink; some green, ice blue and red.   *(See Reproduction Section)*

I have a report of a Hocking factory worker who took home 8 of everything made in Miss America. No big deal?. How would an 8 piece place setting in RED Miss America sound to you! It boggles the imagination, doesn't it? We do know the pattern exists in red because a sugar, creamer, 10 oz. goblets, 3½" wines, 4½" juice glasses, luncheon plates and a curved-in fruit bowl have surfaced already. Watch for it!

The price of the Miss America butter dish has suffered because of the reproductions. Old ones are still quite rare and the crystal is still rarer than the pink. It's EASY to tell the old from the new. (See reproduction section at the back for how to tell old from new). However, casual collectors are content to own the much cheaper reproduction; and some are still fearful of being duped, so they shy away from buying. Except for the butter dish and shakers, nothing else has been reproduced in this pattern.

At present, the odd colors of Miss America have more conversational value than anything else. Should any quantity surface, that might change.

I don't list the tid-bit server in Miss America any longer because too many were being "put together" by drilling through regular plates and adding new hardware. One from the original manufacturer is still a nice piece to own.

If you have pieces that aren't found in the listing below, check English Hobnail. Often these two patterns are confused. Miss America tends to have uniform raying of pieces and three rings around the top of its stemware. English Hobnail, on the other hand, has hexagonally patterned rays and clear glass edges rising directly from the diamond-like pattern.

Demand is still greater than supply for pink Miss America pitchers, candy dishes, the divided relish, goblets and tumblers.

Coasters DO have six raised rays in the bottom. One is pictured on the left above the blue sherbet plate. They're the same size as the 5¾" plate.

The unusual Jadite plate used in the pattern shot was turned in order to clearly show the pattern.

The amethyst sprayed-on goblet makes an interesting conversation piece.

	Crystal	Pink	Green	Red
Bowl, 4½" Berry			7.00	
*Bowl, 6¼" Berry	5.00	9.50	9.00	
Bowl, 8" Curved in at Top	25.00	40.00		225.00
Bowl, 8¾" Straight Deep Fruit	22.50	35.00		
Bowl, 10" Oval Vegetable	9.50	14.00		
**Butter Dish and Cover	187.50	365.00		
Cake Plate, 12" Footed	14.50	22.50		
Candy Jar and Cover, 11½"	45.00	80.00		
Celery Dish, 10½" Oblong	7.00	12.50		
Coaster, 5¾"	12.00	17.50		
Comport, 5"	9.50	13.00		
Creamer, Footed	6.00	10.00		100.00
Cup	7.00	12.50	8.00	
Goblet, 3¾", 3 oz. Wine	14.00	39.50		125.00
Goblet, 4¾", 5 oz. Juice	16.00	40.00		125.00
Goblet, 5½", 10 oz. Water	15.00	30.00		125.00
Pitcher, 8", 65 oz.	47.50	77.50		
Pitcher, 8½", 65 oz. w/Ice Lip	55.00	80.00		
***Plate, 5¾" Sherbet	3.00	4.00	5.00	
Plate, 6¾"			6.00	
Plate, 8½" Salad	4.50	10.00	8.00	52.50
****Plate, 10¼" Dinner	8.50	15.00		
Plate, 10¼" Grill	6.50	10.00		
Platter, 12¼" Oval	9.50	12.50		
Relish, 8¾", 4 Part	6.50	11.50		

	Crystal	Pink	Green	Red
Relish, 11¾" Round Divided	12.50	97.50		
Salt and Pepper, Pr.	20.00	37.50	257.50	
Saucer	2.50	4.00		
Sherbet	6.00	10.50		
Sugar	5.50	10.00		100.00
****Tumbler, 4", 5 oz. Juice	12.50	32.50		
Tumbler, 4½", 10 oz. Water	12.00	19.50	13.50	
Tumbler, 6¾", 14 oz. Iced Tea	19.50	40.00		

*Also has appeared in Cobalt Blue — $100.00
**Absolute mint price
***Also in Ice Blue — $30.00
****Also in Ice Blue — $75.00

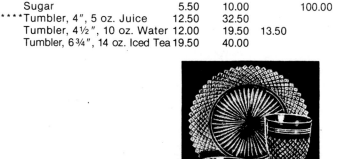

**Glass Luncheon Set
Crystal or Rose Tint**

A practical Luncheon Set with hobnail design — sunburst center. Choice of crystal or rose glass. Set serves 4. Consists of four each of 8½-in. salad plates, footed tumblers 5⅜-in. tall. 3⅜-in. tea cups, 5¼-in. saucers. Shipping weight 15 pounds.

550 A 4906—Crystal.
16-Piece Set......... **$1.29**

550 A 4907—Rose.
16-Piece Set........... **1.29**

Please refer to Foreword for pricing information

116

MODERNTONE, "WEDDING BAND"   HAZEL ATLAS GLASS COMPANY, 1934-1942

Colors: Amethyst, cobalt blue; some crystal, pink and platonite fired-on colors.

A now familiar tune is being sung about this pattern also. "It used to be inexpensive . . .!" Depression Glass has gained some collectors via this Moderntone's cobalt blue color alone. In fact, I had a man ask me the other day why I didn't write a book on "cobalt blue glass"! Heavens! What an undertaking considering the hundreds of companies who've made it over the years and the trillions of pieces it's found in! However, increasingly, there are collectors for things made just in that color. Thus, collectors, you have competition for Moderntone who have never HEARD of Depression Glass.

The blue soup bowls are impossible to find any more; those in amethyst are only scarce!

I've noticed a trend recently toward buying the Platonite pieces---particularly the "Little Hostess Party Set" manufactured for children in the late 40's. Platonite refers to a special heat resistant ware that was marketed by Hazel Atlas and came with various fired-on colors. The child's set consisted of 4 cups, saucers and plates, sugar, creamer and teapot with lid and sells for about $30.00. At present, there seems to be plenty of the Platonite still around. You can get an idea of the range of colors available in Platonite by noticing the shakers lined up at the rear of the photograph.

The butter dish has a ledge for the metal lid to rest around; so don't buy a top seated on the cereal bowl as a "butter" dish. The cheese dish needs the wooden board in order to be labeled a cheese dish, too.

Some items crop up in pink and crystal; unless they're the ash tray, these have little importance.

The tumbler pictured here was made in cobalt, pink, green and crystal. It was not officially listed as Moderntone. However, it was made by the same company in the same color; so collectors have adopted it as the glass for this pattern.

	Cobalt	Amethyst	Platonite Fired On Colors		Cobalt	Amethyst	Platonite Fired On Colors
*Ash Tray, 7¾", Match Holder in Center	87.50			Plate, 5¾" Sherbet	2.50	2.50	.75
Bowl, 4¾" Cream Soup	7.50	8.50		Plate, 6¾" Salad	3.00	3.50	1.00
Bowl, 5" Berry	8.00	6.00	.75	Plate, 7¾" Luncheon	4.50	4.00	1.25
Bowl, 5" Cream Soup, Ruffled	13.50	10.00	1.25	Plate, 8 7/8" Dinner	7.00	6.00	2.00
Bowl, 6½" Cereal	28.50	22.50	1.00	Plate, 10½" Sandwich	12.00	9.00	2.50
Bowl, 7½" Soup	27.50	22.50	1.50	Platter, 11" Oval	12.50	10.00	2.00
Bowl, 8¾" Large Berry	17.50	14.50	3.00	Platter, 12" Oval	22.50	18.00	2.00
Butter Dish with Metal Cover	55.00			Salt and Pepper, Pr.	20.00	25.00	8.00
Cheese Dish, 7" with Metal Lid	65.00			Saucer	2.00	2.00	.75
				Sherbet	5.50	4.00	2.00
Creamer	5.00	5.00	2.00	Sugar	5.00	5.00	2.00
Cup	5.50	4.00	1.00	Sugar Lid in Metal	17.50		
Cup (Handle-less) or Custard	8.00	8.50		Tumbler, 5 oz.			2.50
				Tumbler, 9 oz.	10.00		3.00
				Tumbler, 12 oz.			3.00
				Whiskey, 1½ oz.	8.00		3.00

Please refer to Foreword for pricing information

119

MOONDROPS   NEW MARTINSVILLE, 1932-1940

Colors: Amber, pink, green, cobalt, ice blue, red, amethyst, crystal, dark green, light green, jadite, smoke, black.

Collectors of Moondrops have not increased quite as rapidly as the prices on this pattern! One avid collector wanted a different picture in this book; however, gathering the **variety** of pieces again was practically impossible; and I was reluctant to change just for the sake of changing. Cost factor on the butter dishes alone would be prohibitive! Now, if some of you are willing to LEND your collection for a new photograph . . . .

Moondrops, like Iris, is one of the few Depression Glass patterns where the flat pieces are more difficult to find than any other piece. So, don't pass any by that you find because there will be a market for it either by selling it directly or by trading it.

Collectors favor the covered items, pitchers and the "rocket" and "winged" style pieces. "Bee Hive" items are not quite as fetching.

Crystal Moondrops brings less than prices listed.

One very unusual piece seen recently was a pitcher the same size as the 5½", 12 oz. mug! Are there more--or was this a facotry worker's personal design?

	Blue/Red	All Other Colors		Blue/Red	All Other Colors
Ash Tray	25.00	10.00	Goblet, 5 1/8", Metal Stem Wine	9.50	6.50
Bowl, 5¼" Berry	5.00	3.00	Goblet, 5½", Metal Stem Wine	10.00	6.50
Bowl, 6¾" Soup	9.00	6.00	Goblet, 6¼", 9 oz. Water	15.00	11.00
Bowl, 7½" Pickle	10.00	6.50	Mug, 5 1/8", 12 oz.	20.00	15.00
Bowl, 8 3/8" Footed, Concave Top	13.00	7.50	Perfume Bottle, "Rocket"	35.00	19.00
Bowl, 8½" Three Footed Divided			Pitcher, 6 7/8", 22 oz. Small	85.00	65.00
Relish	12.00	9.50	Pitcher, 8 1/8", 32 oz. Medium	125.00	85.00
Bowl, 9½" Three Legged Ruffled	15.00	9.75	Pitcher, 8", 50 oz. Large with Lip	135.00	90.00
Bowl, 9¾" Oval Vegetable	20.00	15.00	Pitcher, 8 1/8", 53 oz. Large, No Lip	145.00	100.00
Bowl, 9¾" Covered Casserole	65.00	40.00	Plate, 5 7/8" Bread and Butter	3.00	2.50
Bowl, 9¾" Two Handled Oval	30.00	20.00	Plate, 6 1/8" Sherbet	3.00	2.50
Bowl, 11½" Boat Shaped Celery	19.00	14.00	Plate, 6" Round, Off-Center Indent for		
Bowl, 12" Round Three Footed			Sherbet	5.00	3.00
Console	30.00	20.00	Plate, 7 1/8" Salad	5.00	3.00
Bowl, 13" Console with "Wings"	45.00	30.00	Plate, 8½" Luncheon	5.50	4.50
Butter Dish and Cover	350.00	200.00	Plate, 9½" Dinner	10.00	6.00
Candles, 2" Ruffled Pair	20.00	15.00	Plate, 15" Round Sandwich	20.00	12.00
Candles, 4½" Sherbet Style Pr.	15.00	10.00	Plate, 15" Two Handled Sandwich	25.00	15.00
Candlesticks, 5" "Wings" Pr.	45.00	30.00	Platter, 12" Oval	15.00	10.00
Candlesticks, 5¼" Triple Light Pr.	45.00	30.00	Saucer	3.25	2.00
Candlesticks, 8½" Metal Stem Pr.	22.00	15.00	Sherbet, 2 5/8"	8.00	5.00
Candy Dish, 8" Ruffled	15.00	10.00	Sherbet, 4½"	10.00	6.00
Cocktail Shaker, with or without			Sugar, 2¾"	12.00	8.00
Handle, Metal Top	20.00	15.00	Sugar, 4"	10.00	6.00
Comport, 4"	9.00	6.00	Tumbler, 2¾", 2 oz. Shot	8.00	5.00
Comport, 11½"	20.00	12.00	Tumbler, 2¾", 2 oz. Handled Shot	9.00	6.00
Creamer, 2¾" Miniature	12.00	8.00	Tumbler, 3¼", 3 oz. Footed Juice	9.00	6.00
Creamer, 3¾" Regular	10.00	6.00	Tumbler, 3 5/8", 5 oz.	8.00	5.00
Cup	7.50	5.00	Tumbler, 4 3/8", 7 oz.	9.00	6.00
Decanter, 7¾" Small	40.00	30.00	Tumbler, 4 3/8", 8 oz.	10.00	7.00
Decanter, 8½" Medium	45.00	32.50	Tumbler, 4 7/8", 9 oz. Handled	11.00	8.00
Decanter, 11¼" Large	50.00	35.00	Tumbler, 4 7/8", 9 oz.	12.00	9.00
Decanter, 10¼" "Rocket"	65.00	40.00	Tumbler, 5 1/8", 12 oz.	15.00	10.00
Goblet, 2 7/8", ¾ oz. Liqueur	15.00	10.00	Tray, 7½", For Miniature		
Goblet, 4", 4 oz. Wine	12.00	8.00	Sugar/Creamer	20.00	14.00
Goblet, 4¾", "Rocket" Wine	22.00	15.00	Vase, 7¾" Flat, Ruffled Top	40.00	30.00
Goblet, 4¾", 5 oz.	10.00	6.00	Vase, 9¼" "Rocket" Style	75.00	50.00

Please refer to Foreword for pricing information

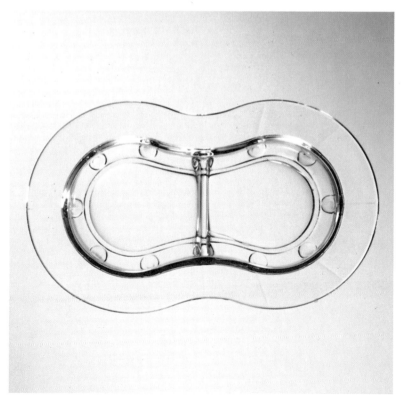

121

MOONSTONE ANCHOR HOCKING GLASS CORPORATION, 1941-1946

Color: Crystal with opalescent hobnails, some green.

The green Moonstone bowl shown in the pattern shot of the last book shook some people. I can now report a whole set of green being found in the original box. It consisted of goblets, cups, saucers, plates, soups and creamer and sugar; it was called "Ocean Green".

Please notice also the four additional pieces that have come from Ohio with the original Moostone stickers (although one of our "helpers" at the photographer's studio turned the label inward on the toothpick)! Only the divided bowl looks like Moonstone as we know it.

A larger 9" vase (shaped like the 5½") has shown up.

The cologne bottle pictured and not priced was made by Fenton Glass Company rather than Anchor Hocking and usually sells for $7.50. Many Moonstone collectors include these with their collections ---as they do pitchers, shakers and stemmed water goblets made by this same company. As you can see, few people would detect any difference; so I see no harm in combining pieces from the two companies if you wish. The listing here is strictly Anchor Hocking's ware, however.

The hobs on Hocking's pieces tend to be somewhat rounder or smoother than do those of Fenton's; and Hocking's flat pieces have raised center rays with a row of hobs just outside the rays.

	Opalescent Hobnail		Opalescent Hobnail
Bowl, 5½" Berry	6.50	Cup	5.00
Bowl, 5½" Crimped Dessert	4.50	Goblet, 10 oz.	12.50
Bowl, 6½" Crimped Handled	6.50	Heart Bonbon, One Handle	6.50
Bowl, 7¾" Flat	7.50	Plate, 6¼" Sherbet	2.50
Bowl, 7¾" Divided Relish	6.50	Plate, 8" Luncheon	6.50
Bowl, 9½" Crimped	10.00	Plate, 10" Sandwich	12.00
Bowl, Cloverleaf	7.50	Puff Box and Cover, 4¾" Round	13.50
Candleholder, Pr.	13.50	Saucer (Same as Sherbet Plate)	2.50
Candy Jar and Cover, 6"	15.00	Sherbet, Footed	5.50
Cigarette Jar and Cover	13.00	Sugar, Footed	5.50
Creamer	5.50	Vase, 5½" Bud	8.50

MT. PLEASANT, "DOUBLE SHIELD"   L.B. SMITH COMPANY, 1920's-1934

Colors: Black amethyst, cobalt blue, green, pink.

The first two colors listed for this pattern insure its being collected! They also assure Depression Glass collectors of keener competition for this glassware!

Mt. Pleasant was never "give away" glassware. It was purchased in better stores. You generally have to look for the "double shield" design, particularly on the black pieces.

Mt. Pleasant is usually spotted by its two distinctive shapes, squared with scalloped edges and round with alternating scallops and points.

The listing here is not complete; so let me hear of your other finds!

That crystal cup has turned up in several boxed luncheon sets; all the other pieces in the set will be black with gold trim.

	Pink, Green	Black Amethyst, Amethyst, Cobalt		Pink, Green	Black Amethyst, Amethyst, Cobalt
Bon Bon, Rolled Up Handles	9.00	14.50	Cup	4.00	6.50
Bowl, 3 Footed, Rolled-In			Plate, 8" Scalloped or Square	6.00	8.50
Edges, As Rose Bowl	12.00	15.50	Plate, 8", Solid Handles	7.00	12.00
Bowl, 8" Scalloped, Two Handles	10.00	14.50	Plate, 10½" Cake with		
Bowl, 8" Two Handled Square	10.00	15.00	Solid Handles	12.50	17.50
Candlesticks, Single Stem Pr.	12.00	15.00	Salt and Pepper Shakers		
Candlesticks, Double Stem Pr.	17.50	27.50	(Two Styles)	15.00	22.50
Creamer (Scalloped Edges)	8.00	12.00	Saucer, Square or Scalloped	2.00	2.50
Cup (Waffle-Like Crystal)	3.00		Sherbet, Scalloped Edges	5.00	9.00
			Sugar (Scalloped Edges)	8.00	12.00

NEW CENTURY, and incorrectly, "LYDIA RAY"   HAZEL ATLAS GLASS COMPANY, 1930-1935

Colors: Green; some crystal, pink, amethyst and cobalt.

Although there are no listings for cups except in green and crystal, a few have to have been made in amethyst and cobalt blue. They've appeared! So, any time you find one of them, buy it.

As far as I can determine, the ash tray is the most difficult piece to locate, with the covered casserole, decanter and cream soup falling close behind.

Prices haven't increased as much in this pattern as others mostly due to its scarcity. Most people hate collecting something they seldom see.

Ovide pattern has been incorrectly called New Century elsewhere. Therefore, you might wish to look at that pattern now to see how completely different it is from New Century. It really matters when you order one and get the other!

	Green, Crystal	Pink, Cobalt, Amethyst		Green, Crystal	Pink, Cobalt, Amethyst
Ash Tray/Coaster, 5 3/8"	25.00		Plate, 7 1/8" Breakfast	5.00	
Bowl, 4½" Berry	4.00		Plate, 8½" Salad	5.50	
Bowl, 4¾" Cream Soup	8.00		Plate, 10" Dinner	8.50	
Bowl, 8" Large Berry	9.50		Plate, 10" Grill	7.50	
Bowl, 9" Covered Casserole	42.50		Platter, 11" Oval	9.50	
Butter Dish and Cover	45.00		Salt and Pepper, Pr.	22.50	
Cup	4.50	8.50	Saucer	2.00	4.00
Creamer	5.50		Sherbet, 3"	5.00	
Decanter and Stopper	37.50		Sugar	4.50	
Goblet, 2½ oz. Wine	10.00		Sugar Cover	8.50	
Goblet, 3¼ oz. Cocktail	12.50		Tumbler, 3½", 5 oz.	7.00	6.50
Pitcher, 7¾", 60 oz. with			Tumbler, 4 1/8", 9 oz.	7.50	6.50
or without Ice Lip	22.50	20.00	Tumbler, 5", 10 oz.	9.00	8.00
Pitcher, 8", 80 oz. with			Tumbler, 5¼", 12 oz.	12.50	10.00
or without Ice Lip	25.00	27.50	Tumbler, 4", 5 oz. Footed	8.00	
Plate, 6" Sherbet	2.00		Tumbler, 4 7/8, 9 oz. Footed	10.00	
			Whiskey, 2½", 1½ oz.	5.50	

Please refer to Foreword for pricing information

NEWPORT, "HAIRPIN"   HAZEL ATLAS GLASS COMPANY, 1936-1940

Colors: Cobalt blue, amethyst, pink, "Platonite" white and fired-on colors.

Prices for cobalt blue items have edged ahead of the amethyst in several instances, not because blue is less scarce, but because there is more demand for it! When did you last see the cereal bowl, shakers, sandwich plate or tumblers?

White shakers for this pattern have been falsely attributed to Petalware pattern. Petalware doesn't have shakers; so, if you don't mind a slight variation in pattern, the color will allow them to blend with Petalware.

I recently met a collector of amethyst Newport who is frantically trying to complete her set before "too many other collectors get in there and raise the prices". Take heed!

	*Cobalt	Amethyst		*Cobalt	Amethyst
Bowl, 4¼" Berry	4.00	4.50	Plate, 11½" Sandwich	12.50	14.00
Bowl, 4¾" Cream Soup	9.00	8.00	Platter, 11¾" Oval	15.00	15.00
Bowl, 5¼" Cereal	9.00	8.50	Salt and Pepper	27.50	30.00
Bowl, 8¼" Large Berry	12.00	12.50	Saucer	2.25	2.50
Cup	4.00	4.50	Sherbet	6.50	6.50
Creamer	5.50	5.50	Sugar	6.00	5.50
Plate, 6" Sherbet	2.50	2.50	Tumbler, 4½", 9 oz.	12.50	12.50
Plate, 8½" Luncheon	5.00	6.00			

*White 60% of Cobalt price.

NORMANDIE, "BOUQUET AND LATTICE"   FEDERAL GLASS COMPANY, 1933-1940

Colors: Iridescent, amber, pink, crystal.

The pink Normandie dinner plate has become one of the most elusive in Depression Glass. I can remember stacks that did not sell at $4.00 each; now that they are $37.50 each, you can't even find one! Also hard to find in pink are the shakers, pitcher and tumblers, and the sugar lid! I last saw that sugar lid in May of 1973! Shades of years gone by!

The only iridescent salad plate I've seen recently sold for $20.00 and the man asked the dealer if he knew of any more! Except for salad plates, the iridized is often seen. Activity in iridescent items is increasing of late. The problem you encounter with that is convincing the unaware that it ISN'T Carnival Glass!

Pink Normandie is relatively rare and desirable. Amber Normandie is still rather hard to sell. I don't expect that shunning to last indefinitely, however.

	Amber	Pink	Iridescent		Amber	Pink	Irdescent
Bowl, 5" Berry	4.00	4.50	4.50	Platter, 11¾"	8.00	12.50	9.50
*Bowl, 6½" Cereal	6.00	7.00	6.50	Salt and Pepper, Pr.	30.00	40.00	
Bowl, 8½" Large Berry	7.50	9.50	8.50	Saucer	2.00	2.50	2.00
Bowl, 10" Oval Veg.	8.50	17.50	12.50	Sherbet	5.00	6.00	5.00
Creamer, Footed	5.00	5.00	5.50	Sugar	4.00	4.00	5.00
Cup	4.00	4.00	4.50	Sugar Lid	57.50	87.50	
Pitcher, 8", 80 oz.	42.50	62.50		Tumbler, 4", 5 oz.			
Plate, 6" Sherbet	2.00	2.00	2.00	Juice	10.50	22.50	
Plate, 8" Salad	5.50	6.00	20.00	Tumbler, 4¼", 9 oz.			
Plate, 9¼" Luncheon	4.50	5.50	6.00	Water	9.50	17.50	
Plate, 11" Dinner	12.50	27.50	12.50	Tumbler, 5", 12 oz.			
Plate, 11" Grill	8.00	9.50	9.50	Iced Tea	13.50	22.50	

*Mistaken by many as butter bottom.

NO. 610, "PYRAMID" INDIANA GLASS COMPANY, 1926-1932

Colors: Green, pink, yellow; some crystal; black, 1974-75 by Tiara.

The art deco design of this pattern has caught on in a big way with collectors. There's been a dramatic increase in the prices on the pitcher, large footed tumbler and the ice bucket and cover in yellow! As far as I can determine, only that yellow ice bucket has a lid and my listing will so indicate.

Speaking of ice buckets, there are collectors about who collect nothing but ice buckets! So, it is not always a fellow Pyramid collector who drives up the price on those.

In crystal Pyramid, I've only seen pitchers---and only two of those! There ought to be other pieces, at least tumblers! This is one Depression pattern where crystal pieces represent quite a find!

Do remember that the black pieces of Pyramid were made by Tiara in 1974 and 1975; thus, when offered black Pyramid, just realize it is not old.

Eleven ounce tumblers are quite rare!

	Crystal, Pink	Green	Yellow
Bowl, 4¾" Berry	10.00	11.50	20.00
Bowl, 8½" Master Berry	15.50	17.50	37.50
Bowl, 9½" Oval	20.00	20.00	39.50
Bowl, 9½" Pickle	20.00	20.00	39.50
Creamer	15.50	16.50	20.50
Ice Tub	55.00	62.50	157.50
Ice Tub and Lid			350.00
Pitcher	95.00	100.00	187.50
Relish Tray, 4 Part Handled	20.00	20.00	42.50
Sugar	15.50	16.50	20.50
Tray for Creamer and Sugar	12.50	15.00	18.00
Tumbler, 8 oz. Footed	15.00	20.50	35.00
Tumbler, 11 oz. Footed	30.00	37.50	47.50

NO. 612, "HORSESHOE" INDIANA GLASS COMPANY, 1930-1933

Colors: Green, yellow; some pink, crystal.

The cost factor for this fancy "Horseshoe" pattern has been so prohibitive on accessory pieces that it's discouraged many people from even trying to collect No. 612--even though they like it! That's probably a mistake. It's possible to get basic pieces to a luncheon service. That way, one could enjoy owning the pattern both aesthetically and monetarily!

At present, the prices for No. 612 have increased only slightly from what they were two years ago! This probably reflects a momentary lack of demand. However, this pattern has a history of pricing spurts and sputters; so, you might look for another spurt in pricing soon!

Several batches of 12 oz. flat tumblers have been discovered in the last year; and although none of the flat tumblers are easily found, this minor deluge has made the smaller 9 oz. flat tumbler the harder one to find.

Novice collectors should know that some plates do not carry the center motif. They're like the platter pictured. Grill plates (sectioned plates) are really scarce!

Candy dishes have plain bottoms. Only the tops have the design, should you be so lucky as to see one.

There ARE three sizes of vegetable bowls: 7½", 8½" and 9½". I've held them and measured them myself. The 8½" size (unlisted on company rosters) is the hardest to locate.

The only pieces I've ever seen in crystal are the sugar and creamer. Let me know if you find something else!

As is true of many Indiana patterns, the company merely gave this glassware a line number (No. 612). Collectors have dubbed it "Horseshoe".

	Green	Yellow		Green	Yellow
Bowl, 4½" Berry	16.50	13.50	Plate, 8 3/8" Salad	5.00	6.00
Bowl, 6½" Cereal	11.50	14.50	Plate, 9 3/8" Luncheon	7.00	7.00
Bowl, 7½" Salad	12.50	14.50	Plate, 10 3/8" Dinner	13.50	14.50
Bowl, 8½" Vegetable	15.00	20.00	Plate, 10 3/8" Grill	16.50	16.50
Bowl, 9½" Large Berry	22.50	25.00	Plate, 11" Sandwich	8.50	10.00
Bowl, 10½" Oval Vegetable	12.50	15.00	Platter, 10¾" Oval	13.00	15.00
Butter Dish and Cover	477.50		Relish, 3 Part Footed	10.50	12.50
Candy in Metal Holder			Saucer	3.00	3.00
Motif on Lid —			Sherbet	9.50	10.50
Also, Pink— ($97.50)	117.50		Sugar, Open	9.00	9.50
Creamer, Footed	10.00	11.00	Tumbler, 4¼", 9 oz.	57.50	
Cup	6.00	7.00	Tumbler, 4¾", 12 oz.	62.50	
Pitcher, 8½, 64 oz.	177.50	197.50	Tumbler, 9 oz. Footed	11.50	12.50
Plate, 6" Sherbet	2.50	4.00	Tumbler, 12 oz. Footed	52.50	62.50

NO. 616, "VERNON" INDIANA GLASS COMPANY, 1930-1932

Colors: Green, crystal, yellow.

Not enough of this pattern is found to give new collectors a chance to collect it! Only luncheon sets seem to be available and what you see pictured is what is possible to own. We used to use a set in crystal and my wife longed for a serving bowl.

You can find crystal pieces trimmed with a platinum band---when you can find them at all. Crystal is turning out to be the most elusive color in this design although yellow and green are most desired by collectors. The yellow, like Lorain, has almost a fluorescent glow!

	Green	Crystal	Yellow
Creamer, Footed	20.00	10.50	17.50
Cup	13.50	5.50	12.00
Plate, 8" Luncheon	6.50	5.50	7.25
Plate, 11" Sandwich	20.00	12.50	18.50
Saucer	4.50	2.75	4.50
Sugar, Footed	19.50	10.00	17.50
Tumbler, 5" Footed	24.00	11.50	22.50

NO. 618, "PINEAPPLE & FLORAL" INDIANA GLASS COMPANY, 1932-1937

Colors: Crystal, amber; some fired-on red, green; Late 60's: avocado.

"Pineapple and Floral", called line No. 618 by Indiana, is an attractive pattern. It "dresses" a table well. However, it does have a drawback. You will find extreme mold roughness (excess glass around the seams of the pieces) to be a general characteristic. I once collected a whole set of the tumblers for my wife to use only to have her give them back because she didn't care for the rough "feel" of the glass! (Those tumblers are tough to find, by the way)!

Green plates, like the one pictured, have shown up several times; but as yet, there've been no other pieces in light green. The avocado green color was made into the 1970's.

The diamond shaped comport has recently appeared in all kinds of flashed and iridized colors at the local dish barns and flea markets. Only the amber and the fired-on red can be assured of possessing any "age".

Bowls, except for the 7", have quietly disappeared into collections.

The vase fits into a metal stand. They were popular in funeral parlors.

	Crystal	Amber, Red		Crystal	Amber, Red
Ash Tray, 4½"	13.00	16.00	Plate, 11½" Sandwich	10.00	11.50
Bowl, 4¾" Berry	17.50	12.50	Platter, 11" Closed Handles	8.00	10.00
Bowl, 6" Cereal	14.50	15.00	Platter, Relish, 11½",		
Bowl, 7" Salad	5.00	8.50	Divided	14.00	8.50
Bowl, 10" Oval Vegetable	14.00	15.00	Saucer	2.50	2.50
Comport, Diamond Shaped	1.50	6.50	Sherbet, Footed	11.50	11.50
Creamer, Diamond Shaped	6.50	8.50	Sugar, Diamond Shaped	6.50	8.50
Cream Soup	15.00	17.50	Tumbler, 4¼", 8 oz.	20.00	22.50
Cup	6.00	6.50	Tumbler, 4½", 10 oz.	20.00	19.00
Plate, 6" Sherbet	2.50	3.50	Vase, Cone Shaped	20.00	
Plate, 8 3/8" Salad	4.50	5.00	Vase Holder (17.50)		
*Plate, 9 3/8" Dinner	8.50	10.00			

*Green — $17.50

Please refer to Foreword for pricing information

OLD CAFE HOCKING GLASS COMPANY, 1936-1938; 1940

Colors: Pink, crystal, ruby red.

The Old Cafe juice and 80 oz. pitchers make their debut in this book on the rare page at the back. I managed to get the Royal Ruby lamp pictured in the 2nd edition Pocket Guide. It's made from an inverted 7¼" vase and was part of Hocking's Royal Ruby promotion of the early '40's. Ruby pieces are still favorites with collectors.

I cannot convince myself that the cookie jar with the "Old Cafe" type panels really belongs to this pattern, particularly with that strange lid with the cross hatching design. However, if you like it, it will blend nicely with this pattern.

Dinner plates and pitchers are the choice items in Old Cafe.

	Crystal, Pink	Royal Ruby		Crystal, Pink	Royal Ruby
Bowl, 3¾" Berry	2.00	4.00	Pitcher, 6", 36 oz.	45.00	
Bowl, 5", One or Two Handles	3.00		Pitcher, 80 oz.	65.00	
Bowl, 5½" Cereal	4.00	8.50	Plate, 6" Sherbet	1.25	
Bowl, 9", Closed Handles	7.00	10.00	Plate, 10" Dinner	10.00	
Candy Dish, 8" Low	5.00	10.00	Saucer	2.00	
Cup	3.00	5.00	Sherbet, Low Footed	3.00	
Lamp	8.50	14.50	Tumbler, 3" Juice	4.00	
Olive Dish, 6" Oblong	3.50		Tumbler, 4" Water	4.50	
			Vase, 7¼"	8.00	12.00

OLD ENGLISH, "THREADING" INDIANA GLASS COMPANY

Colors: Green, amber; some pink, crystal, forest green.

Notice the fan type vase in a forest green color that has never been reported before!

Collectors for Old English are not numerous, as yet; but the ones there are take an absolute DELIGHT in it! They are among THE most ENTHUSIASTIC of any collectors I meet.

There is a major difference in the candy and pitcher lids although they are almost interchangeable in size. There is a notch in the pitcher lid for pouring.

The only goblet I have seen recently had been "converted" to a candy dish by adding some strange lid to it. I would have purchased it anyway except that it was priced as a RARE candy dish in Depression Glass!

That pink sherbet has hardly shown up in abundance either.

There is a cheese and cracker (dip and chip in present lingo) set to be found in this. I consists of a 3½" comport on an indented plate much like the one in Flower Garden and Butterfly pattern. Let me know of any other items of interest to collectors that you find.

	Pink, Green, Amber		Pink, Green, Amber
Bowl, 4" Flat	9.50	Pitcher and Cover	77.50
Bowl, 9" Footed Fruit	17.50	Plate, Indent for Compote	15.00
Bowl, 9½" Flat	20.00	Sandwich Server, Center Handle	22.50
Candlesticks, 4" Pr.	20.00	Sherbet	12.50
Candy Dish & Cover, Flat	35.00	Sugar	9.50
Candy Jar with Lid	32.50	Sugar Cover	16.50
Candy Jar, 9¾", 2 Handles	25.00	Tumbler, 4½" Footed	9.50
Compote, 3½" Tall, 7" Across	12.50	Tumbler, 5½" Footed	17.50
Creamer	10.50	Vase, 5 3/8", Fan Type, 7"	
Fruit Stand, 11" Footed	25.00	Across	20.00
Goblet, 5¾", 8 oz.	15.00	Vase, 12" Footed	27.50

Please refer to Foreword for pricing information

"ORCHID" PADEN CITY GLASS COMPANY, Early 1930's

Colors: Yellow, cobalt blue, green, pink.

Since I've been looking for these "orchids" from Paden City for some time, I'm deciding they aren't too easily found. However, maybe people just don't know it's collectible; so, I elected to include it even with these few pieces. Perhaps I can stimulate you to find more pieces. Please let me know what you find.

You'll immediately notice the similarity of these items to those of 'Peacock Reverse'. Both patterns were etched on the so-called "crow's foot" blanks. Thus, it stands to reason that Orchid might be found in the same pieces as "Peacock Reverse". We'll see!

	Pink, Green, Yellow	Cobalt Blue
Bowl, 4 7/8″ Square	9.00	17.50
Bowl, 8¾″ Square	12.50	30.00
Candlesticks, 5¾″ Pair	22.50	37.50
Creamer	12.50	17.50
Comport, 6¼″	13.50	22.50
Ice Bucket, 6″	27.50	49.50
Mayonnaise, 3 Pc.	17.50	32.50
Sugar	12.50	17.50
Vase, 10″	37.50	67.50

OVIDE, incorrectly dubbed "New Century" HAZEL ATLAS GLASS COMPANY, 1930-1935

Colors: Green, black, white, platonite trimmed with fired-on colors.

Everyone likes the Art Deco decorated pieces in Ovide pattern. I've had letters from a couple of lucky people who've found sets of it. However, this is definitely NOT the normal situation. It appears to be quite scarce.

The futuristic oviform attracts some who enjoy "meaningful simplicity". I have recently had some black brought in at a show to be identified which had sterling floral designs on it. It was attractive; and the people who had brought it did so because they "liked" it.

I found a black Ovide candy dish; but I was disappointed that it didn't have the Cloverleaf design on it! Sorry, Ovide fans; it's just that it would have been such a treasure in Cloverleaf, which, along with Ribbon, has the same shape as Ovide.

There are divers Platonite decorations to be found; so, find a favorite and go from there. Platonite was the specially made, heat resistant ware which came in a kaleidoscope of fired-on colors. (See the Moderntone shakers pictured to get an idea of the various colors made). Some of the plainer dishes you may remember being used by a local restaurant. They were attracted by its heat resistant durability.

	Green	Black, Decorated White		Green	Black, Decorated White
Bowl, 4¾″ Berry		6.50	Plate, 6″ Sherbet	1.00	2.50
Bowl, 5½″ Cereal		6.50	Plate, 8″ Luncheon	1.50	5.00
Bowl, 8″ Large Berry		13.50	Plate, 9″ Dinner		7.00
Candy Dish and Cover	12.50	20.00	Platter, 11″		9.00
Cocktail, Footed Fruit	1.50	5.50	Salt and Pepper, Pr.	7.50	17.50
Creamer	2.50	7.50	Saucer	1.25	3.00
Cup	1.50	5.00	Sherbet	1.50	6.50
			Sugar, Open	2.50	7.50

Please refer to Foreword for pricing information

OYSTER AND PEARL ANCHOR HOCKING GLASS CORPORATION, 1938-1940

Colors: Pink, crystal, ruby red, white with fired-on pink or green.

The Royal Ruby Oyster and Pearl sells very fast at today's prices. That large sandwich plate and fruit bowl are such nice serving pieces that people feel they're getting a real bargain in them!

Besides the red which is still bargain basement priced, other colors in this pattern are reasonable. This is probably due to the fact that you can't collect a "set" in this pattern. However, I'm encountering more and more collectors who are using Oyster and Pearl to fill in the serving piece gaps in other patterns. "After all, it's Depression Glass!" they say. I find that interesting. Ten years ago, people were into collecting PATTERNS. They'd hardly sniff at a piece of Depression Glass that wasn't some particular pattern. Now, more and more, if it's ANY piece of Depression Glass, it merits interest. That's good. We've made progress!

I find little middle ground attitude toward the fired-on pieces in pink and green. People either love them or hate them. One lady, who had a set of both pink and green, told me that they just "did something" for her table when she served in them!

	Crystal, Pink	Royal Ruby	White With Fired On Green Or Pink
Bowl, 5¼" Round or Handled	4.00	8.00	5.00
Bowl, 5¼" Heart Shaped, One Handled	4.50		5.00
Bowl, 6½" Deep Handled	7.50	10.50	
Bowl, 10½" Deep Fruit	12.50	27.50	10.00
Candleholder, 3½" Pr.	12.50	27.50	12.50
Plate, 13½" Sandwich	8.00	25.00	
Relish Dish, 10¼" Oblong	4.50		6.00

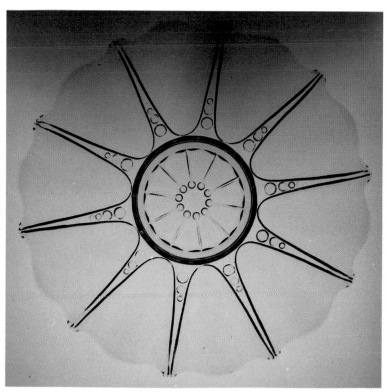

"PARROT", SYLVAN FEDERAL GLASS COMPANY, 1931-1932

Colors: Green, amber; some crystal and blue.

Webster's tells us that a sylvan is one who lives in the woods. By that token, this pattern was appropriately named by Federal. However, we less erudite collectors simply call it "Parrot". Therefore, this pattern's nickname makes the alphabetical listing. (If I placed this pattern under SYLVAN, I'd get letters from collectors wondering why I left it out!)

The "everyday" Depression market is beginning to catch up to the prices on Parrot. They haven't advanced appreciably since the last book. There for a while, only those with a deep pocket were buying Parrot. Too, a few dealers, knowing the desirability, demand and dwindling supply, priced it beyond anyone's sensible means. They had it and they wanted to keep it, I guess, so they wouldn't have to go hunt it any more. I expect activity to pick up in this pattern, however, merely because the market, in general, is advancing.

There are still fewer pieces of amber found than green; however, there are fewer collectors for the amber. Thus, the prices have remained reasonable for the available supply. With four sizes of tumblers around, hope still springs for an amber pitcher. Federal made bushels of amber Madrid pitchers; surely they made a few Parrot ones of like shape!

Unfortunately, that cache of 37 green pitchers found in the basement of an old hardware store has all been swallowed up into collections. I understand at least two have "bitten the dust" due to breakage. Horrors! They're the only ones known so far. However, my wife's grandmother recently attended a ladies' tea and was served from Parrot plates by her friend. Commenting on their being Depression Glass, the lady told her that she'd had the whole set (including pitcher and tumblers) but she'd given them away. Yes, they all had the birds on them. So, there must BE more out there somewhere!

Carefully check the pointed ridges on the cups, sherbets, et cetera. These tend to flake and chip. Prices listed here are for MINT items only.

The amber grill plates are squared whereas the green Parrot grill plates are round.

Indiana Glass Company made some thin green plates with parrots and flowers in an all-over pattern. These are NOT "Parrot". At the moment, they're just round Depression Glass plates.

A **blue** Parrot sherbert has just been found, unfortunately too late to be photographed for this book. Think of it, "Madonna" **blue** Parrot!

	Green	Amber		Green	Amber
Bowl, 5″ Berry	10.00	9.50	Plate, 10¼″ Square	20.00	20.00
Bowl, 7″ Soup	17.50	22.50	Platter, 11¼″ Oblong	20.00	37.50
Bowl, 8″ Large Berry	42.50	47.50	Salt and Pepper, Pr.	147.50	
Bowl, 10″ Oval Vegetable	30.00	35.00	Saucer	7.00	7.00
Butter Dish and Cover	217.50	525.00	Sherbet, Footed Cone	12.50	11.50
Creamer, Footed	15.00	17.50	Sherbet, 4¼″ High	117.50	
Cup	15.00	17.50	Sugar	14.50	13.50
Hot Plate, 5″	277.50		Sugar Cover	45.00	97.50
Pitcher, 8½″, 80 oz.	525.00		Tumbler, 4¼″, 10 oz.	47.50	47.50
Plate, 5¾″ Sherbet	8.50	8.50	Tumbler, 5½″, 12 oz.	62.50	67.50
Plate, 7½″ Salad	12.00		Tumbler, 5¾″ Footed		
Plate, 9″ Dinner	17.50	15.50	Heavy	62.50	77.50
Plate, 10½″ Round Grill	12.50		Tumbler, 5½″, 10 oz.		
Plate, 10½″ Square Grill		12.50	Thin (Madrid Mold)		69.50

PATRICIAN, "SPOKE" FEDERAL GLASS COMPANY, 1933-1937

Colors: Pink, green, amber, yellow.

An art student told me at a show I attended that I had doubled her appreciation of Depression Glass when she came to the introductory paragraph I'd written for Patrician in the fourth edition. "Up until then, I'd just been enjoying reading about the glass and admiring the pieces photographed. After that paragaraph, I went back and studied the various patterns from the aspect of their actual design. Then, I DOUBLY appreciated it!" she explained. After that accolade for our beloved glassware, I feel justified in repeating my small soapbox lecture.

A patrician was a Roman nobleman. I feel we do this particular pattern a disservice when we refer to it simply as "Spoke" because whoever designed Patrician for Federal went to a great deal of trouble to embody some Roman characteristics. His museum preserved chariot wheel is echoed in the center motif. Notice the various types of borders used on the edges of the pattern. Borders were very significant to Romans as well as certain drapings of the toga. A purple border around an elaborately draped toga set a nobelman apart from persons of lower rank. Indeed, borders were so significant that the Roman incorporated them into his buildings and tombs, intricate and beautiful borders such as those seen here on the Patrician pattern. Since the designer so artfully and thoughtfully constructed this design, we owe him at least the tiny homage of recognizing his work by its name, Patrician!

Amber still heads the list of colors collected in Patrician. Federal called it "Golden Glow". Because of the heavy demand, many pieces in amber are in short supply such as pitchers, footed tumblers, cookie jars, cereals and even the large berry bowl. I expect there to be enough dinner plates to go around for some time yet! Whoever promoted those did a superb job! However, the prices for them are slowly creeping upward. So, better buy yours now! I can remember they used to be a dollar each; but as a fellow dealer so frequently says, "There USED TO BE just Indians here, too!

Mint condition sugar lids and cookie bottoms are difficult in all colors. Butter bottoms are less frequently discovered than those heavy tops.

Pitchers with applied handles (shown in crystal) show up less frequently than do those with molded handles. Neither type show their little hexagonal sides very often, however.

If you plan to own tumblers, better get them now. I don't ever expect them to be any "cheaper"; and as the supply dwindles, so do your chances of having them.

This pattern, with dinner plates, can still be collected for prices considered reasonable in Depression Glass! Occasionally, there are bargains still. A pink Patrician shaker for $4.00 was recently purchased in Atlanta!

	Amber, Crystal	Pink	Green		Amber, Crystal	Pink	Green
Bowl, 4¾" Cream Soup	9.50	14.50	15.00	Plate, 9" Luncheon	6.00	5.50	5.50
Bowl, 5" Berry	6.50	9.50	6.50	Plate, 10½" Dinner	4.50	13.50	15.00
Bowl, 6" Cereal	13.50	12.50	12.50	Plate, 10½" Grill	7.00	9.50	9.50
Bowl, 8½" Large Berry	22.50	15.00	15.00	Platter, 11½" Oval	9.50	10.00	12.50
Bowl, 10" Oval Vegetable	15.00	10.00	10.00	Salt and Pepper, Pr.	35.00	67.50	40.00
Butter Dish and Cover	57.50	197.50	77.50	Saucer	4.00	4.00	4.00
Cookie Jar and Cover	45.00		175.00	Sherbet	6.50	9.50	9.50
Creamer, Footed	6.00	7.50	6.00	Sugar	5.00	6.00	6.00
Cup	6.50	6.00	6.00	Sugar Cover	25.00	37.50	37.50
Pitcher, 8", 75 oz.	57.50	97.50	77.50	Tumbler, 4", 5 oz.	17.50	17.50	17.50
Pitcher, 8¼", 75 oz.	57.50	97.50	87.50	Tumbler, 4½", 9 oz.	15.00	14.00	14.00
Plate, 6" Sherbet	6.00	3.00	4.00	Tumbler, 5½", 14 oz.	22.50	30.00	25.00
Plate, 7½" Salad	8.00	12.50	8.00	Tumbler, 5¼", 8 oz.			
				Footed	27.50		37.50

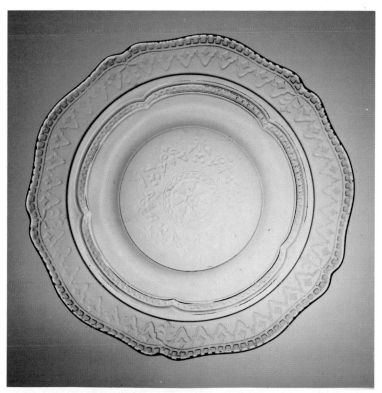

"PEACOCK AND WILD ROSE", LINE #300 PADEN CITY, 1930's

Colors: Pink, green, cobalt blue.

The cup, saucer and luncheon plate HAVE NEVER BEEN SEEN in this pattern before; and the COBALT blue vase was certainly a pleasant surpise! Additional pieces shown this time include candlesticks and the covered candy.

Paden City didn't "name" any of its glassware or their etchings; and they had a strange tendency of putting handles in the center of their serving pieces.

The 10½" plate has two handles; the CAKE plate is actually a cake stand with the foot being only an inch or two tall.

Since there were no complete catalogue listings for this pattern, I include what I have found and their particular measurements. Any additional items, or colors, you may find, please let me know.

Prices encountered on this line since the last book have been quite high; but there seems to be a definite market for it; and the glass IS quite scarce!

	Pink, Green		Pink, Green
Bowl, 8½" Flat	22.50	Candlesticks, 5" Across, Pr.	27.50
Bowl, 8½" Oval Fruit, Footed	30.00	Candy Dish and Cover, 7"	47.50
Bowl, 8¾" Footed	22.50	Comport, 6¼"	19.50
Bowl, 9¼" Footed	25.00	Creamer, 4½" Footed	20.00
Bowl, 9¼" Center Handled	27.50	Cup	50.00
Bowl, 10½" Fruit	30.00	Ice Bucket, 6"	42.50
Bowl, 10½" Footed	30.00	Ice Tub, 4¾"	35.00
Bowl, 10½" Center Handled	27.50	Mayonnaise, 3 Pc.	37.50
Bowl, 11" Console	28.00	Plate, 8"	12.50
Bowl, 14" Console	32.50	Plate, 10½"	17.50
Cake Plate	27.50	Relish, 3 Part	17.50
		Saucer	15.00
		Sugar, 4¼" Footed	20.00
		*Vase, 10"	45.00

*Cobalt blue — $75.00

145

"PEACOCK REVERSE", LINE 412   PADEN CITY, 1930's

Colors: Cobalt blue, red, yellow.

The blue vase pictured in "Peacock and Wild Rose" was purchased sight unseen from Indiana. I was so positive it was "Peacock Reverse" that it took me about a month to realize that bird wasn't looking over his shoulder.

These pieces have what is commonly called "crow's foot" background. Actually, the "crow's foot" is what made this line #412. The reverse peacock etching would have been given a number by the company.

Those few pieces encountered this year have awaited a richer man than I. The $100.00 sherbet plate was the most fantastic item I saw; and no, it hadn't been purchased by the end of the show!

Shown for the first time are the 5¾" candleholders represented to us as Cambridge glassware. A lady in Tennessee brought a pair of black ones with a sterling trim for me to see at a show there recently. They weren't "Peacock Reverse", but they were definitely Paden City and very attractive!

	Red, Blue		Red, Blue
Bowl, 4 7/8" Square	19.50	Plate, 5¾" Sherbet	15.00
Bowl, 8¾" Square	37.50	Sherbet, 4 5/8" Tall, 3 3/8" Diameter	27.50
Bowl, 8¾" Square with Handles	42.50	Sherbet, 4 7/8" Tall, 3 5/8" Diameter	27.50
Candlesticks, 5¾" Sq. Base, Pr.	67.50	Sugar, 2¾" Flat	45.00
Candy Dish, 6½" Squared	39.50	Tumbler, 4", 10 oz. Flat	37.50
Creamer, 2¾" Flat	45.00		

147

PETALWARE   MACBETH-EVANS GLASS COMPANY, 1930-1940

Colors: Pink, crystal, monax, cremax, cobalt and fired-on yellow, blue, green & red.

I said last year that Petalware had begun to "grow on me". I wonder if that's what prompted the deluge of Petalware that's been showered on our Grannie Bear shop of late. Anyone need about 36 of everything (except creme and flat soups, of course)? It's really strange how business "cycles" like that. You won't have any of a pattern for six months; and then six people will want you to buy their glass---and five of the six will have the **same** pattern!

All pieces shown in this picture are in the Monax color. Petalware can also be found in a beige or clam color called Cremax by Macbeth-Evans. This color will turn green under a black light; but that's about the only interesting thing collectors find about it.

Decorated items, like the ones shown, are very popular with some collectors, particularly the red banded items with the flowers. There's a set that comes with a Pennsylvania Dutch bird decoration which is more attractive "live" than there in the picture.

The plates with the fruit and "red ribbon" were decorator pieces. There are eight different fruits and one lovely collector wrote each down so that I'd have them for the book. We looked high and low for that paper that we put "in a safe place", but to no avail! Florence Cherry, I remember; Ord Apple . . . . Help!

There is a cobalt MUSTARD jar, having a saucer ATTACHED which should come with a metal lid. My dear wife bought three sans lids thinking they were a cute kind of sherbet dish!

I get letters constantly about the petalware lamp and chandelier shades. They come in both large and small sizes and in both Monax and Cremax. They're more "interesting" than rare. You usually see at least one at every other flea market.

You will find some pieces having colors of blue, red, green or yellow fired-on. One such "blue" cup was pictured in the 3rd edition. It came on a saucer having several fired-on rings of color encircling the indented cup ring.

There are no salt and pepper shakers for this pattern. Newport shakers in Monax will serve the color specifications.

Plain Monax Petalware sets an attractive table. Various food colors won't clash with the color of the plate as sometimes happens with a Depression pattern; and best of all, this pattern, though NOT all that plentiful (in spite of my six sets), can still be afforded!

	Pink, Crystal	CREMAX, MONAX Plain	Fired-On Decorations		Pink, Crystal	CREMAX, MONAX Plain	Fired-On Decorations
Bowl, 4½" Cream Soup	4.00	5.50	7.50	Plate, 8" Salad	1.75	3.00	5.00
Bowl, 5¾" Cereal	3.50	4.50	6.50	Plate, 9" Dinner	3.00	3.50	5.50
Bowl, 7" Soup		6.00	9.50	Plate, 11" Salver	4.00	5.00	8.50
*Bowl, 8¾" Large Berry	4.00	6.50	12.50	Plate, 12" Salver		6.50	10.00
Cup	2.50	3.00	4.50	Platter, 13" Oval	5.25	7.25	10.00
**Creamer, Footed	2.50	3.50	6.50	Saucer	1.25	1.25	1.75
Lamp Shade (Many Sizes) $5.00 to $10.00				Sherbet, 4" Low Footed	10.00		
Mustard with Metal Cover				**Sherbet, 4½" Low Footed	3.00	4.00	6.50
in Cobalt Blue Only $4.50				**Sugar, Footed	2.50	3.50	6.50
Pitcher, 80 oz. (Crystal				Tidbit Servers or Lazy Susans,			
Decorated Bands)	17.50			Several Styles 11.00 to 17.50			
Plate, 6" Sherbet	1.25	2.00	2.50	***Tumblers (Crystal			
				Decorated Bands) 2.50 to 7.50			

*Also in cobalt at 30.00
**Also in cobalt at 17.50
***Several Sizes

149

"POPEYE & OLIVE", Line #994, PADEN CITY GLASS COMPANY, Early 1930's

Colors: Ruby, cobalt, green and crystal.

The recent movie "Popeye" was around about as long as this elusive pattern! This is collected primarily in cobalt blue and red; but it's found in green in many areas.

The red items pictured here made it through a fire at the photographer's studio with only a water soaking by the fire department. They did develop some interesting mold later; but that washed away with various soakings and some strong detergent.

Candlesticks, the decanter and the 48 oz. pitcher appear to be the hardest items to obtain.

Paden City didn't "name" their glassware; so heaven only knows who first stuck the glass with this "nickname"!

	Green	Blue, Red		Green	Blue, Red
Bowl, 8"	10.00	20.00	Plate, 12"	10.00	20.00
Bowl, 8", 2 Handled Salad	12.50	22.50	Saucer	2.00	3.00
Bowl, 10"	20.00	15.00	Sherbet, High	6.00	11.50
Candlesticks, Pair	17.50	27.50	Sherbet, Low	5.00	10.00
Creamer	8.00	15.00	Sugar	8.00	15.00
Cup	5.00	9.50	Sundae, 7 oz.	7.50	12.50
Decanter	5.00	47.50	Tray, 10½" Center Handled	12.50	22.50
Finger Bowl & Plate	10.00	22.50	Tumbler, 2½ oz. Wine	5.00	9.00
Goblet, 3½ oz. Claret	9.00	15.00	Tumbler, 5 oz.	6.50	10.00
Goblet, 10 oz. Water	7.50	13.50	Tumbler, 9 oz.	7.50	12.50
Pitcher, 48 oz.	25.00	67.50	Tumbler, 12 oz. Iced Tea	8.75	15.00
Plate, 8" Salad	5.00	9.50	Vase, 7"	10.00	22.50
Plate, 10", 2 Handled	10.00	17.50	Vase, 7" Crimped	12.50	27.50

PRINCESS HOCKING GLASS COMPANY, 1931-1935

Colors: Green, 2 yellows, pink; some blue.

Princess, for some unknown reason, does not photograph well! We've tried four different times and none of the pictures do justice to the true beauty of this pattern!

Those FOOTED pink and green pitchers with their matching tumblers are VERY unusual pieces. They have also been found with frosted panels down the sides.

The yellow juice pitcher is one of TWO known thus far; and both of those have surfaced in Kentucky.

You might also take a good look at the crystal sherbet shown on the left. It's Princess SHAPE; but it sports a MAYFAIR design!

The pink Princess shakers with the red plastic tops were bought years ago by a collector in Ohio. I suspect these may have been replacement tops made for shakers of this type.

Naturally, that blue cup and saucer stands out like a sore thumb. In past photographs we've enjoyed a blue cookie jar, one of eight or ten to surface. However, this leads us to another subject murmured among dealers but never discussed in print that I know of. There's a lot of strange glass crossing the border from Mexico, ostensibly from their flea markets down there. As far as I can find out, all of the blue Princess hails from Mexico or Texas. In fact, I just talked to a dealer who turned down an eight place setting in blue Princess at a show in west Texas because it came from Mexico. Other things come to mind, the pink Florentine sherbet from Madrid shaped mold and the blue Florentine pitcher shown on the cover of the 2nd edition, all came from Mexico. A strange crystal bowl stikingly similar to No. 612 has also turned up. As I see it, there are two lines of thought on this; one, it's reproduction; and two, it's very possible that Hocking and other companies cleaned out their storage bins or dumped their experimental or inferiorly made items south of the border. At this point I don't know; but a Mexican vacation is becoming more and more intriguing!

Beginning collectors should know there are two colors of yellow; the most popular is the bright yellow topaz; the other is apricot. The two will not mix well at all. Yellow bowls are particularly hard to locate.

	Green	Pink	Yellow Amber		Green	Pink	Yellow Amber
Ash Tray, 4½"	47.50	57.50	67.50	Plate, 11½" Grill, Closed			
Bowl, 4½" Berry	14.50	9.00	22.50	Handles	6.50	4.50	6.00
Bowl, 5" Cereal or Oatmeal	15.50	9.50	22.00	Plate, 11½" Handled Sandwich	8.50	7.50	8.50
Bowl, 9" Octagonal Salad	19.50	15.00	65.00	Platter, 12" Closed Handles	9.50	9.50	27.50
Bowl, 9½" Hat Shaped	20.00	13.50	67.50	Relish, 7½" Divided	15.00	11.50	45.00
Bowl, 10" Oval Vegetable	12.00	10.00	35.00	Relish, 7½" Plain	47.50		90.00
Butter Dish and Cover	60.00	65.00	400.00	Salt and Pepper, 4½" Pair	32.50	25.00	47.50
Cake Stand, 10"	12.50	10.00		Spice Shakers, 5½" Pair	20.00		
†††Candy Dish and Cover	30.00	32.50		††Saucer (Same as Sherbet Plate)	3.50	2.50	3.00
Coaster	17.50	50.00	65.00	Sherbet, Footed	12.50	9.50	22.50
†Cookie Jar and Cover	30.00	37.50		Sugar	6.00	5.50	7.50
Creamer, Oval	7.50	8.50	8.50	Sugar Cover	10.00	9.50	10.00
††Cup	7.00	4.50	5.50	Tumbler, 3", 5 oz. Juice	15.00	12.50	15.00
Pitcher, 6", 37 oz.	27.50	20.00	375.00	Tumbler, 4", 9 oz. Water	17.50	10.50	15.00
Pitcher, 7 3/8", 24 oz. Footed	375.00	295.00		Tumbler, 5¼", 13 oz. Iced Tea	22.50	14.50	20.00
Pitcher, 8", 60 oz.	32.50	27.50	57.50	Tumbler, 4¾", 9 oz. Sq. Ftd.	45.00	37.50	
Plate, 5½" Sherbet	3.50	2.50	3.00	Tumbler, 5¼", 10 oz. Footed	18.00	14.50	15.00
Plate, 8" Salad	7.00	5.50	6.50	Tumbler, 6½", 12½ oz. Footed	40.00	25.00	47.50
Plate, 9½" Dinner	15.00	8.00	9.00	Vase, 8"	20.00	15.50	
††Plate, 9½" Grill	8.50	5.00	6.00				

†Blue — $375.00
††Blue — $55.00
††† — $400.00

QUEEN MARY (PRISMATIC LINE), "VERTICAL RIBBED"
HOCKING GLASS COMPANY, 1936-1940

Colors: Pink, crystal; some ruby red.

The most frequent question I'm asked about Queen Mary is if the pink shakers really exist, where are they? Well, I got out the fourth edition picture and took a real HARD look at those "pink" shakers shown and couldn't REALLY decide whether they were pink or whether the red tops fooled the camera into giving them an extra pink glow. Next, I consulted with the lady who lent me the pattern who further fuzzied the matter by having gotten rid of said shakers and being uncertain whether they were pink or not. My Hocking information merely refers to "shakers". So, nearly five years from having made that photograph showing pink shakers, I can't recall whether they were really pink or not. Authors don't like to MAKE mistakes; but I would ADMIT to it---if I really knew I had. Frankly, at this point, I don't honestly know. They could have been pink! At any rate, I'll bet you'll remember these are unusual shakers if you find them now in pink, won't you? Please let me know if you own or find them!

There are two size cups found in Queen Mary or Prismatic Line as Hocking referred to it. The smaller cup is the easiest to find and rests on a saucer having a cup ring. The larger cups are found on Hocking's typical "saucer/sherbet" plate, that is, a plate serving both as a saucer and as a sherbet. I'm thinking of using that term throughout the book to indicate those saucers not having rings for the cups.

Hocking made a few pieces of Queen Mary in ruby red for their Royal Ruby promotion during the early 1940's. I've seen the candle holder in Royal Ruby.

In the early 1950's Anchor Hocking made an ash tray in Forest Green from their old Prismatic Line.

	Pink, Crystal		Pink, Crystal
Ash Tray, 2" x 3¾" Oval	2.50	Cup (2 sizes)	4.50
Bowl, 4" One Handle or None	3.00	Plate, 6" and 6 5/8"	2.50
Bowls, 5" Berry, 6" Cereal	3.00	Plate, 8½" Salad	3.50
Bowl, 5½", Two Handles	3.50	***Plate, 9¾" Dinner	6.50
Bowl, 7" Small	4.50	Plate, 12" Relish, 3 Sections	6.00
Bowl, 8¾" Large Berry	6.50	Plate, 12" Sandwich	5.50
*Butter Dish or Preserve and Cover	22.50	Plate, 14" Serving Tray	7.50
**Candy Dish and Cover	19.50	Relish Tray, 12", 3 Part	8.50
Candlesticks, 4½" Double Branch Pr.	10.00	Relish Tray, 14", 4 Part	8.50
Candlesticks, Ruby Red Pr.	27.50	****Salt and Pepper, Pr.	12.50
Celery or Pickle Dish, 5" x 10"	3.50	Saucer	1.50
Cigarette Jar, 2" x 3" Oval	4.50	Sherbet, Footed	3.50
Coaster, 3½"	2.00	Sugar, Oval	4.00
Coaster/Ash Tray, 4¼" Square	4.50	Tumbler, 3½", 5 oz. Juice	2.50
Comport, 5¾"	4.50	Tumbler, 4", 9 oz. Water	4.00
Creamer, Oval	4.00	Tumbler, 5", 10 oz. Footed	12.50

*Pink — 77.50
**Pink — 27.50
***Pink — 12.00
****Pink — 67.50

RADIANCE NEW MARTINSVILLE, 1936-1939

Colors: Red, cobalt & ice blue, amber, crystal.

Radiance was better quality glassware, the kind you bought at the store rather than what you got free with a purchase of gas. This, of course, helps to account for its relative scarcity today. The same can be said for the Moondrops pattern also made by this company.

Punch bowl sets in several colors have been observed at antique shows; but I've never seen any with the original (and very elusive) ladles.

This pattern is very attractive and its colors of red and cobalt alone insure it of being collectible! Further, the shapes are unusual. Butter dishes, pitchers, handled decanters and the 5 piece condiment sets are all considered choice items to possess. A lady in Tennessee who stopped at my table was recently delighted to find "that pretty old blue bottle with a stopper" that her Dad had given her "years ago" was a cobalt Radiance decanter! When told its worth she exclaimed, "My word! I've got that sitting out! I'm going home and put that right up!"

You will find pieces trimmed with gold or platinum. They may or may not be attractive depending on how worn the decoration. It can be removed with a rust removing agent.

Crystal items, unless decorated with platinum or gold, sell for about HALF the prices listed below.

The cobalt pitcher and tumbler are shown on the Rare page.

	Red	Other Colors		Red	Other Colors
Bon Bon, 6"	9.50	5.50	Creamer	9.00	6.50
Bon Bon, 6" Footed	9.50	6.00	Cruet, Individual	25.50	20.00
Bon Bon, 6" Covered	19.50	13.50	Cup	8.00	4.50
Bowl, 5", 2 Handled			Decanter, Handled with		
Nut	9.50	6.50	Stopper	82.50	50.00
Bowl, 7", 2 Part	10.00	7.50	Lamp, 12"	47.50	35.00
Bowl, 7" Pickle	9.50	6.00	Mayonnaise, 3 Pc. Set	22.50	10.00
Bowl, 8", 3 Part Relish	15.00	9.00	*Pitcher, 64 oz.	147.50	100.00
Bowl, 10" Celery	12.50	7.50	Plate, 8" Luncheon	6.50	4.00
Bowl, 10" Crimped	17.50	10.00	Plate, 14" Punch Bowl		
Bowl, 10" Flared	20.00	9.75	Liner	25.00	15.00
Bowl, 12" Crimped	22.50	12.50	Punch Bowl	57.50	35.00
Bowl, 12" Flared	22.00	12.00	Punch Cup	7.00	4.00
Butter Dish		125.00	Punch Ladle	42.50	40.00
Candlestick, 8" Pr.	37.50	15.00	Salt & Pepper, Pr.	32.50	20.00
Candle, 2 Light Pr.	35.00	22.50	Saucer	2.50	2.00
Cheese and Cracker, 11			Sugar	9.00	6.50
Plate Set	25.00	13.50	Tray, Oval	17.50	15.00
Comport, 5"	9.50	6.00	**Tumbler, 9 Oz.	12.50	8.50
Comport, 6"	12.50	7.00	Vase, 10" Flared	32.50	10.00
Condiment Set, 4 Pc. on			Vase, 12" Crimped	45.00	15.00
Tray	97.50	85.00			

*Cobalt blue - $225.00
**Cobalt blue - $25.00

Please refer to Foreword for pricing information

156

157

RAINDROPS, "OPTIC DESIGN" FEDERAL GLASS COMPANY, 1929-1933

Colors: Green, crystal.

I've now looked six years for a mate to this Raindrops shaker. Are they really that rare, or is someone hoarding them?

Raindrops is still often confused with "Thumbprint"/Pear Optic. Raindrops's impressions are **rounded** little hills or bumps occurring on the INSIDES of the pieces and on the undersides of the plates. "Thumbprint"/Pear Optic has **elongated** or pear shaped impressions which are slightly "scooped out" in the middle.

I have now seen TWO other Raindrops sugar lids at shows; so that accounts for THREE lids known to date. That still ranks this sugar lid as one of the rarest in Depression Glass. However, due to lack of demand for this particular pattern, this lid will not command the price accorded a Monax American Sweetheart sugar lid or a Mayfair sugar lid. DEMAND, not necessarily RARITY, determines price in Depression Glass.

	Green		Green
Bowl, 4½" Fruit	2.50	Salt and Pepper, Pr.	42.50
Bowl, 6" Cereal	3.50	Saucer	1.50
Cup	3.00	Sherbet	4.00
Creamer	5.00	Sugar	4.00
Plate, 6" Sherbet	1.50	Sugar Cover	22.50
Plate, 8" Luncheon	2.50	Tumbler, 3", 4 oz.	3.00
		Whiskey, 1 7/8"	3.50

"RIBBON" HAZEL ATLAS GLASS COMPANY, Early 1930's

Colors: Green; some black, crystal, pink.

Yes, I have seen shakers in pink Ribbon pattern! Several people have brought pairs to shows to convince me; so they do exist!

This pattern was made by Hazel Atlas during the same time as their Cloverleaf and Ovide, probably from the same basic molds! You will notice the similarity of shapes. Molds were expensive; but they could be re-designed.

It's possible to gather a set of the green. It'll take time because you generally spot "Ribbon" a piece or two at a time rather than in groups of pieces. Black "Ribbon" is collected mostly by item collectors. They want just the candy dish or shakers.

Obscure patterns like this used to be ignored. However, more and more, I'm encountering a real interest in these lesser patterns. They're still inexpensive due to lack of demand; and one collector said, "Once you've put a set together, it's bound to be more rare than having a set of Mayfair!" That's one school of thought.

	Green	Black		Green	Black
Bowl, 4" Berry	2.50		*Salt and Pepper, Pair	12.00	27.50
Bowl, 8" Large Berry	12.50	17.50	Saucer	1.50	
Candy Dish and Cover	22.50		Sherbet, Footed	3.50	
Creamer, Footed	4.00	10.00	Sugar, Footed	3.50	20.00
Cup	3.50		Tumbler, 5½", 10 oz.	8.50	
Plate, 6¼" Sherbet	1.50		Tumbler, 6½", 13 oz.	12.50	
Plate, 8" Luncheon	2.50	8.50			

*Pink — $15.00

Please refer to Foreword for pricing information

RING, "BANDED RINGS" HOCKING GLASS COMPANY, 1927-1932

Colors: Crystal, crystal w/pink, red, blue, orange, yellow, black, platinum, etc. rings; green, some pink, "Mayfair" blue, red.

Ring, one of the oldest Depression patterns, isn't generally even recognized as Depression Glass by the public! The pattern was produced in numerous items; and once gathered into sets, it's really pretty.

The purist collector will have giant headaches trying to match the order of color on his pieces. Most collectors of Ring cease to even try that. I've recently been shown an ad calling the flamboyantly colored Ring (yellow, orange, green) "New Fiesta". The ad was suitably festooned with sombreros and gaily skirted girls dancing in a party-like atmosphere! It was enough to make you want to dash out and buy this wonderful, frivolous glassware!

Notice the different styles of pitchers shown. These are the commonly found ones. If they were vice versa, that is, a pink one like the green one shown and a green one like the pink one shown, you'd have the harder to find pitchers in Ring.

Thus far, only pitcher and tumblers have been located in pink. Unusual colors of "Mayfair" blue and ruby red have only turned up in luncheon plates.

My wife thinks the platinum banded pieces of Ring, especially the stemware, are "elegant". Thus, Ring affords the collector the unique opportunity to party with the "New Fiesta" or to polish the good silver and serve "elegantly" from the platinum rimmed.

Dealers used to exchange Ring tops for their more prestigious Mayfair shakers. As collectors for Ring increased and they had to find Ring shakers intact, it was discovered that green Ring shakers are few and far between! One is pictured; so memorize it!

Collectors for Ring are on the increase. If you like this, better start to gather it now. One young couple told me they chose this pattern because of the ring name and design. It symbolized, to them, the unending, encircling love they felt for each other. (It shows how newly wed they were, doesn't it; but with the headlines I read daily, I can stand knowing the gentler sentiments yet survive)!

	Crystal	Crystal Decor., Green		Crystal	Crystal Decor., Green
Bowl, 5" Berry	2.00	2.50	Sandwich Server,		
Bowl, 7" Soup	5.50	7.50	Center Handle	9.50	17.50
Bowl, 8" Large Berry	3.50	5.50	Saucer	1.50	2.00
Butter Tub or Ice Bucket	8.00	12.50	Sherbet, Low		
Cocktail Shaker	7.00	12.50	(for 6½" Plate)	4.00	4.50
Cup	2.50	3.00	Sherbet, 4¾" Footed	4.00	5.50
Creamer, Footed	3.00	3.50	Sugar, Footed	3.00	4.00
Decanter and Stopper	13.50	22.50	Tumbler, 3½", 5 oz.	2.50	3.50
Goblet, 7" to 8" (Varies),			Tumbler, 4¼", 9 oz.	3.00	4.00
9 oz.	4.50	9.50	Tumbler, 5 1/8", 12 oz.	3.50	4.50
Ice Tub	8.00	15.00	Tumbler, 3½" Footed		
Pitcher, 8", 60 oz.	8.50	15.00	Cocktail	3.50	4.50
*Pitcher, 8½", 80 oz.	10.50	17.50	Tumbler, 5½" Footed		
Plate, 6¼" Sherbet	1.25	2.50	Water	3.50	4.50
Plate, 6", Off Center Ring	2.50	3.50	Tumbler, 6½" Footed		
**Plate, 8" Luncheon	1.50	2.50	Iced Tea	4.50	8.00
***Salt and Pepper, 3" Pr.	12.50	22.50	Whiskey, 2", 1½ oz.	3.00	5.00

*Also found in Pink. Priced as Green.
**Red — 17.50. Blue — 22.50.
***Green — 57.50.

Please refer to Foreword for pricing information

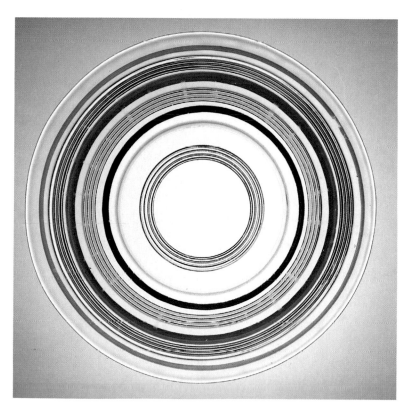

161

ROCK CRYSTAL, "EARLY AMERICAN ROCK CRYSTAL"

McKEE GLASS COMPANY, 1920's and 1930's in colors

Colors: Pink, green, cobalt, red, yellow, amber, blue-green, crystal, etc.

Rock Crystal has many devotees, my wife being one! As you can see from the listing, this pattern was made in many pieces; and I don't pretend that this is ALL you can find. I've tried to give the overall picture, particularly in the various colors. It would take three pages to list ALL the various bowls, etc. made in crystal with their varying heights, ounce capacity and types of edgings. It would be like getting a 15 page computer report. It's MORE than you'd want to know and certainly more than you'd want to wade through in trying to find a price for something!

The large forest green and amber tankards shown on the following page are quite rare in these colors. Since you've already turned the page, notice the canary yellow pitcher just in front of the forest green one. You rarely see that one either. It's so yellow it almost glows; and it's perfectly gorgeous!

I hope you truly enjoy our endeavors to get the prettiest, rarest, most beautiful glassware photographed IN COLOR! Besides being exceptionally costly, it's a MONUMENTAL task, gathering, packing, hauling, coordinating box loads of glass; and that's all BEFORE you get to the photographer's studio to unload it and photograph it!

For pricing purposes, the colors are divided into three columns. However, Rock Crystal colors include the following: four shades of green, aquamarine, vaseline yellow, amber, pink and satin frosted pink, red slag, dark red, red, amberina red, crystal, frosted crystal, crystal with goofus decoration, crystal with gold decoration, amethyst, milk glass, blue frosted or "Jap" blue and cobalt blue.

Cobalt blue has only shown up so far in the large footed fruit bowl and the candlesticks shown.

Red Rock Crystal commands a lot of attention. However, as stated above, there seem to be three distinct shades of red; so getting everything you want in your particular shade of red is sometimes quite a chore.

Hazards of the game, but the crystal small fruit bowl pictured at middle left got broken at the photography session. It belonged to my wife. If you find one of those, I guess I know a buyer. Me!

	Crystal	Green, Amber, Pink	Red & Other Colors
*Bon Bon, 7½" S.E.	6.50	12.50	20.00
Bowl, 4" S.E.	4.00	5.50	10.00
Bowl, 4½" S.E.	4.50	6.00	11.50
Bowl, 5" S.E.	4.50	6.00	12.50
**Bowl, 5" Finger Bowl with 7" Plate, P.E.	8.50	14.50	22.50
Bowl, 7" Pickle or Spoon Tray	8.50	15.00	25.00
Bowl, 7" Salad S.E.	7.00	9.00	15.00
Bowl, 8" Salad S.E.	8.00	10.00	15.00
Bowl, 9" Salad S.E.	9.00	14.00	22.50
Bowl, 10½" Salad S.E.	10.00	15.00	27.50
Bowl, 11½" Two Part Relish	10.00	15.00	27.50
Bowl, 12" Oblong Celery	13.00	20.00	30.00
***Bowl, 12½" Footed Center Bowl	30.00	50.00	115.00
Bowl, 13" Roll Tray	17.50	25.00	40.00
Bowl, 14" Six Part Relish	17.50	30.00	67.50
Butter Dish and Cover	175.00		
Candelabra, Two Lite Pr.	27.50	32.50	47.50
Candelabra, Three Lite Pr.	30.00	35.00	57.50
Candlestick, 5½" Low Pr.	20.00	25.00	40.00
Candlestick, 8½" Tall Pr.	57.50	59.50	75.00
Candy and Cover, Round	20.00	37.50	85.00
Cake Stand, 11", 2¾" High, Footed	15.00	22.00	45.00
Comport, 7"	12.50	17.50	30.00
Creamer, Flat S.E.	15.00		
Creamer, 9 oz. Footed	12.00	20.00	30.00

Please refer to Foreword for pricing information

162

ROCK CRYSTAL, "EARLY AMERICAN ROCK CRYSTAL" (Con't.)

	Crystal	Green, Amber, Pink	Red & Other Colors
Cruet and Stopper, 6 oz. Oil	37.50	50.00	75.00
Cup, 7 oz.	9.00	12.00	20.00
Goblet, 7½ oz., 8 oz. Low Footed	12.00	20.00	32.50
Goblet, 11 oz. Low Footed Iced Tea	12.50	17.50	32.50
Jelly, 5" Footed S.E.	10.00	12.00	22.00
Lamp, Electric	45.00	85.00	175.00
Parfait, 3½ oz. Low Footed	8.00		
Pitcher, Quart S.E.	35.00	75.00	
Pitcher, ½ Gal., 7½" High	55.00	110.00	
Pitcher, 9" Large Covered	95.00	150.00	250.00
Pitcher, Fancy Tankard	75.00	300.00	400.00
Plate, 6" Bread and Butter S.E.	3.00	4.00	7.00
Plate, 7½" P.E. & S.E.	3.50	5.00	12.50
Plate, 8½" P.E. & S.E.	5.50	7.00	15.50
Plate, 9" S.E.	8.00	9.00	20.00
Plate, 10½" S.E.	16.00	13.00	22.50
Plate, 11½" S.E.	17.50	16.00	25.00
Plate, 10½" Dinner S.E. (Large Center Design)	13.50	17.50	25.00
Punch Bowl and Stand, 14"	250.00		
Salt and Pepper (2 styles)	37.50	65.00	
Salt Dip	17.50		
Sandwich Server, Center Handled	15.00	20.00	60.00
Saucer	3.25	4.50	6.50
Sherbet or Egg, 3½ oz. Footed	9.00	12.00	20.00
Spooner	20.00		
Stemware, 1 oz. Footed Cordial	12.00	17.00	30.00
Stemware, 2 oz. Wine	9.00	14.00	25.00
Stemware, 3 oz. Wine	10.00	17.00	30.00
Stemware, 3½" oz. Footed Cocktail	10.00	15.00	27.50
Stemware, 6 oz. Footed Champagne	10.00	15.00	23.50
Stemware, 8 oz. Large Footed Goblet	12.00	20.00	33.00
Sundae, 6 oz. Low Footed	9.00	15.00	23.00
Sugar, 10 oz. Open	9.00	15.00	25.00
Sugar, 10 oz. Covered	25.00	35.00	55.00
Syrup with Lid	40.00		
Tumbler, 2½" oz. Whiskey	7.00	13.00	30.00
Tumbler, 5 oz. Juice	9.00	12.00	25.00
Tumbler, 5 oz. Old Fashioned	10.00	14.00	27.50
Tumbler, 9 oz. Concave or Straight	10.00	14.00	25.00
Tumbler, 12 oz. Concave or Straight	13.50	17.00	32.50
Vase, Cornucopia	25.00	35.00	
Vase, 11" Footed	25.00	37.50	95.00

*S.E. McKee designation for scalloped edge
**P.E. McKee designation for plain edge
***Red Slag — $300.00. Cobalt — $137.50

Please refer to Foreword for pricing information

165

ROSE CAMEO   BELMONT TUMBLER COMPANY, 1931

Color: Green.

Although the patent to Rose Cameo is registered to the Belmont Tumbler Company, there are strong indications that the glass itself may have been manufactured at the Hazel Atlas Plant.

Pictured this time is the tumbler with the slightly flared edges. Previous editions have shown the straight sided tumbler.

The "dirty" looking bowl at the back with the straight sides is a new discovery! That isn't dirt. We powdered the bowl to help the camera pick up the rose design.

This pattern is still confused with Cameo by beginning collectors. Cameo has the dancing girl inside the "Cameo". This pattern has a rose as its name indicates.

Tumblers are the most frequently found pieces. Though a pattern with few pieces, a basic serving set can be acquired, sans cups and saucers. Rose Cameo is attractive. It deserves your consideration.

	Green		Green
Bowl, 4½" Berry	3.00	Sherbet	3.50
Bowl, 5" Cereal	4.50	Tumbler, 5" Footed (2 Styles)	7.50
Bowl, 6", Straight Sides	7.50		
Plate, 7" Salad	4.00		

ROSEMARY, "DUTCH ROSE"   FEDERAL GLASS COMPANY 1935-1937

Colors: Amber, pink, green.

Rosemary has a "history". This is the pattern that ultimately came from Federal's twice changing of its Mayfair pattern after learning that Hocking had beaten them to the patent office with the name "Mayfair".

You will notice that the Rosemary pattern does not have the arches around the base which the "transitional" Mayfair pieces have; nor does it have the arches and waffling around the base that regular Federal Mayfair has; Rosemary has perfectly plain glass at the base of its pieces save for the center Rose motif.

Amber is the most plentiful color in Rosemary; so, naturally, pink and green are most in demand. Pink supplies seem to be dwindling faster than the green.

Rosemary sports a handle-less sugar bowl; this piece causes more consternation with new collectors than any other. It's not a tumbler and it's not a sherbet. It's the sugar bowl!

Bowls (cream soup, oval vegetable, cereal) seem the hardest items to locate; next come tumblers.

	Amber	Pink, Green		Amber	Pink, Green
Bowl, 5" Berry	2.00	4.00	Plate, Dinner	3.50	8.50
Bowl, 5" Cream Soup	6.00	12.50	Plate, Grill	3.50	5.50
Bowl, 6" Cereal	5.00	10.00	Platter, 12" Oval	6.00	11.50
Bowl, 10" Oval Vegetable	6.50	12.00	Saucer	1.25	2.00
Creamer, Footed	5.50	7.50	Sugar, Footed	5.50	7.50
Cup	3.00	4.50	Tumbler, 4¼", 9 oz.	7.50	12.00
Plate, 6¾" Salad	2.00	3.50			

167

ROULETTE, "MANY WINDOWS"   HOCKING GLASS COMPANY, 1935-1939

Colors: Pink, green.

To 'roulette' something means to mark it with a series of incisions. Thus, this pattern was aptly named by Hocking.

As with Princess, Roulette has been extremely difficult to capture on film. The colors seem to disappear before your eyes. The pattern is much more attractive than this photograph shows it to be!

Notice that the rouletting on the pitcher occurs toward the upper third of the piece. There is a pitcher with a cubed like design at the bottom. This ISN'T Roueltte pattern. Too, there is a cobalt tumbler which has an embossed rather than an impressed design which resembles Roulette. This isn't Roulette either.

Shot glasses, tumblers and saucers are few and far between.

Green is more often seen than pink as you can see from the picture!

	Pink, Green, Crystal
Bowl, 9" Fruit	8.00
Cup	3.50
Pitcher, 8", 64 oz.	20.00
Plate, 6" Sherbet	2.00
Plate, 8½" Luncheon	3.50
Plate, 12" Sandwich	7.50
Saucer	2.00
Sherbet	4.00
Tumbler, 3¼", 5 oz. Juice	4.00
Tumbler, 3¼", 7½ oz. Old Fashioned	5.50
Tumbler, 4 1/8", 9 oz. Water	10.00
Tumbler, 5 1/8", 12 oz. Iced Tea	10.00
Tumbler, 5½", 10 oz. Footed	9.00
Whiskey, 2½", 1½ oz.	6.50

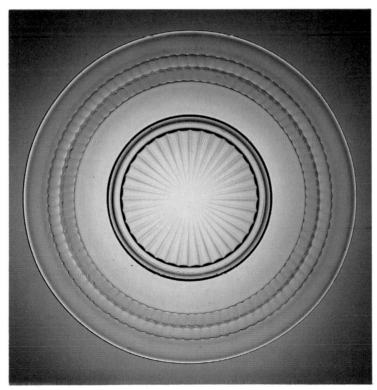

"ROUND ROBIN" MANUFACTURER UNKNOWN, Probably early 1930's

Colors: Green, iridescent.

If you round off the top of the creamer and place a handle on the vacant side, you'll know what a sugar bowl in Round Robin looks like. We photographed one for the old black and white pictures in the first and second books; but since we went to color pictures, I've not found a sugar bowl!

However, I HAVE finally found a sherbet in this pattern---directly after we photographed for this book, of course. There were six of them---more pieces of "Round Robin" than I have seen at once!

Notice the FOOTED cup. That's very unusual in Depression Glass.

The drip tray for the creamer is also rather special. Round Robin has this item in common with Cameo! Supposedly, you could ring the creamer with sugar cubes and thus eliminate the sugar bowl "mess" alltogether. Cubes on my cereal just don't "cut it", however!

	Green	Iridescent		Green	Iridescent
Bowl, 4" Berry	3.00	3.50	Plate, 8" Luncheon	2.50	3.00
Cup, Footed	3.00	3.50	Plate, 12" Sandwich	3.50	4.50
Creamer, Footed	4.50	5.00	Saucer	1.50	1.50
Domino Tray	17.50		Sherbet	3.50	4.00
Plate, 6" Sherbet	1.50	1.50	Sugar	4.50	5.00

ROXANA HAZEL ATLAS GLASS COMPANY, 1932

Colors: Yellow, white, crystal.

I am still of the conviction that Roxana and Bowknot should be married. With Bowknot's saucerless cup and Roxana's cupless saucer, it should be an ideal match.

I have met a few ladies who collect this because it's their namesake. Otherwise, I suspect that writers of books are the only other people who ever seek it---not because it isn't an attractive little pattern, but because there's so very little of it!

The sherbet is footed but not stemmed. One was pictured in my first and second editions.

	Yellow	White		Yellow
Bowl, 4½" x 2 3/8"	5.00	10.00	Plate, 6" Sherbet	2.50
Bowl, 5" Berry	3.50		Saucer	2.50
Bowl, 6" Cereal	5.50		Sherbet, Footed	3.50
			Tumbler, 4", 9 oz.	6.00

ROYAL LACE   HAZEL ATLAS GLASS COMPANY, 1934-1941

Colors: Pink, green, crystal, blue, amethyst.

Once again the cycle of cobalt Royal Lace has repeated. There'll be a period of FRENZIED buying and then the prices increase and collectors turn elsewhere for a time; and cobalt Royal Lace will sit at shows with no takers. Then, prices on other things will "catch up" and there'll be another scurry to buy cobalt Royal Lace. This "cycling" happens with other Depression patterns, also; but in the eleven years I've been in this business, cobalt Royal Lace is the classic example of this phenomenon.

Collectors for crystal Royal Lace have put such a dent in the supply of pieces in that color that it now sells for the same prices as the pink---except for the butter dish.

We had such an array of pitchers to photograph that we had to make two pictures in order to include everything. I've had people tell me that they purposely mixed crystal and cobalt in their sets. You know, they may have something! It looks nice, doesn't it?

I want to thank Shelby and Kathy for sending me a picture of their ruffled cream soup in pink Royal Lace. It's like those in Moderntone and Florentine, patterns also made by Hazel Atlas. It is definitely the most unusual item I've seen in Royal Lace lately.

You might notice the amethyst toddy set pictured. It comes with a ladle having that cherry red knob at the end and poking through the metal lid at the ascribed notch. We placed three of the roly-poly tumblers on that ledge, two cobalt and one amethyst. The amethyst, in the middle, merged with its background. Notice that one of the cobalt tumblers has a tiny white ship design. Originally, the toddy sets came with eight of those roly-poly cups. The cookie jar base is the toddy set insert.

Beginners, pay attention to those butter dishes and shakers. You wouldn't want any of those to slip by you! By the way, a 1930's advertisement for Royal Lace shows you could buy that butter dish for 15¢---or a FORTY-FOUR PIECE SET for $2.99!

Those are what some call "the good old days"!

You won't know it by these photographs but pitchers aren't easily found, particularly the bulbous types.

Green Royal Lace seems in shorter supply than any of the other colors.

	Crystal	Pink	Green	Blue	Amethyst
Bowl, 4¾" Cream Soup	7.50	9.50	22.50	18.50	
Bowl, 5" Berry	6.00	10.00	15.00	19.50	
Bowl, 10" Round Berry	10.00	11.50	17.50	27.50	
Bowl, 10", 3 Leg Straight Edge	12.50	14.50	27.50	32.50	
Bowl, 10", 3 Leg Rolled Edge	75.00	15.00	57.50	147.50	
Bowl, 10", 3 Leg Ruffled Edge	17.50	15.00	35.00	42.50	
Bowl, 11" Oval Vegetable	12.50	14.50	18.50	27.50	
Butter Dish and Cover	47.50	90.00	215.00	327.50	
Candlestick, Straight Edge Pair	17.50	22.50	37.50	67.50	
Candlestick, Rolled Edge Pair	35.00	27.50	47.50	87.50	
Candlestick, Ruffled Edge Pair	20.00	30.00	47.50	72.50	
Cookie Jar and Cover	22.50	32.50	47.50	187.50	
Cream, Footed	7.00	8.00	15.00	22.50	
Cup	4.50	6.00	14.50	17.50	
Pitcher, 54 oz., Straight Sides	27.50	35.00	60.00	65.00	
Pitcher, 8", 68 oz.	37.50	35.00	72.50	85.00	
Pitcher, 8", 86 oz.	40.00	52.50	90.00	97.50	
Pitcher, 8½", 96 oz.	42.50	57.50	117.50	137.50	
Plate, 6" Sherbet	2.00	3.00	5.50	7.50	
Plate, 8½" Luncheon	3.50	5.50	8.50	20.00	
Plate, 10" Dinner	6.50	7.50	15.00	24.00	
Plate, 9 7/8" Grill	5.50	8.00	12.50	18.50	
Platter, 13" Oval	12.00	15.00	22.50	30.00	
Salt and Pepper, Pr.	30.00	35.00	97.50	157.50	
Saucer	2.00	3.00	4.50	6.50	
Sherbet, Footed	5.50	7.00	15.00	20.00	
Sherbet in Metal Holder	3.50	3.50		18.00	22.50
Sugar	5.00	6.50	14.00	18.50	
Sugar Lid	10.00	10.00	22.50	57.50	
Tumbler, 3½", 5 oz.	6.50	10.00	17.50	24.50	
Tumbler, 4 1/8", 9 oz.	7.50	9.50	16.00	22.50	
Tumbler, 4 7/8", 12 oz.	10.00	12.50	22.50	30.00	
Tumbler, 5 3/8", 13 oz.	12.00	16.00	22.50	35.00	
Toddy or Cider Set: Includes Cookie Jar, Metal Lid, Metal Tray, 8 Roly-Poly Cups and Ladle				95.00	100.00

Please refer to Foreword for pricing information

ROYAL RUBY   ANCHOR HOCKING GLASS COMPANY, 1939-1960's; 1977

Color: Red.

Royal Ruby refers solely to the red glassware made by Anchor Hocking. Their initial promotion started in 1938. Some people tend to throw all red glassware into the Royal Ruby category regardless of what company made it. Strictly speaking, Royal Ruby was the term coined by Anchor Hocking to describe the red glassware issued during its late 30's early 40's Royal Ruby Promotion.

I happened upon an abundance of the ball stemmed goblets via my Grannie Bear Antique Shop connections. They were from an old grocery store, still in the original boxes of 36, and most of them still have the original stickers on them!

The 5¼" round bowl behind the round dinner plates was sold as a popcorn bowl. A 10" bowl and six of these smaller ones comprised the set!

The small ball vase shown in the pattern shot still has the citronella candle in it which was used as a deterrent for bugs as you sat on the patio. This probably explains why you see SO MANY OF THESE!

Not all footed sugars will take the slotted lid!

Squared items you find in red are a 1950's issue which came along about the same time as the "Forest Green" pieces of the same shape.

In 1977 Hocking re-introduced 4½" and 8" bowls in Bubble; 7, 9, 12 and 16 oz. plain tumblers; an ivy ball vase; a punch cup and a square ash tray. They supposedly carry the anchor trademark of the company. Generally speaking, the pieces were lighter in weight and color than the older glassware.

	Red
Ash Tray, 4½" Square	2.50
Bowl, 4¼" Berry	3.50
Bowl, 5¼"	6.00
Bowl, 7½" Soup	8.00
Bowl, 8" Oval Vegetable	10.00
Bowl, 8½" Large Berry	9.50
Bowl, 10" Deep	12.50
Creamer, Flat	5.00
Creamer, Footed	6.00
Cup (Round or Square)	3.50
Goblet, Ball Stem	6.50
Lamp	17.50
Pitcher, 22 oz. Tilted or Upright	17.50
Pitcher, 3 qt. Tilted	22.50
Pitcher, 3 qt. Upright	25.00
Plate, 6½" Sherbet	1.50
Plate, 7" Salad	2.50
Plate, 7¾" Luncheon	3.50
Plate, 9" or 9¼" Dinner	6.00
Punch Bowl and Stand	32.50
Punch Cup	2.50
Saucer (Round or Square)	1.50
Sherbet, Footed	5.50
Sugar, Flat	6.50
Sugar, Footed	6.00
Sugar Lid	5.00
Tumbler, 2½ oz. Footed Wine	7.50
Tumbler, 3½ oz. Cocktail	5.50
Tumbler, 5 oz. Juice, 2 Styles	4.00
Tumbler, 9 oz. Water	4.00
Tumbler, 10 oz. Water	5.00
Tumbler, 13 oz. Iced Tea	7.00
Vase, 4" Ball Shaped	3.50
Vase, 6½" Bulbous, Tall	7.50
Vases, Several Styles (Small)	5.00
Vases, Several Styles (Large)	9.50

Please refer to Foreword for pricing information

"S" PATTERN, "STIPPLED ROSE BAND"   MACBETH-EVANS GLASS COMPANY, 1930-1933

Colors: Crystal; crystal w/trims of platinum, blue, green, amber; pink, some amber, green, red and white.

You are looking at three rarely seen items in "S" Pattern, the pink and green pitchers and the 13" amber cake plate.

For the first time you can see the actual blue trim on that plate which looked orchid in the last book's picture because of the reflection from the rare red "S" Pattern plate pictured.

There are two distinct shades of yellow just as in Princess pattern. There's a very light, pretty yellow and a darker amber shade.

Because "S" Pattern is so delicate looking in crystal, the various colored trims really enhance the pieces; and, of course, the platinum trimmed always goes well with the good silver!

As in Dogwood, there are two sizes of cake plates in "S" Pattern. Unlike Dogwood, the harder to find is the 13" rather than the 11". That amber cake plate is the only non-crystal one I have ever seen in "S" Pattern. I always have hoped for a green one to turn up!

The green pitcher and tumblers and the pink pitcher may be all you ever see in these colors. I once left a $2.50 pink creamer at a show in Michigan because it didn't have a sugar bowl with it! Probably some creamer and sugar collector latched onto that before the show ended! I trust there are pink tumblers to match the pitcher. They can't all have broken!

Pictured in the last book were the "normal" "S" Pattern pitcher with the fat shape of the American Sweetheart pitcher, the tid-bit server, and the unusual Monax plate.

	Crystal	Yellow, Amber, Crystal With Trims
*Bowl, 5½" Cereal	2.50	3.50
Bowl, 8½" Large Berry	6.50	12.50
*Creamer, Thick or Thin	4.00	5.50
*Cup, Thick or Thin	2.50	3.00
Pitcher, 80 oz. (Like "Dogwood") (Green or Pink 450.00)	35.00	67.50
Pitcher, 80 oz. (Like "American Sweetheart")	45.00	50.00
Plate, 6" Sherbet (Monax: 14.00)	1.50	1.75
**Plate, 8" Luncheon	2.00	2.50
Plate, 9¼" Dinner	3.00	4.50
Plate, Grill	2.50	4.50
Plate, 11" Heavy Cake	27.50	30.00
***Plate, 13" Heavy Cake	45.00	52.50
*Saucer	1.25	1.50
Sherbet, Low Footed	3.00	4.50
*Sugar, Thick and Thin	3.50	5.50
Tumbler, 3½", 5 oz.	2.50	4.50
Tumbler, 4", 9 oz. (Green: 57.50)	3.00	5.50
Tumbler, 4¼", 10 oz.	3.50	6.00
Tumbler, 5", 12 oz.	4.50	6.50

*Fired-on red items will run approximately three times price of amber.
**Deep Red — $62.50.
***Amber — $57.50

Please refer to Foreword for pricing information

177

SANDWICH HOCKING GLASS COMPANY, 1939-1964; 1977

Colors:

Crystal	1950's-1960's	Pink	1939-1940	Forest Green	1950's-1960's
Amber	1960's	Royal Ruby	1939-1940	White (opaque)	1950's

Thankfully, the Sandwich pattern most collected is that of Anchor Hocking. (When you turn the page, you'll understand that statement a little better). Crystal is the color most sought with Forest Green presently running a close second. The green is difficult to find in all but five pieces which were packaged in Mother's Oats. Those five pieces found nation wide include: the 5 oz. juice, 9 oz. water, 4 7/8" berry bowl, and the custard cup and liner.

For those who want the story behind the scarcity of the pitcher in Forest Green, read the 3rd and 4th editions. I won't bore previous readers by repeating it. It boiled down to crossed purposes in marketing.

Though some factory workers believe they remember lids being made for the green cookie jar, it's generally agreed there were none because the company sold this green bottom as a vase rather than a cookie jar.

The opaque white (some gold trimmed) egg nog sets sold in my area for $1.79 with an oil change and lube at Ashland Oil. Presently, they sell for about $20.00-25.00 if you can find someone who really wants one!

The liner (small plate) for the CRYSTAL custard is considered to be a treasure! Those green liners are plentiful (thanks to Mother's Oats).

Anchor Hocking got briefly into the re-issue business by making a Sandwich cookie jar again. The newer version is larger than the old, however; so there's no reason to mistake the two. The newer one has a height of 10¼", a 5½" opening and a 20" circumference at its largest part. The old Sandwich cookie jar is 9¼" tall, has a mouth of 4 7/8" and is only 19" in circumference.

You might notice the iridized blue cup and saucer of unknown origin.

On the subject of re-issues, I would like to state the following:

It's only my opinion, of course, but I feel companies only hurt themselves with re-issues. They sacrifice their integrity or the "trust" factor they have with the collecting public which numbers in the millions; and they sabotage all that free prideful publicity the collectors give them when bragging to friends about their collections made by thus and so glass company during such and such years. That's got to be PRICELESS material (feed-back) to that company since it's BOUND to make persons hearing that "testimony" sit up and take notice of any other glassware that company advertises or is historically associated with. Really, it's beyond me to understand the reasoning behind re-issues. If they absolutely HAVE to use old molds, they should always make pieces in **untried** colors. That way, the pieces MIGHT become collectible and thus would be marketable to larger numbers of people. Trying for old colors, besides showing no imagination, just destroys everybody's taste for any of it! What's being accomplished? A large scale destruction of an invaluable reputation for making fine, collectible, valuable glassware, a reputation which was being built free of charge! Where's the sense ("cents") in that? Excuse me, ladies, but a former boss called that logic "pinching pennies to blow hell out of dollars".

	Crystal	Desert Gold	Ruby Red	Forest Green	Pink		Crystal	Desert Gold	Forest Green
Bowl, 4 7/8" Berry	2.50	2.50	8.50	1.50	2.50	Pitcher, 6" Juice	35.00		77.50
Bowl, 5¼"			10.00			Pitcher, ½ gal. Ice Lip	40.00		157.50
Bowl, 6" Cereal	10.00	5.00				Plate, 7" Dessert	5.00	2.50	
Bowl, 6½" Smooth						Plate, 8"	2.00		
or Scalloped	4.50	5.50		17.50		Plate, 9" Dinner	8.50	4.00	30.00
Bowl, 7" Salad	5.50			25.00		Plate, 9", Indent			
Bowl, 8" Smooth						For Punch Cup	2.50		
or Scalloped	5.00		25.00	27.50	7.50	Plate, 12" Sandwich	6.00	7.50	
Bowl, 8¼" Oval	4.50					Punch Bowl & Stand	25.00		
Butter Dish, Low	27.50					Punch Cup	2.00		
Cookie Jar and Cover	25.00	27.50		16.00†		Saucer	1.25	3.00	4.00
Creamer	4.00			13.50		Sherbet, Footed	4.00		
Cup, Tea or Coffee	1.50	3.50		12.00		Sugar and Cover	9.50		13.50†
Custard Cup	2.50			1.50		Tumbler, 5 oz. Juice	4.50		2.00
Custard Cup Liner	6.00			1.25		Tumbler, 9 oz. Water	5.00		2.50
						Tumbler, 9 oz. Footed	11.50		

†(No Cover)

Please refer to Foreword for pricing information

SANDWICH INDIANA GLASS COMPANY, 1920's-1980's

Colors:

| Crystal | Late 1920's-Today | Pink | Late 1920's-Early 1930's | Teal Blue | 1950's |
| Amber | Late 1920's-1970's | Red | 1933-1970's | Lt. Green | 1930's |

THIS GLASSWARE IS FAST BECOMING VIRTUALLY UNCOLLECTIBLE. READ ON!

If you haven't already read it, please read the last paragraph on the preceding page. I didn't have room on this page for all my opinions.

The big "news" is that Indiana has made for Tiara a butter dish which is extremely close to the old teal color made in the 1950's. It's available as a hostess gift item for selling X number of dollars of glass.

Because of the new Sandwich being made today by Indiana, I'm dropping crystal from my listing. It's become a collectors' pariah! The list is too long to examine each piece to tell the difference between old and new. In many cases, there is little difference since the same molds are being used. Hopefully, somebody at Indiana will wise up and stop making the old colors as I was told they would do after the "pink Avocado" fiasco in 1974. Instead of trying to entice collectors to new wares, they are stuck on trying to destroy the market for the old glassware which has been collectible for years but which may never be again. Perhaps you could start collecting Hocking Sandwich if you like the pattern. Sure, they re-made a cookie jar, but they carefully made it different from the old which showed their awareness of collectors in the field!

For those of you who have collected the crystal Indiana Sandwich or the teal butter dish and have a sizable investment involved, I can only say that time will tell as to the future collectiblity of this pattern. At present, it doesn't look too promising.

The really maddening thing is that all this "new" Sandwich is being touted to prospective buyer as glass that's going to be worth a great deal in the future based on its past history---and the company is steadily destroying those very properties they're using to sell the new glass! Supreme irony!

I can vouch for three items in red Sandwich dating from 1933, i.e. cups, creamers and sugars. May we assume a saucer accompanied the cup? I know this because these specific items are found with inscriptions for the 1933 World's Fair. However, in 1969, Tiara Home Products produced red pitchers, 9 oz. goblets, cups, saucers, wines, wine decanter, 13" serving tray, creamers, sugars and salad and dinner plates. Now, if your dishes glow yellow under a black light or if you KNOW that your Aunt Sophie held her red dishes in her lap while fording the swollen stream in a buggy, then I'd say your red Sandwich pieces are old. Other than that, I know of no way to tell if they are or aren't. NO, I won't even say that all old red glass glows under black light. I know SOME of it does because of a certain type ore they used then. However, I've seen some newer glass glow; but Tiara's 1969 red Sandwich glass does not.

Presently, the only two colors remotely worth having are pink and green; and who knows but what the company will make those tomorrow!

	Pink, Green	Teal Blue	Red		Pink, Green	Teal Blue	Red
Ash Tray Set (Club, Spade, Heart, Diamond Shapes) $2.50 each	15.00			Pitcher, 68 oz.	77.50		
				Plate, 6" Sherbet	2.50	4.00	
Bowl, 4¼" Berry	3.00			Plate, 7" Bread and Butter	3.50		
Bowl, 6"	3.50			Plate, 8" Oval, Indent for Sherbet	5.00	7.50	
Bowl, 6", 6 Sides		6.50		Plate, 8 3/8" Luncheon	4.50		
Bowl, 8¼"	10.00			Plate, 10½" Dinner	12.50		
Bowl, 9" Console	15.00			Plate, 13" Sandwich	12.50		
Bowl, 10" Console	18.00			Sandwich Server, Center Handle	27.50		
*Butter Dish and Cover, Domed	150.00	187.50		Saucer	2.50	3.50	6.00
Candlesticks, 3½" Pr.	13.00			Sherbet, 3¼"	5.00	6.00	
Candlesticks, 7" Pr.	35.00			Sugar, Large Open	8.50		27.50
Creamer	6.50		27.50	Tumbler, 3 oz. Footed Cocktail	15.00		
Cruet, 6½ oz. and Stopper		117.50		Tumbler, 8 oz. Footed Water	12.50		
Cup	4.50	4.50	20.00	Tumbler, 12 oz. Footed Iced Tea	22.50		
Creamer and Sugar on Diamond Shaped Tray		27.50					
Decanter and Stopper	67.50			Wine, 3", 4 oz.	17.50		
Goblet, 9 oz.	13.50						

*Beware new Teal

Please refer to Foreword for pricing information

SHARON, "CABBAGE ROSE" FEDERAL GLASS COMPANY, 1935-1939

Colors: Pink, green, amber; some crystal.   *(See Reproduction Section)*

Sharon is one of the most popular patterns in Depression Glass; it's also one of the most durable. You seldom find chips; scratches, yes, from YEARS of use! I was told by one lady that she remembered the drummer coming around selling this pattern. He'd put a plate on the floor and stand on it to show you what good service you'd get from the dishes. I asked her if she bought a set and she said, "Yes, **Mama** did!" (Whoops! I never was very good about guessing ages)!

Because of its popularity, Sharon is one of those patterns that has been hassled by reproductions. However, all the new is recognizable from the old; so the prices for Sharon have never been jeopardized. Shakers are the latest item reproduced. Read the section at the back of this book on reproductions in Sharon. They should aid you in telling new pieces from old.

There has always been a difference in the prices of the green Sharon pitchers, one with an ice lip and one without. However, we're beginning to see the same pricing differential in the other colored pitchers.

There ARE green footed iced teas in Sharon. I once owned six!

Thin tumblers were always the choice tumblers; however, collectors are now turning to the thick variety, too; and you'll see some pricing changes there.

There is less amber Sharon than pink; yet pink is more in demand. Therefore, the prices for pink are generally higher than those for amber. Green has always commanded the highest prices of the three colors.

Three pieces have been found in crystal Sharon thus far: three 7½" salad plates, many footed tumblers (both plate and tumbler are pictured) and a few thousand cake plates.

The differences between legitimate butter and cheese dishes are as follows: the BUTTER bottom was made from the 1½" deep jam dish (pictured behind the green shakers) ONTO WHICH the company added a tiny ledge of glass for the butter top to rest around. This ridge is so tiny in most cases that if you tried to scoot the butter dish across the table using the knob, you'd scoot the top off the butter bottom. (The pink covered dish pictured is a butter dish). The CHEESE dish bottom was made by adding a rim to the regular salad plate (pictured in front of the shakers) INTO WHICH the dish top would fit. The cheese dish rim remains OUTSIDE of the top once the top is placed on the dish. If you look closely, you can see the glass ridge outside the top of the amber cheese dish pictured.

The 2" high soup bowl is pictured behind the pink shakers. Beginners tend to confuse this with the 1½" jam dish shown beside it.

A unique Sharon lamp is pictured.

	Amber	Pink	Green
Bowl, 5" Berry	5.00	6.00	6.50
Bowl, 5" Cream Soup	12.50	25.00	25.00
Bowl, 6" Cereal	9.00	12.50	12.50
Bowl, 7½" Flat Soup, 2" Deep	22.50	22.00	
Bowl, 8½" Large Berry	3.75	10.00	15.00
Bowl, 9½" Oval Vegetable	8.50	12.50	14.00
Bowl, 10½" Fruit	14.50	15.00	18.50
Butter Dish and Cover	35.00	37.50	62.50
*Cake Plate, 11½" Footed	14.50	19.50	40.00
Candy Jar and Cover	26.50	32.50	100.00
Cheese Dish and Cover	147.50	500.00	
Creamer, Footed	6.50	9.50	10.50
Cup	7.50	8.50	9.00
Jam Dish, 7½"	22.50	65.00	30.00
Pitcher, 80 oz. with Ice Lip	85.00	97.50	287.50
Pitcher, 80 oz. without Ice Lip	87.50	90.00	325.00
Plate, 6" Bread and Butter	2.50	3.50	3.50
Plate, 7½" Salad	8.00	13.50	11.50
Plate, 9½" Dinner	8.00	10.00	10.00
Platter, 12½" Oval	8.50	12.00	15.00
Salt and Pepper, Pr.	30.00	35.00	52.50
Saucer	3.00	4.50	4.50
Sherbet, Footed	7.00	8.50	17.50
Sugar	6.00	8.50	9.50
Sugar Lid	14.50	17.50	22.50
Tumbler, 4 1/8", 9 oz. Thick or Thin	17.50	18.50	30.00
Tumbler, 5¼", 12 oz. Thin	22.50	27.50	42.50
Tumbler, 5¼", 12 oz. Thick	22.50	40.00	47.50
**Tumbler, 6½", 15 oz. Footed	40.00	29.50	

*Crystal: $ 4.50
**Crystal: $12.50

Please refer to Foreword for pricing information

SIERRA, "PINWHEEL" JEANNETTE GLASS COMPANY, 1931-1933

Colors: Pink, green.

There has been a big difference in prices occurring between the pink and the green in several pieces of Sierra. This is why I price colors separately in this book. If I lumped everything under one heading, you'd never know which were the better pieces.

This is a pattern where you must check every little serration for chips. Sierra is the Spanish word for "saw"; and because of this saw-toothed design, it damages easily.

Sierra is mainly noted for its "Adam-Sierra" combination butter dish. There are numerous collectors who'd love to own this little oddity. It's pictured here in pink. If you look closely at the picture, you'll see the Adam pattern motif imprinted on the outside of the butter while you can see the saw-toothed Sierra design molded into the inside of the butter top. The top will then fit the bottom of the butter dish in either pattern. If you turn back to Adam, you'll see one pictured on the Adam butter bottom.

Watch your cups when buying. Some people will set any paneled cup atop a Sierra saucer. It must have the saw-tooth serrations before the clear rim! Notice, too, that the cup, tumbler and pitcher all have smooth, rather than serrated edges. This was done, of course, so you can drink or pour from them! I know of one dealer who hadn't thought that far ahead and was concerned that he'd not found any cups with serrated edges to match his saucers! Cups ARE more difficult to find than the saucers.

Green pitchers and tumblers have disappeared from the market.

Sierra is not jumping out at you by any means; but a set can be put together still with patience and careful searching. Besides, you like challenges, don't you? Didn't your grandmother tell you that things gained easily weren't worth having?

	Pink	Green		Pink	Green
Bowl, 5½" Cereal	5.50	6.50	Plate, 9" Dinner	6.00	8.50
Bowl, 8½" Large Berry	9.00	12.50	Platter, 11" Oval	11.50	14.50
Bowl, 9¼" Oval Vegetable	12.50	17.50	Salt and Pepper, Pr.	22.50	27.50
Butter Dish and Cover	40.00	42.50	Saucer	3.00	3.50
Creamer	8.50	10.50	Serving Tray, 2 Handles	7.00	8.50
Cup	6.00	8.50	Sugar	6.00	7.00
Pitcher, 6½", 32 oz.	32.50	57.50	Sugar Cover	8.50	9.50
			Tumbler, 4½", 9 oz. Footed	17.50	22.50

SPIRAL HOCKING GLASS COMPANY, 1928-1930

Colors: Green.

New to the business and extremely knowledgeable, I would blithely tell everyone that the difference between Hocking's Spiral and Imperial's Twisted Optic was the direction of the spirals. Hocking's went left, or with the clock; Imperial's went right, or counterclockwise. IN GENERAL, that's true. Yet, Imperial's candy jar appears to go left---unless you turn it upside down; and Spiral's center handled server goes right---unless you look through the bottom! The difference is relatively unimportant, except to purists, in these minor patterns. Dealers tend to lump all companies' spiraling patterns together anyway as "one of those spiraling patterns", thus broadening your range of choice.

Some people are gathering luncheon sets in this because it's inexpensive.

	Green		Green
Bowl, 4¾" Berry	4.00	Plate, 8" Luncheon	2.00
Bowl, 7" Mixing	4.00	Preserve and Cover	15.00
Bowl, 8" Large Berry	6.00	Salt and Pepper, Pr.	15.50
Creamer, Flat or Footed	4.00	Sandwich Server, Center Handle	13.50
Cup	3.00	Saucer	1.00
Ice or Butter Tub	12.50	Sherbet	2.50
Pitcher, 7 5/8", 58 oz.	17.50	Sugar, Flat or Footed	4.00
Plate, 6" Sherbet	1.00	Tumbler, 3", 5 oz. Juice	2.50
		Tumbler, 5", 9 oz. Water	3.50

Please refer to Foreword for pricing information

STARLIGHT   HAZEL ATLAS GLASS COMPANY, 1938-1940

Colors: Crystal, pink; some white, cobalt.

Since very little of the cobalt has turned up, only in bowls, I'm putting those prices with the pink. The rarer pink prices are comparable to those presently being seen on the Starlight cobalt bowls.

A number of people buy this pattern to supplement the absence of bowls in other patterns. I still remember one lady who told me the large 11½" salad bowl was an absolute must at their family reunions! It's large enough to serve as a punch bowl, particularly when seated on that 13" Sandwich plate.

Notice the pink salad set in the metal holder. That's always been a favorite of mine. I'm intrigued by the way the serving pieces are held at ready for you.

The pieces shown in white are the only ones found thus far. Let me know if you find others.

This is a pattern that is usually found a single piece at a time.

	Crystal, White	Cobalt, Pink		Crystal, White	Cobalt, Pink
Bowl, 5½" Cereal	2.50	3.50	Plate, 9" Dinner	3.50	5.50
Bowl, 8½", Closed			Plate, 13" Sandwich	4.00	7.00
Handles	3.00	8.50	Relish Dish	2.50	4.50
Bowl, 11½" Salad	10.00	17.50	Salt and Pepper, Pr.	12.50	
Plate, 6" Bread and			Saucer	1.00	2.00
Butter	2.00	2.50	Sherbet	3.50	
Creamer, Oval	3.00		Sugar, Oval	3.00	
Cup	2.50	3.00			
Plate, 8½" Luncheon	2.00	3.00			

STRAWBERRY   U.S. GLASS COMPANY, Early 1930's

Colors: Pink, green, crystal; some iridized.

Looking at this picture, you might surmise that pitchers and butter dishes in this pattern are easily found. You'd be wrong. Further, since there are three of each type pitcher, Strawberry and "Cherryberry", you might think one is as readily found as the other. Sorry; wrong again. The "Cherryberry" picking is a lot harder to do than Strawberry picking---particularly where pitchers, tumblers and butter dishes are concerned! Notice I priced these pieces separately.

The 6¼", 2" deep bowl listed last edition is pictured here in "Cherryberry". I originally found it in the Strawberry design and photographed it for the pattern shot in the last book (which was edited out)!

Notice the large handle-less sugar and lid. The lid is not common; and when found lidless, the sugar is often mistaken for a spooner.

Neophyte collectors should know that the butter bottom is very plain, having only a rayed design in the bottom of the dish. Only the top carries the Strawberry or "Cherryberry" design.

Since there is some pricing differential on some pieces of the two designs, dealers nicknamed the Cherry design "Cherryberry" as a quick means of identification.

I was glad to notice recently that another writer conclusively confirmed my educated guess of three years ago concerning the company who manufactured Strawberry.

	Crystal, Irridescent	Pink, Green		Crystal, Irridescent	Pink, Green
Bowl, 4" Berry	4.50	6.00	Pickle Dish, 8¼" Oval	7.00	8.50
Bowl, 6¼", 2" Deep	20.00	32.50	**Pitcher, 7¾"	150.00	127.50
Bowl, 6½" Deep Salad	7.50	9.50	Plate, 6" Sherbet	3.50	4.00
Bowl, 7½" Deep Berry	9.50	12.50	Plate, 7½" Salad	6.50	8.50
*Butter Dish and Cover	97.50	117.50	Sherbet	5.50	6.50
Comport, 5¾"	8.00	11.50	Sugar, Small Open	10.00	12.50
Creamer, Small	8.00	10.00	Sugar Large	9.00	11.50
Creamer, 4 5/8" Large	10.00	14.00	Sugar Cover	12.50	17.50
Olive Dish, 5" One			***Tumbler, 3 5/8", 9 oz.	13.50	20.00
Handled	6.50	8.50			

  *Cherry Motif — 137.50
 **Cherry Motif — 127.50
***Cherry Motif — 16.00

Please refer to Foreword for pricing information

SUNFLOWER JEANNETTE GLASS COMPANY

Colors: Pink, green, some delphite.

Take a look at that delphite creamer used as a pattern shot. Has anyone got the sugar bowl to match? It would be nice to photograph the two pieces together.

The price for the Sunflower cake plate which we used to disdain continues to spiral. It's still the most plentiful piece in the pattern due to its having been given away inside twenty pound sacks of flour during the Depression. I once saw 25 of these at a garage sale for 50¢ each--and only bought ten which I nearly never got rid of in the shop! Live and learn! I believe I could have "afforded" to hold them a few years!

The rarely found trivet is 7" across and has a slightly raised edge. It's pictured in the back on the page showing the 2nd edition book cover picture. We often pictured rarely found items in Depression Glass on the covers of the past books. It seemed a shame to "waste" these pictures. So, we included them at the end of the book so you'd still have the opportunity to see some of the really rare items in Depression Glass that we have managed to "capture" on film, at least. I include that lengthy explanation because one gentleman told me he never understood what I meant by "2nd edition cover".

The odd mustard and mayonnaise colored pieces of Sunflower shown are unique to my knowledge. No one has ever found anything else like them. Ash trays have turned up in delphite.

	Pink, Green		Pink, Green
*Ash Tray, 5" Center Design Only	7.00	Saucer	2.50
Cake Plate, 10", 3 Legs	7.50	Sugar (Opaque $75.00)	6.50
**Creamer (Opaque 75.00)	7.50	Tumbler, 4¾", 8 oz. Footed	12.50
Cup	6.50	Trivet, 7", 3 Legs, Turned Up Edge	97.50
Plate, 9" Dinner	7.50		

*Found in ultramarine $16.50
**Delphite 40.00

SWANKY SWIGS 1930's-1950's

Swanky Swigs originally came with a Kraft cheese product. In fact, the last Swanky in the bottom photograph still contains "Old English Sharp" cheese (and I'll bet it is--sharp, that is). It was priced 27¢ and was packed in 1954 paper.

There are many new additions since the 4th edition; and you will notice that several of these are getting quite expensive due to demand and relative scarcity.

Top Picture

Top Row	Band No. 1	Red & Black	3 3/8″	1.50 - 2.50
		Red & Blue	3 3/8″	2.00 - 3.00
		Blue	3 3/8″	2.50 - 3.50
	Band No. 2	Red & Black	4¾″	3.00 - 4.00
		Red & Black	3 3/8″	2.00 - 3.00
	Band No. 3	Blue & White	3 3/8″	2.00 - 3.00
	Circle & Dot:	Blue	4¾″	5.00 - 7.50
		Blue	3½″	4.00 - 5.00
		Red, Green	3½″	2.50 - 3.50
		Black	3½″	4.00 - 5.00
		Red	4¾″	5.00 - 7.50
	Dot	Black	4¾″	6.00 - 8.00
		Blue	3½″	4.00 - 5.00
2nd Row	Star:	Blue	4¾″	4.00 - 5.00
		Blue, Red, Green, Black	3½″	2.50 - 3.50
		Cobalt w/White Stars	4¾″	10.00 - 12.00
	Centennials:	W. Va. Cobalt	4¾″	12.50 - 15.00
		Texas Cobalt	4¾″	12.50 - 15.00
		Texas Blue, Black, Green	3½″	5.00 - 7.50
	Checkerboard	Blue, Red	3½″	12.50 - 15.00
3rd Row	Checkerboard	Green	3½″	15.00 - 17.50
	Sailboat	Blue	4½″	10.00 - 15.00
		Blue	3½″	8.00 - 10.00
		Red, Green	4½″	10.00 - 12.50
		Green, Lt. Green	3½″	8.00 - 10.00
	Tulip No. 1	Blue, Red	4½″	5.00 - 6.00
		Blue, Red	3½″	2.50 - 3.50
	Tulip No. 1	Green	4½″	5.00 - 6.00
		Green, Black	3½″	2.50 - 3.50
		Green w/Label	3½″	4.00 - 5.00
	Tulip No. 2	Red, Green, Black	3½″	8.00 - 10.00
	Carnival	Blue, Red	3½″	2.50 - 3.50
		Green, Yellow	3½″	8.00 - 10.00
	Tulip No. 3	Dk. Blue, Lt. Blue	3¾″	1.00 - 2.00

Second Picture

1st Row	Tulip No. 3	Red, Yellow	3¾″	1.00 - 2.00
	Posey: Tulip	Red	4½″	8.00 - 10.00
		Red	3½″	2.00 - 3.00
		Red	3¼″	6.00 - 8.00
	Posey: Violet, Jonquil, Cornflower No. 1		4½″	8.00 - 10.00
	Posey: Violet, Jonquil, Cornflower No. 1		3½″	2.00 - 3.00
	Cornflower No. 2	Lt. Blue, Dk. Blue	3½″	1.50 - 2.50
2nd Row	Cornflower No. 2	Red, Yellow	3½″	1.50 - 2.50
	Forget-Me-Not	Dk. Blue, Blue, Red, Yellow	3½″	1.00 - 2.00
		Yellow w/Label	3½″	3.00 - 4.00
	Daisy	Red & White; Red, White, & Green	3¾″	1.00 - 1.50
	Bustling Betsy	Blue	3¾″	1.00 - 2.00
		Blue	3¼″	4.00 - 5.00
		Green, Orange	3¾″	1.00 - 2.00
3rd Row	Bustling Betsy	Yellow, Red, Brown	3¾″	1.00 - 2.00
	Antique Pattern:			
	Clock & Coal Scuttle	Brown	3¾″	1.00 - 2.00
	Lamp & Kettle	Blue	3¾″	1.00 - 2.00
	Coffee Grinder & Plate	Green	3¾″	1.00 - 2.00
	Spinning Wheel & Bellows	Red	3¾″	1.00 - 2.00
	Coffee Pot & Trivet	Black	3¾″	1.00 - 2.00
	Churn & Cradle	Orange	3¾″	1.00 - 2.00
4th Row	Kiddie Cup:			
	Squirrel & Deer	Brown	3¾″	1.00 - 2.00
	Bear & Pig	Blue	3¾″	1.00 - 2.00
	Cat & Rabbit	Green	3¾″	1.00 - 2.00
	Bird & Elephant	Red	3¾″	1.00 - 2.00
	Bird & Elephant w/Label		3¾″	3.00 - 4.00
	Duck & Horse	Black	3¾″	1.00 - 2.00
	Dog & Rooster	Orange	3¾″	1.00 - 2.00
	Dog & Rooster w/Cheese			6.00 - 8.00

Please refer to Foreword for pricing information

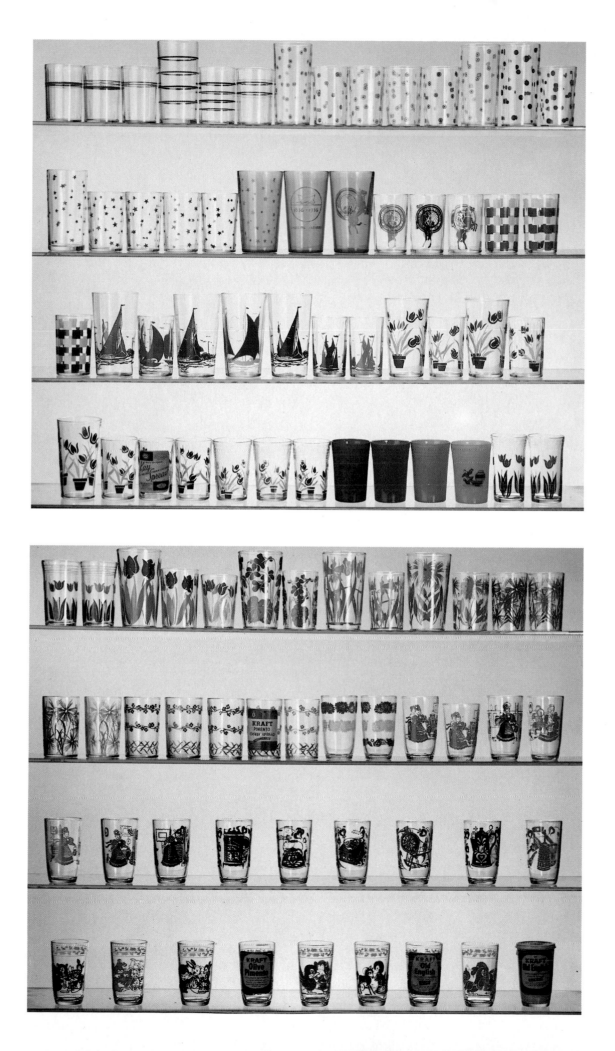

SWIRL, "PETAL SWIRL"   JEANNETTE GLASS COMPANY, 1937-1938

Colors: Pink, ultramarine, delphite, some amber, ice-blue.

The ultramarine Swirl pitcher is shown for the first time in color. It turned up in the Pittsburg area. This is one of the finest designed pieces in Depression Glass. It's a pity more were not made.

The major difficulty for collectors of the ultramarine color is matching the various shades. Many of the pieces have a green tinge to them; and these type seem to be in shorter supply.

Pink Swirl collectors have no shakers as yet; and their candy dishes, lug soups and butter dishes are seldom seen.

You will find both round and fluted edged plates in this pattern. Coasters will have only the concentric rings shown in the center of the ultramarine plates. These coasters are also found with small General Tires around them having been used as advertising ash trays.

Watch for the flat iced tea tumblers. They're tough to locate!

	Pink	Ultra-marine	Delphite
Ash Tray, 5 3/8″	6.00		
Bowl, 5¼″ Cereal	5.00	7.50	8.50
Bowl, 9″ Salad	9.00	14.00	15.00
Bowl, 10″ Footed, Closed Handles		22.50	
Bowl, 10½″ Footed Console	12.50	17.50	
Butter Dish	127.50	197.50	
Candleholders, Double Branch Pr.	22.50	24.00	
Candleholders, Single Branch Pr.			75.00
Candy Dish, Open, 3 Legs	5.00	7.50	
Candy Dish with Cover	50.00	62.50	
Coaster, 1″ x 3¼″	5.50	6.50	
Creamer, Footed	6.00	8.00	7.50
Cup	3.50	6.00	5.00
Pitcher, 48 oz. Footed		650.00	
Plate, 6½″ Sherbet	2.00	3.00	3.00
Plate, 7¼″	4.50	6.50	
Plate, 8″ Salad	4.50	8.50	4.50
Plate, 9¼″ Dinner	5.50	8.50	5.50
Plate, 10½″			10.00
Plate, 12½″ Sandwich	6.50	12.00	
Platter, 12″ Oval			19.50
Salt and Pepper, Pr.		22.50	
Saucer	1.75	2.50	2.25
Sherbet, Low Footed	5.50	8.50	
Soup, Tab Handles (Lug)	12.50	12.50	
Sugar, Footed	5.00	7.50	7.50
Tumbler, 4″, 9 oz.	7.00	10.50	
Tumbler, 4 5/8″, 9 oz.	9.50		
Tumbler, 4¾″, 12 oz.	14.50	25.00	
Tumbler, 9 oz. Footed	11.00	17.50	
Vase, 6½″ Footed	10.00	15.00	
Vase, 8½″ Footed		16.50	

Please refer to Foreword for pricing information

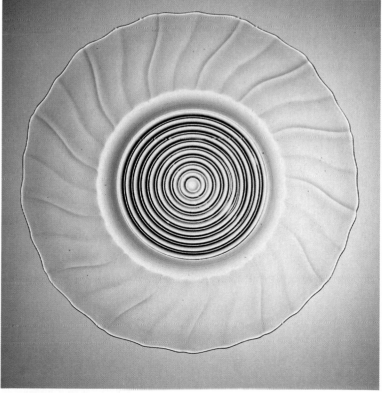

TEA ROOM INDIANA GLASS COMPANY, 1926-1931

Colors: Pink, green, amber, some crystal.

Tea Room in absolutely mint condition has increased in value considerably since the last book. However, I'm speaking of absolutely MINT items, those having no chips, cracks or scratches on those jutting ridges. This pattern is notorious for roughness. I once examined 96 pieces in their original sealed-from-the-factory state and found only 8 in mint condition!

Tea Room, as its name suggests, was designed to be used in the "tea rooms" and "ice cream parlors" of the times. That's why you find so many soda fountain type pieces in the pattern. Plates, cups and saucers seem few and far between.

Prices on Tea Room at the various shows I've attended throughout the country tend to be regional. They're rather high in the Indiana area where it was originally distributed and in the New York area where there are strong leanings toward Art Deco type things. Surprisingly, the lowest prices encountered were at the extremes of the country, Florida and California. Yes, I know; you thought everything was higher there. Evidently, the demand is less there for this particular pattern. That's one reason I try to travel to all sections of the country. I feel I can get a better overall idea of price if I schedule my shows north, south, east, west, and central. I can give you better information that way.

There are four different sugar and creamer sets in Tea Room. There are two sized footed sets, 3½" and 4½"; the 3½" is found on a center handled tray. The third type is represented by the rectangular pair shown to the left of the ice bucket. These are rather hard to find and the tray they sit on is more difficult still. The fourth type has a covered sugar without handles and is shaped like that lidless mustard shown in front of the pink shakers. It's bigger than that, of course. By the way, the mustard lid has a notch in it to accommodate a spreader.

Collectors for Tea Room, like Pyramid, are practically fanatic in their devotion to it! Other people can't stand it. So, there isn't much middle feeling here. You either adore the pattern or you dislike it intensely.

	Pink, Green		Pink, Green
Bowl, 7½" Banana Split	12.50	*Plate, 8¼" Luncheon	17.50
Bowl, 8½" Celery	14.50	Plate, 10½", Two Handled	21.50
Bowl, 8¾" Deep Salad	32.50	Relish, Divided	8.50
Bowl, 9½" Oval Vegetable	35.00	Salt and Pepper, Pr.	32.50
Candlestick, Low Pr.	27.50	*Saucer	9.50
Creamer, 4" (Amber $40.00)	10.00	Sherbet, Three Styles	11.50
Creamer, 4½" Footed	12.00	Sugar, 4" (Amber $40.00)	9.50
Creamer, Rectangular	10.00	Sugar, 4½" Footed	12.00
Creamer and Sugar on Tray, 3½"	37.50	Sugar, Rectangular	10.00
*Cup	15.00	Sugar, Flat with Cover	32.50
Goblet, 9 oz.	22.50	Sundae, Footed	15.00
Ice Bucket	30.00	Tumbler, 8½ oz.	17.50
Lamp, 9" Electric	27.50	Tumbler, 6 oz. Footed	12.00
Mustard, Covered	45.00	Tumbler, 9 oz. Footed (Amber $45.00)	12.00
Parfait	17.00	Tumbler, 11 oz. Footed	15.00
**Pitcher, 64 oz. (Amber $200.00)	77.50	Tumbler, 12 oz. Footed	22.50
Plate, 6½" Sherbet	9.50	Vase, 6" Ruffled Edge or Straight	22.00
		Vase, 9" Ruffled Edge or Straight	25.00
		Vase, 11" Ruffled Edge or Straight	25.00

*Prices for absolute mint pieces.
**Crystal — $175.00

195

THISTLE   MACBETH-EVANS, 1929-1930

Colors: Pink, green, some yellow, crystal.

That 10¼" bowl in Thistle is even harder to find than its counterpart in Dogwood! Buying that, SHOULD you find it, will probably dent your wallet.

I've seen very few grill plates in either pink or green.

Pink is more in demand than the green, particularly in serving pieces. This is possibly due to the fact that basic luncheon items (cups, saucers, plates) are easier to find in the pink.

The cereal bowl shown is the only piece to be found thus far in yellow.

Beginning collectors will notice this pattern strongly resembles Dogwood. The same basic molds were used for both patterns. Dogwood does have a pitcher and tumblers. We're still hoping for those in Thistle.

The heavy pink butter dish being frequently found is a new copy of an old Pattern Glass butter dish and is not a part of this pattern even though it has a thistle design on it. Of the 350 or so letters I receive a month, one concerns this butter dish! (By the way, I no longer answer letters which don't have a self-addressed and STAMPED envelope enclosed. When the postage meter hit $275.00 for unstamped letters, I got mercenary and ceased to feel guilty about not answering your questions. While I'm on this, please keep letters brief and restrict them to patterns listed in this book. I do travel a lot; don't be impatient for a reply.

	Pink	Green		Pink	Green
Bowl, 5½" Cereal	10.00	13.50	Plate, 8" Luncheon	7.00	9.50
Bowl, 10¼" Large Fruit	127.50	77.50	Plate, 10¼" Grill	11.50	11.50
Cup, Thin	12.50	14.50	Plate, 13" Heavy Cake	65.00	60.00
			Saucer	7.00	7.00

197

TROJAN FOSTORIA GLASS COMPANY, 1929-1944

Colors: "Rose" pink, "Topaz" yellow officially; some green.

My catalogue listings from Fostoria speak only of the pink and yellow colors; however, as I've seen some green pieces recently, I know some green exists.

Scarcity of pink has made it equal in price to the more plentiful yellow. Yellow is the color most usually collected.

Pitchers and shakers are much in demand. However, there are pieces more difficult to locate than these items, namely the footed oils and the combination bowl having the candle holders at each end.

This, as stated before, is considered Depression ERA glass. It wasn't cheap then---or free in sacks of flour. Considering its age, beauty and the cost of NEW glassware, Trojan has reasonable investment potential!

	Rose, Topaz		Rose, Topaz
Ash Tray, Large	27.50	Mayonnaise Plate	8.00
Ash Tray, Small	22.50	Mint Dish	10.00
Baker, 9"	30.00	Oil, Footed	175.00
Bon Bon	12.00	Oyster Cocktail	20.00
Bouillon, Footed	15.00	Parfait	22.50
Bowl, 5" Fruit	14.00	Pitcher	225.00
Bowl, 6" Cereal	16.00	Plate, 6" Bread & Butter	5.00
Bowl, 7" Soup	20.00	Plate, 7" Salad	7.50
Bowl, Large Handled Dessert	18.00	Plate, 8" Luncheon	10.00
Bowl, 10"	25.00	Plate, 9" Dinner	14.00
Bowl, Combination w/Candleholders	75.00	Plate, 10" Dinner	20.00
Bowl, 12" Centerpiece, Several Styles	32.50	Plate, 10" Grill	25.00
Cake Plate, 10" Handled	20.00	Plate, 13" Chop	30.00
Canape Plate	10.00	Platter, 12"	30.00
Candlesticks, 2" Pair	20.50	Platter, 15"	40.00
Candlestick, 3" Pair	25.00	Relish, 8½"	12.00
Candlesticks, 5" Pair	32.50	Relish, 3 Part	15.00
Candy, ½ lb. w/Cover	60.00	Sauce Boat	30.00
Celery, 11½"	20.00	Sauce Plate	10.00
Cheese & Cracker Set	35.00	Saucer, After Dinner	6.00
Comport, 6"	20.00	Saucer	4.00
Cream Soup, Footed	15.00	Shaker, Footed Pair	60.00
Cream Soup Plate, 7"	5.00	Sherbet, High	17.50
Creamer, Footed	15.00	Sherbet, Low	14.00
Creamer, Tea	17.50	Sugar, Footed	15.00
Cup, After Dinner	22.00	Sugar Cover	40.00
Cup, Footed	14.00	Sugar Pail	70.00
Finger Bowl	12.00	Sugar, Tea	17.50
Goblet, Claret	30.00	Sweetmeat	10.00
Goblet, Cocktail	22.00	Tray, 11" Center Handled	26.00
Goblet, Cordial	35.00	Tray, Service	26.00
Goblet, Water	25.00	Tray, Service & Lemon	30.00
Goblet, Wine	26.00	Tumbler, 2½ oz. Footed	24.00
Grapefruit	30.00	Tumbler, 5 oz. Footed	20.00
Grapefruit Liner	25.00	Tumbler, 9 oz. Footed	14.00
Ice Bucket	60.00	Tumbler, 12 oz. Footed	18.00
Ice Dish	20.00	Vase, 8"	40.00
Ice Dish Liner (Tomato, Crab, Fruit)	5.00	Whipped Cream Bowl	10.00
Lemon Dish	10.00	Whipped Cream Pail	70.00
Mayonnaise	20.00		

Please refer to Foreword for pricing information

199

"THUMBPRINT", PEAR OPTIC FEDERAL GLASS COMPANY, 1929-1930

Color: Green.

See the explanation under Raindrops in order to distinguish between the two patterns.

The sugar and creamer in Pear Optic are similar in style to those of Georgian in the larger size. These are not easily found; so don't be fooled by the listed price into believing they're common. There just are few collectors for this pattern; and thus, little demand is expressed for its pieces.

	Green		Green
Bowl, 4¾" Berry	2.00	Salt and Pepper, Pr.	15.00
Bowl, 5" Cereal	2.00	Saucer	1.00
Bowl, 8" Large Berry	5.50	Sherbet	4.00
Creamer, Footed	4.50	Sugar, Footed	4.00
Cup	2.50	Tumbler, 4", 5 oz.	3.00
Plate, 6" Sherbet	1.25	Tumbler, 5", 10 oz.	3.50
Plate, 8" Luncheon	2.00	Tumbler, 5½", 12 oz.	4.00
Plate, 9¼" Dinner	3.50	Whiskey, 2¼", 1 oz.	3.00

TWISTED OPTIC IMPERIAL GLASS COMPANY, 1927-1930

Colors: Pink, green, amber, blue, canary yellow.

A medium blue sherbet was recently found on an off center sherbet plate. The plate measured 7½" x 9" and was found in a Kentucky shop. These same items have also been found in a canary yellow color.

The center handled server pictured here actually belongs to Spiral. Twisted Optic's center handled server has an opened space in the handle for gripping; it's Y shaped. The spirals go left, also, which is the wrong direction (generally) for this pattern. (See Spiral explanation).

	All Colors		All Colors
Bowl, 4¾" Cream Soup	5.50	Plate, 8" Luncheon	2.00
Bowl, 5" Cereal	2.00	Preserve (Same as Candy but with	
Bowl, 7" Salad or Soup	5.00	Slot in Lid)	17.50
Candlesticks, 3" Pr.	9.00	Sandwich Server, Center Handle	12.50
Candy Jar and Cover	14.50	Sandwich Server, Two Handled	5.50
Creamer	4.50	Saucer	1.00
Cup	2.50	Sherbet	4.00
Pitcher, 64 oz.	15.00	Sugar	4.50
Plate, 6" Sherbet	1.50	Tumbler, 4½", 9 oz.	4.50
Plate, 7" Salad	2.00	Tumbler, 5¼", 12 oz.	6.50
Plate, 7½" x 9" Oval with Indent	3.50		

Please refer to Foreword for pricing information

VERSAILLES, FOSTORIA GLASS COMPANY, 1928-1944

Colors: Blue, yellow, pink, green.

Versailles and June are presently in a race as to which is the most collectible of the Fostoria patterns. Versailles may have a slight edge. Time will tell which takes first honors.

Versailles represents Depression ERA glassware rather than Depression Glass per se. This glass sold in the finer department stores of the times.

Shown here are all four pitchers as well as two of the rare footed oils pictured in the pattern shot. These pieces are among the elite in this elegant Versailles.

The handled cake plate is shown in yellow just in front of the green candy. You will notice it is a flat plate, not footed. Notice the fleur-de-lis handles on the candy dish and the center handled tray, a further echo of France in this Versailles christened pattern.

The two handled bowl on the left is the whipped cream bowl. The style of the whipped cream pail can be noted in the picture with Fairfax. The pail has a nickel plated handle.

Notice that the stemware has crystal stems and colored bowls.

	Pink, Green	Blue	Yellow		Pink, Green	Blue	Yellow
Ash Tray	24.00	30.00	27.50	Lemon Dish	10.00	14.00	12.00
Baker, 9"	30.00	45.00	40.00	Mayonnaise	30.00	40.00	35.00
Bon Bon	10.00	14.00	12.00	Mayonnaise Liner	4.00	6.00	5.00
Bouillon, Footed	16.00	20.00	18.00	Mint	12.00	16.00	14.00
Bowl, 5" Fruit	14.00	17.50	15.00	Oil, Footed	200.00	300.00	250.00
Bowl, 6" Cereal	20.00	24.00	22.00	Oyster Cocktail	20.00	24.00	22.00
Bowl, 7" Soup	24.00	28.00	26.00	Parfait	25.00	30.00	27.50
Bowl, Large Dessert, 2				Pitcher	237.50	385.00	295.00
Handled	26.00	30.00	28.00	Plate, 6" Bread & Butter	3.00	5.00	4.00
Bowl, 10"	30.00	34.00	32.00	Plate, 7" Salad	6.00	8.00	7.00
Bowl, 11" Centerpiece	30.00	34.00	32.00	Plate, 8" Luncheon	8.00	10.00	9.00
Bowl, 12" Centerpiece,				Plate, 9" Dinner	12.00	16.00	14.00
Several Styles	30.00	34.00	32.00	Plate, 10" Dinner	22.00	30.00	25.00
Bowl, 13" Oval Centerpiece	40.00	45.00	42.50	Plate, 10" Grill	20.00	30.00	25.00
Cake Plate, 10" Handled	26.00	34.00	30.00	Plate, 13" Chop	29.00	35.00	32.00
Candlestick, 2" Pair	26.00	34.00	30.00	Platter, 12"	30.00	40.00	35.00
Candlestick, 3" Pair	32.00	40.00	36.00	Platter, 15"	38.00	50.00	42.00
Candlestick, 5" Pair	36.00	44.00	40.00	Relish, 8½"	30.00	40.00	35.00
Candy, ½ lb. w/Cover	52.00	80.00	60.00	Salad Dressing Bottle	200.00	300.00	250.00
Candy, 3 Part w/Cover	35.00	45.00	40.00	Sauce Boat	35.00	45.00	40.00
Celery, 11½"	30.00	40.00	35.00	Sauce Plate	10.00	15.00	12.50
Cheese & Cracker Set	40.00	50.00	45.00	Saucer, After Dinner	4.00	6.00	5.00
Comport, 6"	22.00	30.00	26.00	Saucer	4.00	6.00	5.00
Comport, 7"	25.00	35.00	30.00	Shaker, Footed Pair	70.00	100.00	85.00
Comport, 8"	30.00	40.00	35.00	Sherbet, High	20.00	24.00	22.00
Cream Soup, Footed	16.00	24.00	20.00	Sherbet, Low	20.00	24.00	22.00
Cream Soup Plate, 7"	4.00	6.00	5.00	Sugar, Footed	12.50	17.50	15.00
Creamer, Footed	12.50	17.50	15.00	Sugar Cover	60.00	100.00	80.00
Creamer, Tea	15.00	20.00	17.50	Sugar Pail	70.00	90.00	80.00
Cup, After Dinner	17.50	35.00	27.50	Sugar, Tea	25.00	20.00	17.50
Cup, Footed	16.00	20.00	18.00	Sweetmeat	10.00	14.00	12.00
Decanter	100.00	150.00	125.00	Tray, 11" Center Handled	20.00	30.00	25.00
Finger Bowl	16.00	20.00	18.00	Tray, Service	30.00	40.00	35.00
Goblet, Claret	30.00	40.00	35.00	Tray, Service & Lemon	30.00	40.00	35.00
Goblet, Cocktail	25.00	30.00	28.00	Tumbler, 2½ oz. Footed	26.00	35.00	32.50
Goblet, Water	25.00	30.00	28.00	Tumbler, 5 oz. Footed	20.00	24.00	22.00
Goblet, Wine	30.00	42.00	35.00	Tumbler, 9 oz. Footed	18.00	22.00	20.00
Grapefruit	36.00	50.00	40.00	Tumbler, 12 oz. Footed	22.00	26.00	24.00
Grapefruit Liner	25.00	40.00	32.50	Vase, 8"	67.50	115.00	97.50
Ice Bucket	60.00	75.00	67.50	Vase, 8½" Footed Fan	30.00	50.00	40.00
Ice Dish	16.00	20.00	18.00	Whipped Cream Bowl	10.00	14.00	12.00
Ice Dish Liner (Tomato,				Whipped Cream Pail	70.00	90.00	80.00
Crab, Fruit)	4.00	6.00	5.00				

Please refer to Foreword for pricing information

"VICTORY" DIAMOND GLASS-WARE COMPANY, 1929-1932

Colors: Amber, green, pink; some cobalt blue; black.

Most pieces found in "Victory" seem to come from the Ohio - Pennsylvania area.

The only other piece to turn up in cobalt blue (besides the sandwich server used for the pattern shot in the 4th edition) is a cup and saucer! However, I've talked to people who say they have six and eight place settings in cobalt Victory. None have been willing to part with them yet, however.

So far, the most desirable "piece" to own is the gravy with platter.

This was better glassware, sold in the department stores rather than being given away free. That probably accounts for its relative scarcity.

Most pieces have ground bottoms rather than molded ones.

	Pink, Green	Amber, Blue
Bowl, 6½" Cereal	5.50	7.00
Bowl, 8½" Flat Soup	8.50	9.50
Bowl, 9" Oval Vegetable	15.00	22.50
Bowl, 12" Console	15.00	25.00
Candlesticks, 3" Pr.	13.50	22.50
Cheese & Cracker Set, 12" Indented Plate & Compote	17.50	
Comport, 6" Tall, 6¾" Diameter	8.50	10.00
Creamer	6.50	9.50
Cup	4.50	5.00
Goblet, 5", 7 oz.	12.00	17.50
Gravy Boat and Platter	77.50	87.50
Mayonnaise Set: 3½" Tall, 5½" Across, 8½" Indented Plate w/Ladle	22.50	32.50
Plate, 6" Bread and Butter	2.00	3.00
Plate, 7" Salad	3.50	5.50
Plate, 8" Luncheon	4.00	5.00
Plate, 9" Dinner	6.50	8.50
Platter, 12"	15.00	20.00
Sandwich Server, Center Handle	15.00	32.50
Saucer	2.00	4.00
Sherbet, Footed	7.50	9.50
Sugar	6.00	9.50

VITROCK, "FLOWER RIM" HOCKING GLASS COMPANY, 1934-1937

Colors: White and fired-on colors, usually red or green.

The two decaled pieces don't belong here. Upon closer examination, they're Indiana Custard from the 1950's. We had eight people at the studio frantically shifting glass from one set up to the next. So, I had so much help I didn't know what I was doing!

We turned the cream soup so you could see the pattern. Since I've had collectors question its existence, I thought we'd better get it photographed.

Collectors often call these flower bedecked items Vitrock. Actually, Hocking referred to their whole line of white glassware as Vitrock--not just one particular pattern. "Flower Rim" might be the better name.

This doesn't appear to be too plentiful; however, there may be just too few people who know its collectible.

	White		White
Bowl, 4" Berry	2.50	Plate, 8¾" Luncheon	2.00
Bowl, 5½" Cream Soup	3.50	Plate, 9" Soup	2.50
Bowl, 6" Fruit	3.00	Plate, 10" Dinner	3.00
Bowl, 7½" Cereal	2.00	Platter, 11½"	4.50
Bowl, 9½" Vegetable	4.50	Saucer	1.00
Creamer, Oval	3.00	Sugar, Oval	3.00
Cup	1.50		
Plate, 7¼" Salad	1.50		

Please refer to Foreword for pricing information

WATERFORD, "WAFFLE"   HOCKING GLASS COMPANY, 1938-1944

Colors: Crystal, pink; some yellow, white; 1950's, forest green.

We have a difficult time keeping either crystal or pink Waterford stocked in our Grannie Bear Antique Shop! This pattern has caught on like a house afire!

Yes, the 13½" relish tray was made in Forest Green in the 1950's. It's been selling for about $5.00; but it hasn't been selling fast. It was made with inserts; but you usually see the tray by itself. I don't know what people did with those inserts!

There have been no new reports of the Miss America styled pieces being found in Waterford. Four items have been found so far: a crystal creamer and sugar, a pink water goblet complete with three rings encircling the top, and a 3½", 5 oz. juice tumbler in pink.

Notice the unusual yellow plate shown on the left and the white ash tray we overturned so you could see the design. The interior of that ash tray is "Dusty Rose" color (found in Oyster and Pearl fired-on candlesticks).

Cereal bowls, pitchers and butter dishes are very difficult to find in pink Waterford!

Notice the Post Cereals advertising ash tray lent by Ronnie Calhoun and used in the pattern shot!

	Crystal	Pink
Ash Tray, 4"	2.50	5.50
Bowl, 4¾" Berry	3.50	5.50
Bowl, 5½" Cereal	6.00	10.00
Bowl, 8¼" Large Berry	6.00	10.50
Butter Dish and Cover	17.50	177.50
Coaster, 4"	1.50	4.00
Creamer, Oval	2.50	7.50
Creamer (Miss America Style)	6.50	
Cup	3.50	9.50
Goblets, 5¼", 5 5/8"	8.50	
Goblets, 5½" (Miss America Style)	20.00	37.50
Lamp, 4" Spherical Base	22.50	
Pitcher, 42 oz. Tilted Juice	14.00	
Pitcher, 80 oz. Tilted Ice Lip	22.50	107.50
Plate, 6" Sherbet	1.50	3.50
Plate, 7 1/8" Salad	2.00	3.50
Plate, 9 5/8" Dinner	4.00	8.50
Plate, 10¼" Handled Cake	4.00	8.50
Plate, 13¾" Sandwich	4.50	7.50
Relish, 13¾", 5 Part	12.50	
Salt and Pepper, 2 Types	7.50	
Saucer	1.00	3.50
Sherbet, Footed	2.50	6.50
Sugar	2.50	6.50
Sugar Cover, Oval	2.50	8.50
Sugar (Miss America Style)	7.00	
Tumbler, 3½", 5 oz. Juice		20.00
Tumbler, 4 7/8", 10 oz. Footed	6.00	9.50
Vase, 6¾"	8.50	

WINDSOR, "WINDSOR DIAMOND"   JEANNETTE GLASS COMPANY, 1936-1946

Colors: Pink, green, crystal; some delphite, amberina red.

I missed listing the two handled bowl shown in green last time. Sorry. Pieces in green are not easily found; so I got letters about that bowl.

The candlestick shown in crystal is difficult to locate in pink. Also hard to find in pink is the 4½", 16 oz. juice pitcher. Neither of these items appear to have been made in green.

The berry bowls come in both a round and flanged edge variety.

Cups, saucers and plates have now turned up to match that red pitcher and tumbler.

The rather unique Windsor punch bowl was photographed in the 4th edition. It consists of the large bowl resting atop an inverted comport. It was meant to do this as they fit into one another. As it was packaged with 12 cups, that explains why there are so many cups sans saucers!

The comport with a beaded edge is of recent vintage. It's found in crystal or with sprayed on colors.

	Crystal	Pink	Green
*Ash Tray, 5¾"	11.50	27.50	40.00
Bowl, 4¾" Berry	2.00	4.00	4.50
Bowl 5" Pointed Edge		6.50	
Bowl, 5" Cream Soup	4.50	10.00	12.50
Bowl, 5 1/8", 5 3/8" Cereals	3.00	9.00	10.00
Bowl, 7 1/8", Three Legs	4.00	12.50	
Bowl 8" Pointed Edge		15.00	
Bowl, 8", 2 Handled	4.50	8.50	11.50
Bowl, 8½" Large Berry	4.50	8.50	9.50
Bowl, 9½" Oval Vegetable	5.00	10.00	11.50
Bowl, 10½" Salad	5.00		
Bowl, 10½" Pointed Edge		65.00	
Bowl, 12½" Fruit Console	9.50	47.50	
Bowl, 7" x 11¾" Boat Shape	10.00	17.50	19.50
Butter Dish	20.00	32.50	67.50
Cake Plate, 10¾" Footed	5.00	9.50	12.00
Cake Plate, 13½" Thick	5.00	9.50	9.50
Candlesticks, 3" Pr.	11.50	47.50	
Candy Jar and Cover	7.50	17.50	
Coaster, 3¼"	2.50	4.50	
Comport	3.00	7.50	
Creamer	3.00	6.50	7.50
Creamer (Shaped as "Holiday")	3.00		
Cup	2.00	5.00	6.50
Pitcher, 4½", 16 oz.	17.50	75.00	
Pitcher, 5", 20 oz.	5.00		
Pitcher, 6¾", 52 oz.	10.00	17.50	42.50
Plate, 6" Sherbet	1.50	2.50	3.00
Plate, 7" Salad	2.50	7.50	8.50
**Plate, 9" Dinner	2.50	7.00	8.50
Plate, 10¼" Handled Sandwich	3.50	7.50	8.50
Plate, 13 5/8" Chop	7.00	12.50	12.50
Plate, 15½" Serving	5.00		
Platter, 11½" Oval	4.00	7.50	8.50
Relish Platter, 11½" Divided	5.00	57.50	8.50
Salt and Pepper, Pr.	12.50	22.50	32.50
Saucer	1.50	2.00	2.50
Sherbet, Footed	2.50	5.00	6.50
Sugar and Cover	4.50	12.50	15.00
Sugar and Cover (Like "Holiday")	4.00		
Tray, 4" Square	2.00	4.00	6.00
Tray, 4 1/8" x 9"	3.00	6.00	6.50
Tray, 8½" x 9¾", w/Handles	5.00	17.50	18.00
Tray, 8½" x 9¾", No Handles		47.50	
Tumbler, 3¼", 5 oz.	3.50	8.50	9.00
Tumbler, 4", 9 oz.	4.50	7.50	9.50
Tumbler, 5", 12 oz.	4.50	12.50	17.50
Tumbler, 4" Footed	4.50		
Tumbler, 7¼" Footed	6.50		

*Delphite — 37.50
**Blue — 37.50
**Red — 50.00

Please refer to Foreword for pricing information

209

NEW "AVOCADO" INDIANA GLASS COMPANY Tiara Exclusives Line, 1974 . . .

Colors: Pink, frosted pink, yellow, blue, red amethyst, green?

In 1979 a green Avocado pitcher was supposedly made. It was supposed to be darker than the original green and was to be limited to a hostess gift item. I was supposed to get one for photographing purposes. However, I've never seen said pitcher. Did they make it?

The pink they made was described under the pattern. It tends to be more orange than the original color. The other colors shown pose little threat as these colors were not made originally.

I understand that Tiara sales counselors tell potential clientelle that their newly made glass is collectible because it is made from old molds. I don't share this view. I feel it's like saying that since you were married in your grandmother's wedding dress, you will have the same happy marriage for the fifty-seven years she did. All you can truly say is that you were married in her dress. I think all you can say about the new Avocado is that it was made from the old molds. TIME, SCARCITY and PEOPLE'S WHIM determine collectibility in so far as I'm able to determine it. It's taken nearly fifty years or more for people to turn to collecting Depression Glass---and that's done, in part, because EVERYONE "remembers" it; they had some in their home at one time or another; it has universal appeal. Who is to say what will be collectible in the next hundred years. If we all knew, we could all get rich!

If you like the new Tiara products, then by all means buy them; but don't do so DEPENDING upon their being collectible just because they are made in the image of the old! You have an equal chance, I feel, of going to Las Vegas and DEPENDING upon getting rich at the Black Jack table.

NEW "CAMEO" Privately Produced, 1981

As we go to press, we understand that a private individual is having Cameo shakers made in pink and possibly green! They're supposedly being scheduled for production at the factory within the week. If there's any possible way to get a description or a photograph in the book BEFORE this page is run, we'll do it. If not, watch the DAZE and other glass publications for further information!

Picture unavailable at press time.

NEW "CHERRY BLOSSOM" Privately Produced first in 1973 . . .

Colors: Pink, green, blue, delphite.

I could write a book on the differences between old and new scalloped bottom, AOP Cherry pitchers. The easiest way to tell the difference is to turn the pitcher over. My old Cherry pitcher has nine cherries on the bottom. The new one only has seven. Further, the branch crossing the bottom of my old Cherry pitcher LOOKS like a branch. It's knobby and gnarled and has several leaves and cherry stems directly attached to it. The new pitcher just has a bald strip of glass halving the bottom of the pitcher. Further, the old cherry pitchers have a plain glass background for the cherries and leaves in the bottom of the pitcher. In the new pitchers, there's a rough, filled in, straw-like background. You see no plain glass. (My new Cherry pitcher just cracked sitting in a box by my typing stand --- another tendency which I understand is common to the new)!

As for the new tumblers, the easiest way to tell old from new is to look at the ring dividing the patterned portion of the glass from the plain glass lip. The old tumblers have three indented rings dividing the pattern from the plain glass rim. The new has only one. (Turn back and look at the red cherry tumbler pictured with Cherry Blossom pattern). Further, as in the pitcher, the arching encircling the cherry blossoms on the new tumblers is very sharply ridged. On the old tumblers, that arching is so smooth you can barely feel it. Again, the pattern at the bottom of the new tumblers is brief and practically nonexistent in the center curve of the glass bottom. This was sharply defined on most of the old tumblers. You can see how far toward the edge the pattern came on the red cherry tumbler pictured with the pattern. The pattern, what there is, on the new tumblers mostly hugs the center of the foot.

The Cherry child's dishes first made in 1973 are discussed under the pattern heading.

Pictured are the colors made so far in the butter dishes and shakers begun in 1977. Some shakers were dated '77 on the bottom and were marketed at the ridiculous price of $27.95, a whopping profit margin! Shortly afterward, the non dated variety appeared. How can you tell new shakers from old--- should you get the one in a million chance to do so?

First, look at the tops. New tops COULD indicate new shakers. Next, notice the protruding ledges beneath the tops. They are squared off juts rather than the nicely rounded scallops on the old (which are pictured under Cherry Blossom pattern). The design on the newer shakers is often weak in spots. Finally, notice how far up inside the shakers the solid glass (next to the foot) remains. The newer shakers have almost half again as much glass in that area. They appear to be ¼ full of glass before you ever add the salt!

Butter dishes are naturally more deceptive in pink and green since that blue was not an original color. The major flaw in the new butter is that there is ONE band encircling the bottom edge of the butter top; there are TWO bands very close together along the skirt of the old top. Using your tactile sense, the new top has a sharply defined design up inside; the old was glazed and is smooth to touch. The knob on the new is more sharply defined than the smoothly formed knob on the old butter top.

Reproductions (Con't.)

NEW "MAYFAIR" Privately Produced 1977 . . .

Colors: Pink, green, blue.

Only the shot glass (which is rare in the original) has been made in this pattern. The green (totally wrong color) and blue are no problem since the shot glasses have never been found in these colors originally. The difficulty comes with the pink.

Generally speaking, the newer shot glass has a heavier over-all look. The bottom area tends to have a thicker rim of glass. Often, the "pink" coloring isn't right; it may be too light, it may be too orange. However, if these cursory examinations fail, there are other points to check.

First, notice the stem of the flower. You have a single stem in the new flower. At the base of the stem in the old glass, the stem separates into an "A" shape. Further, look at the leaves on the stem. In the new design, the leaf itself is hollow with the veins molded in. In the old glass, the leaf portion is molded in and the veining is left hollow. In the center of the flower, the dots (anther) cluster entirely to one side of the old design and are rather distinct. Nothing like that occurs in the newer version.

NEW "MISS AMERICA" Privately Produced, 1977 . . .

Colors: Crystal, green, pink, ice blue, red amberina.

The new butter dish in "Miss America" design is probably the best of the newer products; yet there are three distinct differences to be found between the original butter top and the newly made one. Since the value of the butter dish lies in the top, it seems more profitable to examine it.

In the new butter dishes pictured, notice that the panels reaching the edge of the butter bottom tend to have a pronounced curving, skirt-like edge. In the original dish, there is much less curving at the edge of these panels.

Second, pick up the top of the new dish and feel up inside it. If the butter top knob is filled with glass so that it is convex (curved outward), the dish is new; the old inside knob area is concave (curved inward).

Finally, from the underside, look through the top toward the knob. In the original butter dish you would see a perfectly formed multi-sided star; in the newer version, you see distorted rays with no visible points.

Shakers have been made in green, pink and crystal. The shakers will have new tops; but since some old shakers have been given new tops, that isn't conclusive at all. Unscrew the lid. Old shakers have a very neatly formed ridge of glass on which to screw the lid. It overlaps a little and has neatly rounded off ends. Old shakers stand 3 3/8" tall without the lid. New ones stand 3¼" tall. Old shakers have almost a forefinger's depth inside (female finger) or a fraction shy of 2½ inches. New shakers have an inside depth of 2", about the second digit bend of a female's finger. (I'm doing finger depths since most of you will have those with you at the flea market, rather than a tape measure). In men, the old shaker's depth covers my knuckle; the new shaker leaves my knuckle exposed. New shakers simply have more glass on the inside of the shaker---something you can spot from twelve feet away! The hobs are more rounded on the newer shaker, particularly near the stem and seams; in the old shaker these areas remained pointedly sharp!

Reproductions (Con't.)

NEW SANDWICH (Indiana)   INDIANA GLASS COMPANY Tiara Exclusive Line, 1969 . . .

Colors: Amber, blue, red, crystal.

The smoky blue and amber shown here are representative of Tiara's line of Sandwich which is presently available. (See Sandwich pattern for older amber color).

The bad news is that the crystal has been made now and there are only minute differences in this new and the old. I will list the pieces made in crystal and you can make yourself aware of these re-issues if you collect the crystal Sandwich.

Ash Tray Set
Basket, Handles, 10½"
Bowl, 4" Berry
Bowl, 8"
Butter Dish & Cover
Candlesticks, 8½"
Cup, 9 oz.
Cup (Fits Indent in 6 oz. Oval Sandwich Plate)
Decanter & Stopper, 10"
Goblet, 5¼", 8 oz.
Pitcher, 8" Tall, 68 oz. Fluted Rim
Plate, 10" Dinner
Plate, 8" Salad
Plate, 8½" x 6¾" Oval Sandwich
Sandwich Tray, Handled
Saucer, 6"
Sherbets
Tray, 10" (Underliner for Wine
   Decanter & Goblets)
Tumbler, 6½" High, 12 oz.

I discussed the red color made in 1969 under the Sandwich heading, Page 180.

See last two paragraphs of text under New Avocado.

NEW "SHARON"   Privately Produced 1976 . . .

Colors: Blue, dark green, light green, pink, burnt umber.

While there is a hair's difference between the height, mouth opening diameter, and inside depth of the old Sharon shakers and those newly produced, I won't attempt to upset you with those sixteenth and thirty seconds of a degree of difference. Suffice it to say that in physical shape, they are very close. However, as concerns design, they're miles apart. The old shakers have true appearing roses. The flowers really LOOK like roses. On the new shakers, they look like poorly drawn circles with wobbly concentric rings. The leaves are not as clearly defined on the new shakers as the old. However, forgetting all that, in the old shakers, the first design you see below the lid is a ROSE BUD. It's angled like a rocket shooting off into outer space with three leaves at the base of the bud (where the rocket fuel would burn out). In the new shakers, this "bud" has become four paddles of a windmill. It's the difference between this 🌿 and this. 🌼

A blue Sharon butter turned up in 1976 and turned my phone line to a liquid fire! The color is Mayfair blue---a fluke and dead giveaway as far as real Sharon is concerned.

When found in similar colors to the old, pink and green, you can immediately tell that the new version has more glass in the top where it changes from pattern to clear glass, a thick, defined ring of glass as opposed to a thin, barely defined ring of glass in the old. The knob of the new dish tends to stick up more. In the old butter dish there's barely room to fit your finger to grasp the knob. The new butter dish has a sharply defined ridge of glass in the bottom around which the top sits. The old butter has such a slight rim that the top easily scoots off the bottom.

In 1977 a "cheese dish" appeared having the same top as the butter and having all the flaws inherent in that top which were discussed in detail above. However, the bottom of this dish was all wrong. It's about half way between a flat plate and a butter dish bottom, bowl shaped; and it is over thick, giving it an awkward appearance. The real cheese bottom was a salad plate with a rim for holding the top. These "round bottom cheese dishes" are but a parody of the old and are easily spotted. We removed the top from one in the picture so you could see its heaviness and its bowl shape.

First Edition Cover

Amethyst	Right Center: Royal Lace Sherbet
Blue	Center Front: Princess Cup
	Right Rear: Mayfair Pitcher
Green	Center Middle: Cherry Shakers
	Left Rear: Mayfair Pitcher
Pink	Left Front: Cameo Wine
	Right Front: Cameo Water Tumbler
	Right Front: Cameo Creamer
	Center Middle: Mayfair Footed Bowl
Yellow	Center Rear: Mayfair Pitcher

Second Edition Cover

Amber	Left Center: Madrid Gravy Boat and Platter
	Left Rear: Parrot Footed and Flat Iced Teas
Amethyst	Left Foreground: Iris Demi-Tasse Cup and Saucer
Blue	Right Foreground: Iris Demi-Tasse Cup and Saucer
	Center: Floral Sherbet
	Right Rear: Princess Cookie Jar and Florentine Pitcher
Custard	Left Center: Sunflower Sugar
Green	Left Front: Sunflower Trivet
	Left Center: Number 612, 9 and 12 oz. Flat Tumblers
	Center: Cherry Opaque Bowl
	Left Rear: Floral Juice Pitcher and Mayfair Cookie Jar
	Right Rear: Princess Footed Pitcher and Tumbler: Mayfair Liqueur
Iridescent	Right Foreground: Iris Demi-Tasse Cup and Saucer
Mustard	Right Center: Sunflower Creamer
Orange	Right Center: Cherry Opaque Bowl (Reddish with yellow rim)
Pink	Center Foreground: Cameo Ice Tub
	Left Foreground: Adam-Sierra Butter Dish
	Center: Cameo Shakers
	Rear Center: Waterford Lamp by Westmoreland (pattern not included) in book, but shown to differentiate from Miss America and English Hobnail)
Red	Left Foreground: Iris Demi-Tasse Cup and Saucer
	Center: Miss America Goblet
Yellow	Center: Cherry Vegetable Bowl
	Right Center: Dogwood Cereal Bowl; Adam 8″ Plate, Cup and Saucer
	Left Rear: Mayfair Juice Pitcher
	Right Rear: Mayfair Shakers

Third Edition Cover

Amber	Center: Moondrops Etched Butter
	Right Front: Victory Gravy Boat and Platter
	Left Middle: Cherry Blossom Child's Cup and Saucer; Florentine No. 2 Footed Tumbler
Blue	Left Front: Windsor Delphite Ash Tray
	Left Center: Heritage Berry Bowl
	Left Rear: English Hobnail Handled Bowl
	Right Center: Floral Delphite Tumbler
	Right Rear: Rock Crystal Berry on Silver Pedestal
Green	Left Center: Rock Crystal Shaker
	Left Rear: American Pioneer Lamp
	Right Center Front: Heritage Berry Bowl
	Right Center: American Sweetheart Shaker
	Right Rear: Floral Ice Tub
Iridescent	Center: Louisa Carnival Rose Bowl
Pink	Left Rear: Floral Ice Tub
	Right Middle: American Pioneer Covered Jug
Red	Left Middle: Windsor Tumbler
	Center: Cherry Blossom Bowl
	Center Rear: Rock Crystal Fruit Bowl
Yellow	Right Rear: Pyramid Pitcher

Fourth Edition Cover Description

Amber	Center Front: Radiance Butter Dish
	Center Middle: English Hobnail Pitcher
	Center Back: Tea Room Pitcher
Blue, Light Cobalt	Center Left: Fire King Dinnerware Juice Pitcher
	Center Right: Radiance Handled Decanter
Crystal	Center Back: Tea Room Pitcher
Green	Center Front: Mayfair Butter Dish
	Left Front: Floral Eight Sided Vase
	Left Center: Floral Dresser Set
	Right Center: Mayfair Juice Pitcher
	Left Rear: Rock Crystal 64 oz. Pitcher
Pink	Left Front: Mayfair Footed Shaker, 1 oz. Liqueur & Round Cup and Saucer
	Left Rear: Colonial Bead Top Pitcher
	Right Rear: Princess Footed Pitcher
Red	Center Middle: English Hobnail Pitcher
Yellow	Right Front: Mayfair Sugar and Lid
	Right Front: Cameo Butter Dish and Lid
	Right Rear: Footed Pitcher

Rare Page

Amber	Left: Lincoln Inn Pitcher
Blue	Left Rear: June Pitcher
	Center Back: Radiance Pitcher
	Radiance Tumbler
	Right: Fire King Dinnerware Pitcher
	Caprice Daulton Pitcher
	Center: Versailles Footed Oil
Crystal	Left Front: Floral Vase and Frog
	Left Center: Floral Juice Pitcher
	Cameo Pitcher
	Right Center: Madrid Juice Pitcher
	Mayfair 80 oz. Pitcher
Green	Front: Floral Vase and Frog
	Left Rear: Doric Footed Pitcher
Pink	Left: Old Cafe Juice Pitcher
	Left Center: Coronation Pitcher
	Right Front: Iris Fruit Bowl
	Right Middle: Old Cafe Water Pitcher
Red	Right: Colonial Water Tumbler
Ultramarine	Right Rear: Swirl Pitcher
Yellow	Center: Versailles Footed Oil

Publications I recommend

DEPRESSION GLASS DAZE

THE ORIGINAL NATIONAL DEPRESSION GLASS NEWSPAPER

Depression Glass Daze, the Original, National monthly newspaper dedicated to the buying, selling & collecting of colored glassware of the 20's and 30's. We average 60 pages each month filled with feature articles by top notch columnists, readers "finds", club happenings, show news, a china corner, a current listing of new glass issues to beware of and a multitude of ads!! You can find it in the DAZE! Keep up with what's happening in the dee gee world with a subscription to the DAZE. Buy, sell or trade from the convenience of your easy chair.

Name _____ Street _____

City_____ State_____ Zip_____

☐ 1 year-$12.00   ☐ Check enclosed   ☐ Please bill me

☐ MasterCard   ☐ VISA (Foreign subscribers - please add $1.00 per year)

Exp. date_____ Card No._____

Signature _____

Orders to D.G.D., Box 57GF, Otisville, MI 48463 - Please allow 30 days

GLASS review

A colorful magazine devoted to keeping glass collectors informed about all kinds of glass - antique to contemporary collectibles. Filled with articles, pictures, price reports, ads, research information and more! 10 "BIG" issues yearly.

Name _____ Street _____

City_____ State_____ Zip_____

☐ New   ☐ 1 year-$12.50   ☐ Single Copy $2.00

☐ Renewal   ☐ 1 Yr. Canada or Foreign $15.00 (U.S. Funds please)

Orders to P.O. Box 542, Marietta, OH 45750

Depression glass has long been a popular collectible in this country. Many glass enthusiasts have turned to kitchen glassware of the same period as a natural "go-with". These kitchen containers, gadgets, and utensils can be found in many of the same shades as the tableware that has become so highly collectible. Nostalgic and colorful, Depression kitchen glassware is now the subject of an authoritative identification and value guide.

Hundreds of pieces of glass are featured in full color in this large format, 8½" x 11" hardbound volume. It includes canisters, salt and peppers, reamers, straw holders, containers, pitchers and many other miscellaneous kitchen pieces. This book is filled with information about the glass, including manufacturers, sizes, colors, and current values. It also includes a section of catalog reprints and many catalog illustrations showing how the glass was originally sold.

Gene Florence is one of the country's best known glass authors. He has written several books in the antiques field including two on Depression glass, *The Collector's Encyclopedia of Depression Glass* and *Pocket Guide to Depression Glass*. This new volume on Depression kitchen glassware will be welcomed by Depression glass lovers everywhere.

Item #1281, 8½" x 11", 128 Pgs., HB **$17.95**

Additional Books By Gene Florence

Kitchen Glassware of the Depression Years   **$17.95**
Pocket Guide to Depression Glass   **$ 8.95**

Add $1.00 postage for the first book, $.35 for each additional book.

Copies of these books may be ordered from:

Gene Florence
P.O. Box 22186
Lexington, KY 40522

COLLECTOR BOOKS
P.O. Box 3009
Paducah, KY 42001